Praise fo

"It was said in the lore and legends of Norse mythology that people who got interested in Odin, the god of hunters, warriors, and oracular seers were "seized" by this deity, fascinated by this multifarious character. Diana Paxson, author of historical novels and short stories on themes from Norse and Celtic mythology was clearly seized, somewhat to her own surprise. She here beautifully retells some classic stories from this mythic complex and relates how they are reflected in the ceremonial practices of the contemporary Neo-Pagan revival. I recommend *Odin* highly."

—Ralph Metzner, PhD, author of *The Well of Remembrance*

"Diana Paxson is both a scholar and a storyteller, which shows in her exhaustive yet enthralling *Odin: Ecstasy, Runes, and Norse Magic*. The figure of Odin, God of battles, but also of inspiration and poetry, lord of the slain, looms through the background of Western culture, affecting everything from our conception of kingship—Queen Elizabeth is descended from him through the Saxon kings of Wessex—to the figure of Gandalf in Tolkien's work. Paxson takes us back to the original and shows the archetypic, mythic power of this figure."

—S. M. Stirling, author of the *Emberverse* series

"*Odin: Ecstasy, Runes, and Norse Magic* is a journey through personal histories of encounters with Odin, a weaving of old lore and modern thought and a guide to practices that deepen your connection to his mysteries. Even if you don't work with Odin or this pantheon, this book is a treasure house of ideas for anyone who is serious about working with goddesses and gods. Moreover, there are people that are dear to me that work with Odin and this book has given me insight into the whys and wherefores of their spiritual path. This remarkable book is at times ribald and reverent, world-wise and innocent, pragmatic and idealistic, as needed to masterfully show the ways of a very complex god."

—Ivo Domiguez Jr., author of *Keys to Perception*

"Diana Paxson's wonderful book *Odin: Ecstasy, Runes, and Norse Magic* follows the trail of Odin, a wandering god, from his misty origins to his current manifestations. Paxson explores Odin's history, as well as the poetry, literature, and other entertainments that he has inspired and in which he stars, both ancient and modern, from the Eddas to *American Gods* and from Tolkien to Wagner and Marvel. A god for the ages, Odin's veneration remains vital and active. Paxson, a priestess, provides songs, rituals, magical exercises, and sound, practical advice to help you develop your own personal relationship with the Lord of Runes and Ecstasy. There is no one in the world that I'd rather learn about Odin from than Diana L. Paxson. Highly recommended."

—Judika Illes, author of *Encyclopedia of Spirits,*
Encyclopedia of 5000 Spells and other books
devoted to the magical and spiritual arts

"Reading Diana Paxson's most excellent book, *Odin: Ecstasy, Runes, and Norse Magic*, whilst listening to Wardruna. This is perhaps the most comprehensive book ever written about Odin. Written with sound scholarship allied to intuitive perception. Capturing the best of both, and a sense of humour to boot. Each chapter is ended by a list of suggestions for working with him. Apart from the scholarship and poetic vision, it is also a most pleasant read! Recommended for everyone interested in Odin. Very, very helpful to students, but also rich in details and associations from other good books. which are listed in the bibliography. All in all, a very worthwhile work and, as such, equally useful to old timers like me."

—Freya Aswynn, author of *Northern Mysteries*
and Magick: Runes & Feminine Powers

Odin

ODIN

Ecstasy, Runes &
Norse Magic

DIANA L. PAXSON

WEISER BOOKS

This edition first published in 2017 by Weiser Books an imprint of
Red Wheel/Weiser, LLC
With offices at:
65 Parker Street, Suite 7
Newburyport, MA 01950
www.redwheelweiser.com

Excerpts from pp. 22, 119, 12-3 (339 words) from AMERICAN GODS by NEIL
GAIMAN. COPYRIGHT © 1999 by NEIL GAIMAN. Reprinted by permission of
HarperCollins Publishers.

Excerpts from Egilssaga, translated by E. R. Eddison and published in 1930 by Cambridge
University Press.

Every effort has been made to trace copyright holders and to obtain their permission for
the use of copyright material. The publisher apologizes for any errors or omissions and
would be grateful if notified of any corrections that should be incorporated in future
reprints or editions of this book.

ISBN: 978-1-57863-610-5
Library of Congress Cataloging-in-Publication Data

Names: Paxson, Diana L., author.
Title: Odin : ecstasy, runes, and Norse magic / Diana L. Paxson.
Description: Newburyport : Weiser Books, 2017. | Includes bibliographical
  references.
Identifiers: LCCN 2017010497 | ISBN 9781578636105 (6 x 9 tp : alk. paper)
Subjects: LCSH: Odin (Norse deity) | Mythology, Norse.
Classification: LCC BL870.O3 P39 2017 | DDC 293/.2113--dc23
LC record available at https://lccn.loc.gov/2017010497

Cover design by Jim Warner
Interior by Steve Amarillo / Urban Design LLC
Typeset in Adobe Garamond Pro, Aon Cari Celtic, Adobe Bembo, Open Sans Italic

Printed in Canada
MAR
10 9 8 7 6

To all those who have heard Odin calling—
my fellow travelers on this road.

"One word led on to another word,
One work led on to another work . . ."

—*Hávamál* 141

Contents

Acknowledgments   XI

INTRODUCTION   XV
        Interlude: King Gylfi Visits the Hall of Hár

CHAPTER ONE   **Will the Real Odin Stand Up, Please?**   2
        Interlude: "Wanderer"

CHAPTER TWO   **The Wanderer**   25
        Interlude: The Second Merseberg Charm

CHAPTER THREE   **Master of Magic**   44
        Interlude: "Rune Song"

CHAPTER FOUR   **Rider of the Tree**   63
        Interlude: The Building of Bifrost

CHAPTER FIVE   **All-father**   91
        Interlude: "In Gunnlödh's Bed"

CHAPTER SIX   **Desired One**   123
        Interlude: "Head-Ransom"

CHAPTER SEVEN   **Battle God**   150
        Interlude: Bölverk and the Thralls

CHAPTER EIGHT   **Bale-Worker**   176
                      Interlude: "Wodan's Hunt"

CHAPTER NINE   **God of the Dead**   196
                      Interlude: At Mimir's Well

CHAPTER TEN   **God of Ecstasy**   225

APPENDIX I   **Rituals**   251

APPENDIX II   **Music**   261

BIBLIOGRAPHY   277

Acknowledgments

I offer my profound thanks to all those who shared their experiences, their poetry, and their songs, especially my kin in the Troth and Hrafnar kindred. Where not otherwise attributed, poems, translations, and music are my own. Since I first began to learn about Odin, the availability of sources, both in translation and the original, has increased a thousandfold.

Scholarship is always a work in progress, and I have tried to work with both old interpretations and new. I am grateful to Dr. Stephan Grundy for helping me with the facts, and to my beta readers for helping me make them comprehensible.

For more information on what I am doing, go to *www.diana-paxson.com*. For news about Hrafnar kindred, see *www.hrafnar.org*.

Odin

Introduction

It's March 2013, and my friend Lorrie and I are sitting in her living room watching the eagerly awaited first episode of the History Channel's *Vikings!* On a wild hillside, warriors battle in a scene that could have come from any of the sagas. Better still, as the battle ends, ghostly valkyries carry off the spirits of the slain. Ragnar Lothbrok, a young warrior with glinting blue eyes, stands as victor, but he is clearly thinking that there must be something more to life than endless battles that serve other men's aims. Ravens soar overhead, and then, half-seen through the mists, we glimpse a dark-clad figure with a broad hat and a tall spear. *That* is what we were waiting for.

The Lord of the Ravens challenges Ragnar to become a leader and seek a wider world. He challenges us as well.

But who is he?

Odin—god of words and wisdom, runes and magic, giver of battle fury and death but also transformer of consciousness, trickster who teaches truth, and wise old man—appears in many guises and has more names than any other god. In the Middle Ages, his worship was suppressed, but in the Icelandic Eddas, his legends endured. In the 19th century, he made a comeback in the *Ring* operas of Richard Wagner. In the 20th, Carl Jung blamed him for the rise of the Nazis. In the universe of Marvel comics, Odin is a warrior king. We can see his reflection in J. R. R. Tolkien's Gandalf and perceive a modern aspect in Mr. Wednesday, an "American God" from Neil Gaiman's novel.

Odin is also among the most popular gods in the contemporary Heathen revival, and has become notorious for spontaneously claiming the attention of people who might not ever even have heard of him.

For example:

> Somewhere around late 1986 or early 1987 I was at an emotional low ebb. One night I dreamed I was being attacked by something and Odin showed up. I was not Asatru at the time and in fact wouldn't encounter the word Asatru for well over a year, but my recognition of Odin was instant and without any doubt whatsoever. This certainty was key to the way in which the dream was to affect me over the years.
>
> In the dream, Odin pointed Gungnir past me so vividly that I felt like I could touch it. The meaning was clear. From this point forward I could handle my problems on my own. And from that moment my life took a turn for the better. I have never known if this was an energy infusion or simply a reminder that I should recognize the strength of my human soul and start acting accordingly.
>
> Then he gave me a nod and the image disintegrated. I awoke with a start. Even though no words were exchanged I understood the meaning of the nod. Maybe it was tele-pathic. It meant "follow." (Freyburger 2009, 14)

People who encounter Odin often find that the only way to express what has happened is through poetry, as in the poem "Odin's Call," by my friend from the Troth, Jennifer Lawrence.

Like the spider spinning his web in a high wind,

You were persistent, tapping again and again

At the door to my heart and head, until I listened,

Opened the door, and let you in.

I thought I had nothing to do with the gods of the North,

Preferring to walk another path, thinking my life

Already too complicated and confused to warrant

Following any others.

But you would not accept my refusal, sending

Little signs and omens: two ravens following

My car, a gray cat adopted on Wednesday who wanders

And will not shut up: so like you.

What need had I for your guidance? I was stubborn,

Did not want to take the steps to meet you,

Knowing how much you would demand of me,

Not knowing whether I could give it.

After a hard lifetime, I tend to think myself unworthy

Of such attention, and you confused me, chasing after

Me so relentlessly; I preferred to think I only imagined it,

Because what would you want with one such as myself?

I don't ask those questions anymore—or if I do, I know

That, while I might not be able to answer them, you must

Have your reasons. Better, then, to serve you as best I can,

Though what gifts I have to offer are little enough.

These verses will win me no friends. Your followers are a

Bold and boasting lot, whereas I have always striven to be

Meek and mild, hiding my lights away, better to go
unnoticed,

Better to avoid strife, sorrow, and conflict.

But hiding from you did not work, and so I am here,

Hoping that someday I will understand why you
wanted me,

Knowing because you did that there must be more that I
can offer

Than the nothing I believe myself to be.

Not all of those who find themselves involved with Odin already think of themselves as Pagan. Psychotherapist Ralph Metzner observes:

> The old legends say that the followers of Odin were "seized" by the god, and often I felt as though I was seized, or inspired. I would think of Odin and get insights or answers to my questions, including questions about the meaning of certain myths. Or I would suddenly find pertinent myths that I had not known before. Strange though it may sound, I would have to say that much of what I am relating in this book [*The Well*

of Remembrance] has been directly given to me by Odin.
(Metzner 1994, 10)

I had the same feeling when I was working on the lectures that eventually turned into my book, *Taking up the Runes,* and I have a sense of Odin's presence as I am writing now. I certainly never anticipated the way my life would change after my first close encounter with the god.

As I explored feminist spirituality in the seventies, I saw him as just one more blustering patriarchal deity. I was quite content to focus on the goddesses until one weekend in August 1987 when I attended a shamanic workshop led by Michael Harner. For some time, I had been having good results with the practices in his book *The Way of the Shaman.* I went to the workshop hoping to improve what I was doing and pick up some new techniques, but my long-term desire was to learn traditional Northern European magical and spiritual skills.

Here is how I wrote about my experience two years after the workshop:

> I am walking through a gray land . . . a world of mist that swirls among mighty stones. The raven flies ahead of me, not dark as she was in the Underworld, but brilliant as the image of the sun against closed eyelids, bright/dark/ bright wings flashing against the shadowed stones.
>
> "Where are you leading me?" I ask, and try to go faster.

I was aware of faint sounds from the world that I had left behind me, but wrapped in my gray cloak, I was insulated from both the noises and the chill of the building where the workshop was being held. Long practice helped me control my breathing and sink back into trance, to trust myself to Michael Harner's steady drumming, and let it thrust me into the vision again.

The brown stones stand like pylons to either side, their rough surfaces inscribed with scratches whose meaning has been worn away by the winds of countless years. The raven alights on one of them, wings twitching impatiently. Clearly, she considers me rather stupid, but she waits for me to catch up again.

"You asked for a teacher—" she tells me. "That's where I'm taking you."

I don't argue. I would never have dared to claim a raven as an ally. Especially not this one, this Grandmother of ravens, whose tongue is as sharp as her pointed beak.

But I thought that *she* was going to teach me what I want to know . . .

Grandmother Raven had turned up on the first day of the workshop and insisted upon being part of the action. That first interaction is described in my book, *Trance-Portation*. For the second journey, Harner told us to go into the Upper World and look for a teacher in human form. What I had not anticipated was what would happen when someone I trusted was doing the drumming, and I was not distracted by responsibility for others. Already, what had begun as active imagination, a visualized journey, was approaching a level of involvement that I had never experienced before. But could I believe what was coming through?

Knowledge is a two-edged tool. Since childhood, I had been a student of mythology, and a graduate degree and years of esoteric study and practice made me familiar with the great myths of Europe and their meaning; but I suffer from the separation between knowledge and gnosis that plagues the educated Westerner—the perception of personal experience as less valid than textbook knowledge or even the life-learning of "natural" man.

And I had a further reason for suspicion. I am a writer, a crafter of archetypes and images and those symbols we call words. When I sought a power animal in the Underworld, I understood the significance of the raven who came to me. But just because I recognized her, it was easy to suspect myself of wishful thinking. If I had been inventing an ally for a character in one of my novels, I might have chosen a raven. That, too, was a reason to doubt what I was hearing. I make my living writing. Was I inventing one now?

> "Did anybody ever tell you that you think too much? Shut up and come along!" The raven flaps away.

> The way is hard, but I have journeyed too far, waited too long, desired this too fervently to turn tail now. I have no choice. I have to follow her.

> The pillars lead to an arena of rock, and Someone is waiting there, a broad hat pulled down. The folds of his grey cloak seem to flow from the stone. He turns and I see the spear in his hand, the greying hair, the missing eye . . .

> No. Oh no. Raven, what are you trying to do to me?

The goddess Freyja, or maybe Heide the wisewoman—these were Powers I might have expected and welcomed. But at that moment, I was finally convinced that what was happening to me was not a daydream, because I recognized the god. I've always been the cautious type, and no sensible person would *ask* to learn magic from Odin.

My reasons for this reaction require some background. To Richard Wagner, composing his operas in the 19th century, the god was Wotan, brooding on destiny and the ring of power. To Snorri Sturlusson, writing in the 13th with one eye on the priests and the other on the poets, he was the All-father, patron of kings and the skjalds who sang their praises. To the writers of the sagas, he was the untrustworthy Lord of Battles, giving victory or harvesting heroes for Valhalla. Who would choose a god like that for a teacher?

But in the collection of poems called the Elder Edda, another image emerges. There we see Odin the seeker after knowledge—rune master, spell singer, whose eight-legged steed Sleipnir bears him even to the land of the dead. When Snorri continued his attempt to euhemerize the gods in the *Ynglingasaga*, he portrayed Odin as a master of a very particular kind of magic.

Odin was many things to the Teutonic peoples, but before anything else, he was a god of ecstasy. He is accompanied by two ravens who bring him knowledge from all over the world. He won the runes and the mead of poetry. For a drink from the well of wisdom, he traded one of his eyes.

Odin's gifts to humankind are the gifts of an expanded consciousness. For those with the courage to learn his lessons, Odin is the great teacher of magic.

The exact nature of this knowledge must be deduced from the somewhat elliptic references in the Eddas (the *Poetic Edda*, a collection of early poetry, and the *Prose Edda*, a mixture of poetry and prose summaries written by Snorri Sturlusson to explain them) and sagas. Norse literature features a kind of poetic shorthand of metaphor and allusion that assumes that the listener already knows the stories to which they refer, not all of which have survived.

According to Snorri, Odin's warriors went into battle intoxicated by battle frenzy. Those who fought joyfully received their reward in Valhalla. Those who tried to deny the god the lives they had dedicated to him came to sticky ends. Perhaps the kings who found Odin untrustworthy did not understand the kind of commitment the god requires and the kind of help he is able to give. Perhaps this is what happened to the Nazis, who took (and perverted) what they wanted from the ancient tradition, sent those rune masters who did not agree with them to the concentration camps, and eventually perished in their own Ragnarök. That is the fate of all who try to bend the god to their own purposes and to use his magic for their own advantage instead of for the good of the world.

I believe that this is, finally, the secret of Odinic magic—its attraction, and also its terror. The story of Odin demonstrates the truth that those who would follow his path can hold back nothing, must be willing to sacrifice themselves for the sake of wisdom. This is Odin. This was the power—whether you want to call him the archetype of the Wise Old Man or a god—who had chosen me . . .

Knowing this, I faced him.

> The raven is sitting on one of the stones, watching me as a mother watches her child begin to walk. Am I willing to suffer what Odin may require? I fear him, but I understand him. The Runes speak to me. The culture from which he comes is the closest parent to my own.
>
> I know that if I refuse this, I'll lose her as well.
>
> The god looks at me. "Why have you come here? What do you want of me?"
>
> "I want to learn Northern magic—"
>
> He lifts his spear.

Through all the years of patient practice in meditation, visualization, and the rest, I had yearned for something unexpected and overpowering to happen to me. When it did, I was grateful for every discipline I had ever learned. My perception was that the spear stabbed through my solar plexus and with it came a great flood of light. Physical tremors surged through my body. I lay twitching and whimpering, almost beyond thought, consciousness clinging to the steady beat of the drum.

When the drum speeded up to bring us back to the world of sensory reality, it was a battle to return. I managed to control the rhythm of my breathing and used it to calm and relax my body. When I was able to open my eyes, I had to spend more time grounding before I could walk well enough to go get some food. A turkey-and-cheese sandwich completed the process of linking spirit and body again.

ଚତ୍ୟତତ

Since then, I have found other people who have encountered Odin's spear, some stabbed in the solar plexus and some through the heart. What I didn't expect was that once installed in my head, the god would stay there. He does not object to my contacts with other gods; indeed, through me, he seems eager to meet them, but he is my *fulltrui,* the fully trusted one, with whom (or perhaps I should say *for* whom) I have now worked for thirty years.

What do I mean when I say that I work with a god? Today the word has a variety of meanings, some of them mutually exclusive. In Christian theology, *God* with a capital G is a supernal being who is *omni*-everything. For an excellent discussion of the problems with traditional monotheism, see *A World Full of Gods* by John Michael Greer. Any human words we can use to talk about this Being inevitably limit it. Except when we are in a highly altered and abstract state of consciousness, connection with the divine requires us to filter our perception through a concept of personhood that we can understand. The polytheist solution to this problem is to subdivide divinity into separate gods.

Thus, Odin, despite the magnificence of some of his titles, is not all-powerful. He knows more, and differently, than we do, but he is not omniscient. When he speaks through seers in trance, it is clear that he has his own opinions and agenda. His true nature may extend into dimensions we can scarcely imagine, but for useful contact to take place, that immensity must be channeled through our human perceptions. We experience him as a person.

There are certain questions that get discussed late at night around the fire at Pagan festivals. One of them is whether the gods create us or we create them. Most people seem to feel that the answer is "yes." Odin and his companions may not have literally shaped humans out of logs of wood, but I believe that divine energies "created" us by influencing physical matter to evolve and grow. At the same time, our changing cultures provide us with images through which to express the ways in which we perceive the divine. We associate the image of an older man with a gray beard with wisdom, so when we try to visualize the god of wisdom, that is how he appears.

A related question is whether the gods are *immanent,* located within us and our world, or *transcendent,* having their being in a dimension beyond ours. The answer to this question is "yes," as well. They are "out there," in the sense that we move into an altered state of consciousness to contact them, but we also sense their presence within.

We humans cannot even fully know one another, so how can we expect to fully understand a god? In the discussions that follow, remember that what we are talking about is neither the totality of the divine energy nor even the entire part of it that is Odin, but rather the aspects of his nature that serve his purposes and meet our needs.

∾⬠∾⬠∾⬠

This book does not aim to be the definitive scholarly analysis of Odin. For that, you should go to the work of scholars such as H. M. Chadwick, Jan DeVries, Karl Hauck, or, more recently, Neil Price's *The Viking Way* and Stephan Grundy's *The Cult of Odin*. I will, however, try to include enough background to put you on a solid footing regarding his nature and function. We call Heathenry "the religion with homework" for a reason. You may want to pick up copies of the Eddas so you can look up the references and read further. I recommend Andy Orchard's translation of the *Poetic Edda* and Anthony Faulkes's translation of the Prose (titled simply *Edda*) for clarity. For more depth, explore the other sources in the bibliography.

You can, of course, simply read this book straight through. But reading only speaks to a part of the psyche. To understand Odin in your heart and soul, you need to seek him in the world and to open the doors of your spirit through spiritual practice. If you choose to go deeper, skim through to the end, then return to the beginning and work your way through the chapters, one per month. At the end of each chapter, you will find suggestions for things you can do. A selection of songs and rituals are included in the appendices.

Approach these chapters as an introduction to Odin's nature and the ways in which he acts in our world, both in the lore, the primary sources from the past, and through the testimony of those who work with him today. Inevitably, a great deal of the content is from my own perspective. But over the years, I have met many others who have encountered Odin, and they have allowed me to share some of their experiences.

A term that has become popular in the contemporary Heathen community is "UPG"—"unsupported personal gnosis"—which refers to insights and opinions derived from meditation, dream, or logic for which there is no explicit evidence in the lore. If other people independently come up with the same idea, it may acquire the status of a "community gnosis," and if after several centuries it becomes generally accepted, it might even qualify as lore. Scholarly conclusions drawn from old texts and archaeology provide a valuable baseline from which to evaluate contemporary inspiration, but Odin is a living Power, and we can also learn from those who encounter him today. As long as we distinguish clearly between these kinds of knowledge, both have value.

As we shall see, no single view of this god is entirely wrong—or right. Odin is complicated. The aspect you encounter will depend on your background and perceptions, what you are looking for, and what you, or the god, thinks you need.

In kindness to the reader, I have dropped the nominative endings of Old Norse words, giving us Frey instead of *Freyr*. I have also used modern English spellings, thus instead of *Óðinn*, we see Odin. The Norse letter ð, "edh," is represented by "dh." The letter "thorn," þ, by "th." In pronouncing the name of the god, the "o" sound should be somewhat drawn out—"aow," and the "dh" in the second syllable pronounced as a hard "th" sound, as in "*th*em," clipping the name off short after the final "n."

Odin and Odinism:

From time to time the media mentions "Odinism," often, unfortunately, in connection with a crime. This term for Heathen religion is popular in prisons and groups that require European ancestry. This attitude is not shared by all in Heathenry. In the lore, Odin insists that the other gods also be honored, and I have met people from all races and genders who clearly have strong and productive relationships with this god.

King Gylfi Visits the hall of hár

This is an excerpt from a play I wrote based on *Gylfaginning*, presented by Hrafnar kindred at PantheaCon in 2009.

The room is arranged theater style. In front, three seats of varying height have been arranged, one above the other. Three cloaked figures are sitting there. Gylfi (a king disguised as a poor traveler) knocks on the door frame.

Steward: Who's there? *(she pulls open the door)*

Gylfi: My name's, um, Gangleri. I've come a long way.

Can you give me a lodging for the night?

Steward: I suppose we can do that. There's room and to spare in this hall.

Gylfi: *(comes into the room to stand before the three figures, sitting one above another on stacked chairs)*

I believe you. I see people eating and drinking,

Playing games and fighting with swords.

There's a little of everything here.

Who's the master of this hall?

Steward: I can take you to him and you can see for yourself.

Gylfi: *(aside)* I'd better look sharp. Like the old verse says,

When you go through a door

Look round with care,

Don't know what foes

Wait for you there.

Gylfi: *(looks at the figures and whispers to steward)* Who are they?

Steward: The one on the lowest throne is called Hár, the High One. He's a king. The next is Jafnhár, Just-as-High. He's a king as well.

Gylfi: And the third?

Steward: Is the Third, Thridhi. He's—

Gylfi: I can guess, he's a king too.

Hár: Now that you know who we are, do you need anything else? If not, sit down and have some food . . .

Gylfi: Well actually, I do have a few questions. Is there a well-informed man in this hall?

Hár: *(laughs)* Unless you're even better informed, you won't leave this hall alive.

While you ask, stand forward please,

The answerer shall sit at ease.

So—what would you like to know?

Fig. 1: Ritual banner depicting Odin, embroidered by Diana Paxson

CHAPTER ONE

Will the Real Odin Stand Up, Please?

High One, Just as High and Third

These are his names as we have heard,

Wide of Wisdom counsel gives,

Odin, Oski, Omi lives,

We call on Wodan, Vili, Vé,

to All-father, Sigfather, Gandfather pray.

—"Namechant," by Diana L. Paxson

The man was in a blue cloak, and called himself Grimnir (the masked, or hidden one); he said nothing else about himself, though he was asked.

—*Grimnismál,* prologue

Those who have grown up with the straightforward definitions of gods that you find in Dungeons and Dragons manuals may find themselves frustrated when they try to explain Odin, who is "the god of . . ." a lot of things. One place to start is by looking at the names and titles he has been given over the years. The "Namechant" quoted above gives a few of them (for the music, see appendix 2 at the end of this book).

In Neil Gaiman's *American Gods*, Shadow asks, "Who are you?" His companion offers "Mr. Wednesday," since it is his day. When Shadow insists on his "real" name, Mr. Wednesday answers, "Work for me long enough and well enough . . . and I may even tell you that" (Gaiman 2001, 22). For many who work with, or for, Odin, that is indeed the goal.

In "The Lay of Hárbard," Thor, worn out from fighting giants, arrives on the shore of a fjord and calls to the ferryman to come over and take him to the other side. Apparently he is too far away to realize that the man at the ferry is his father. Odin seems to be in a quixotic mood. When the exchange of pleasantries works its way around to introductions, the god replies, "I am called Hárbard, I seldom hide my name . . ." (*Hárbardhsljódh* 10).

This may be the only joke Odin makes in the entire body of the lore. The point, of course, is that Odin has more names than anyone else in Asgard, and never gives his own name when a byname will do. He is the ferryman Hárbard ("Hoar-Beard") when he teases his son at the shore. As the wanderer Vegtam, he conjures the seeress from her grave-mound to give him answers, and as Grímnir, the Hidden One, he withstands being "roasted" by King Geirrod. Still other epithets, bynames, and hypostases may be found elsewhere. In *The Viking Way*, Neil Price lists 204 names used for Odin in the lore.

Why does he have so many names? In the section of the Younger Edda called *Skáldskaparmál*, Snorri Sturlusson, writing for young poets, explains that in poetry you can call a thing by its name, substitute another word, or use a descriptive kenning. Given that kings needed praise poems to spread their fame, poets had to find a lot of terms for the patron of kings. The other reason, of course, is that Odin is interested in a great many things. Those who work with him today may refer to him as "the Old Man," or sometimes, "You bastard." How many names Odin really has ranks with his last words to Baldur as one of the great unanswerable questions in the lore.

Some years ago, my friend Lorrie Wood got a post from someone who was trying to understand the relationship between Odin's many aspects. This is how she replied:

> The aspects of Odin that are in one or another "name clump" may resonate more with me, and others with another, but none of them aren't Odin. The aspects of Lorrie that might be collected under the aspect of "lwood"—the parts of me that directly pertain to having been a systems administrator for fifteen years—have friends to whom that's the way they know me. The folk who know me as "Clewara," a community organizer for a certain poly-MMORPG gaming guild primary based in EVE Online, see a different side of me. Our enemies within that game see me and my alternate characters, which only means to them I'm a target, or I'm gathering reconnaissance on them because THEY are—well, we are to one another, ultimately. That's another group of folks who know me after that fashion. Both of those me's aren't the same me as the Lorrie who's been chugging along in service to the Troth for a decade and a half. That's another batch. The Lorrie that stands at Diana's side running Hrafnar isn't the same and hasn't the same friends as the foregoing either.
>
> They all intersect and overlap: the Linux administrator learned how to handle groups of people and both know how to do a good turn in desktop publishing and so on. They all gather data and see patterns and weave threads and tease sense from them and all that happy fun stuff. Those are all me!
>
> So how much less could Odin be Odin, whether I'm

calling him Vegtam or Valfodr? Those address the god in different places, but they're the same god. Who is the Far-Crier? Who is the Way-Tamer? Who is the Hooded One? Who is the Old Man? Who is Frost-Beard and Horsehair-Mustache and Fire-Eyed and Dead-Eyed? Who is Woe-Worker and Desired One?

Yes.

In this chapter, you will encounter a summary of Odin's names and history that will give you a context for the more detailed discussion of his major aspects in the chapters that follow.

Aliases and Aspects

The name by which we know Thor's father best is Óðinn, anglicized as "Odin." In Old English, he is Woden, in German, Wotan, or the archaic *Wodanaz*. The root word can be translated as "frenzy," "voice," "poetry," "vision," "excitation," or "mind." As you shall see in chapter 10, these terms derive from a state of mental exaltation that can indeed manifest as either inspiration or berserk fury. To me, the fervor of excitement one feels in the throes of creative achievement of any kind captures the essence of Odin's primary name.

In the earliest myths, Odin is accompanied by two other gods. We don't know much about his companions, and for this reason, scholars sometimes identify them as "hypostases" of Odin, or other "persons" sharing the same nature. In *Völuspá 4*, we learn that Midgard was made by the "sons of Bor," identified by Snorri Sturlusson in *Gylfaginning* 5 as Odin, Vili, and Vé. If one loosely translates these as "Mind," "Will," and "Holiness," they make up a useful creative trinity.

In verse 18, Odin, Hœnir, and Lódhur create the first humans from logs of wood found on the shore. Hœnir does appear elsewhere in the mythology. Lódhur is unknown, though some have speculated that this is another aspect of Loki. In the *Prose Edda*, Snorri Sturlusson offers us a more explicit trinity. When King Gylfi enters Valhall, he sees three thrones, one above the other, and is told that "the one that sat in the lowest throne was king and was called High, next to him the one called *Jafnhár* (Just-as-high), and the one sitting at the top was called *Thridhi* (Third)" (Sturlusson 1987, *Gylfaginning* 2). Given that the "words of the High One" (*Hávamál*) are ascribed to Odin, it is pretty clear that Jafnhár and Thridhi can be identified as Odin as well.

But three names don't begin to cover Odin's multiplicity of roles. After roasting in silence for nine nights between King Geirrod's fires (*Grimnismál*), Odin responds to receiving a horn of beer from the king's son with fifty stanzas of lore, in the final section of which he gives fifty-four names by which he has been known during various adventures. He was *Grimnir*, the masked, or concealed one, when he came in disguise to Geirrod's hall, but when he leaves, he is *Ódhinn*, "best of gods."

Elsewhere in the lore, other names appear. Each one tells us something about the god. Drawing from all sources, we see Odin in many roles—the great sovereign and creator, the master of magic, the winner of the runes, the god of destruction and frenzy, the god of ecstasy, the god who loves women, who speaks to the dead, and gives defeat or victory.

Although he can take many forms, Odin's bynames give us a pretty good idea what people thought he looked like. When he wanders the world, he appears as a lean man wrapped in a blue or shaggy cloak, with a broad-brimmed hat pulled down over one eye, leaning on a staff that might also be a spear. His symbol is the Valknut.

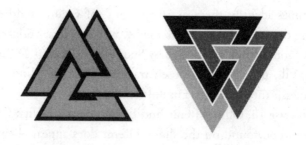

Fig. 2: Unicursal and tricursal interlaced Valknuts

Colors associated with him are black, gray, and blue, and his numbers are three or nine. If the hat comes off, we see him with an eye-patch, half-blind beneath the bristling brows, or if angered, with a blazing eye. Beard and moustache are long, and he is lean and pale. Generally, he appears as old, but in one reference (*Bárdharsaga Snaefellsáss* 18), his hair is still red, which would explain where Thor gets *his* ruddy hair.

We should also not be surprised that Odin also has names derived from the creatures with whom he is associated, *Bjorn*, the bear, and of course the ravens (*Hrafnagudh*). Surprisingly, we have no wolf names, unless *Hildolf* ("Battle-Wolf") should be counted here, instead of under his warrior epithets.

Odin through the Ages—Who Odin Is and How He Got That Way

Odin's names as we find them in the lore tell us a great deal about how he was seen at the end of the Viking Age. But gods, or our concept of them, evolve over time. For a more extensive discussion of Heathen history, see volume 1 of *Our Troth: History and Lore,* compiled by Kveldulf Gundarsson.

One question that is sometimes debated is whether Odin was part of the original Indo-European pantheon, migrated northward from the Middle East, or evolved from a god of death to become the god of kings. Lyonel Perabo (2015), a student of Scandinavian studies at the University of Iceland, characterizes Odin as a divine "vacuum cleaner" who sucked up the characteristics and powers of a number of other deities as he evolved.

Indo-European Origins

Nineteenth century scholars thought that the cult of Odin might have originated outside the Germanic area, among the Gauls or possibly on the Danube, and reached the north sometime between the 4th and 8th centuries CE (Common Era).

In the prologue to the Younger Edda, Snorri Sturlusson makes Odin a *descendant* of Thor who foresees that his destiny is in the north and migrates first to Germany and then to Sweden. Like other medieval historians who were inspired by Virgil's epic of the founding of Rome to link the legendary founders of their royal lines to Troy, Snorri says that Troy was the original home of the Æsir, and thus, the Aesir came from *Asia*. On the other hand, in the *Ynglingasaga* (2–5), he says that during Roman times, Odin led his people to Russia from somewhere east of the river Don, then to Germany, and finally to Scandinavia. Clearly, the present is not the first time that Europe has received an influx of immigrants from the east.

To find Odin's origins, how far back must we go?

Although the most likely explanation for Snorri's attempts to connect the Æsir with Troy is medieval literary fashion, it is tempting to see a possible source in folk memories of the migration of the Yamnaya culture from the steppes of the Caucasus and Urals into northern Europe four or five thousand years ago. A genetic survey reported in the June 2015 issue of *Nature* indicates that steppe herders whose background included Near Eastern elements moved west at this time (Callaway 2015). They joined with the hunter-gatherer and Middle Eastern farming populations that had arrived earlier to become the late-Neolithic Corded Ware people.

By the Bronze Age, a vital culture was flourishing in northern Germany and Scandinavia, enjoying vigorous trade with the eastern Mediterranean. These people spoke the Proto-Indo-European language, which diverged over time into the Baltic, Germanic, Italic, and Celtic language families. Other groups had moved east and south from the original homeland, carrying their language to Eastern Europe, the Mediterranean, and what are now Turkey, Armenia, India, and Iran.

What did these early Indo-Europeans believe? The French scholar Georges Dumézil is best known for his "tripartite" theory, the idea that just as Indo-European society was divided into three classes (preserved in the Hindu caste system and reflected in the Eddic poem *Rígsthula*, which tells how the god Heimdall established social classes), the gods of all Indo-European–descended cultures can be divided into three groups. We have the gods of physical well-being, who would include Frey, Njordh, and most of the goddesses; the gods of physical prowess, especially Thor; and the gods who maintain cosmic and juridical order, namely, Odin and Tyr

(Dumézil 1973). This idea has been vigorously criticized by more recent Heathen scholars, who point out that to lump all the Vanir into the third function seriously unbalances the pantheon, and, among other problems, ignores the importance of Frey as the patron of the Swedish Yngling kings.

However, Dumézil's analysis of Odin in relation to the deities of India is worth considering.

> The gift of shape-changing so characteristic of the former [Varuna] coincides with the *maya* that the latter employs so abundantly. The immediate and irresistible catch that Varuna makes, expressed by his lines and his knots, is also Odin's mode of action. On the battlefield he has the gift not only of blinding, deafening, and benumbing, but literally the gift of binding his enemy with an invisible line. (Dumézil 1973, 40)

Varuna is associated with the night, and the stars are the thousand eyes with which he sees all; however, as Indian religion evolved, he became a god of the sea, and the dead who are in his charge are those who drown. For Kris Kershaw (2000, ch. 11), it is Rudra, deadly leader of the Vedic equivalent of the *mannerbunde* who danced in animal skins over black clothing, who seems the closest analogue to Odin.

In *The Cult of Oðinn: God of Death?*, Stephan Grundy explores the possibility that Odin's original role may have been that of a god of death and the dead. Three major functions are ascribed to him in Old Norse literature—battle god, god of kingship, and god of magic and poetry. As a god of war, he does not actually take part in conflict, but rather (via his valkyries) is the chooser of the slain. His major battle skill is to demoralize the enemy. As a god of kingship, he connects the living ruler with his ancestors in the grave-mound. As a god of magic and poetry, he chants charms to speak with the dead and travels through the worlds. In later chapters, we will see more about all these skills.

Is Odin a shaman? Grundy and other critics of this theory point out that properly speaking, a "shaman" operates in a tribal cultural context quite different from the world of the Viking Age, much less our own. Certainly Odin's *other* functions argue for a very different identity. However, if we look at Odin's roles as a god of magic and battle, it is possible to see him at an earlier period as the shaman who migrated with the tribes, working magic to encourage their warriors and terrify their foes.

Odin and Rome

Most of our written information on the origins of Scandinavian culture comes from sources such as the Eddas, *The Lives of the Norse Kings* (*Heimskringla*) by Snorri Sturlusson, and the history of the Danes by Saxo Grammaticus, all written down in the 12th to 13th centuries. These sources begin with events from the Migrations Period (4th through 7th centuries), when many different Germanic tribes were moving south and west into Europe. We also have a few references in chronicles and inscriptions from the Roman Empire. Even at that date, there is evidence for what H. M. Chadwick calls "the crafty, magical, bardic side [of Odin] on the one hand, and the warlike side on the other" (Chadwick 1899, 29).

The Romans dealt with the abundance of deities they encountered as the Empire expanded by the *interpretatio Romana*—identifying the native gods as local forms of whatever Roman god they most resembled. Germans who served with the Roman army and the Romano-German population living along the border of Germania felt that the Roman equivalent of *Wodanaz* was the Roman Mercurius (who himself overlaps, but is not quite the same, as the Greek Hermes). Mercurius is associated with travel, commerce, and communication and was also a psychopomp who conducted the souls of the dead to the Otherworld. In Cologne, the cathedral was built on the ruins of a Roman temple to Mercurius Augustus. The temple was erected to honor the Emperor Titus, but if I were trying to describe Odin's role as a god of kings in Roman terms, this aspect of Mercurius is the name I would use.

According to Tacitus, a Roman historian who collected information from officers who had served in Germania, the chief god of the

Germans was "Mercurius" (Tacitus 1964, *Germania* 9), who was given human sacrifices. The Greek Hermes and the Roman Mercurius are gods of communication, guides for the dead, magicians, and tricksters—categories that certainly apply to Odin. However, Hermes generally facilitates, rather than originating, action. The messages he carries are those of Zeus and other gods, not his own, whereas Odin speaks to the dead and sometimes is responsible for their deaths rather than serving as a guide. Mercurius and Hermes come closer to Odin in his aspect as Hermes Trismegistus, who in the Hellenistic period was master of esoteric wisdom, though Hermetic magic tends to be far more ceremonial than the skills attributed to Odin in the *Ynglingasaga*. Finally, the tricks played by Odin have a deeper purpose, and often a deadlier result, than the relatively innocent pranks ascribed to Hermes.

My own explorations have led me to speculate on links between Odin and the deities Apollo and Lugos. His Irish incarnation, Lugh Samildanach, is good at everything. In his Gaulish form, Lugos sent ravens to guide his people to found the city of Lugdunensis (Lyons). I am not the only one to have noted these similarities. In *The Quest for Merlin*, Nikolai Tolstoy proposes that Merlin may have been a priest of Lugh/ Odin. Before acquiring his associations with the sun, Apollo was a god of poetry and healing. A plate found at Delphi shows him accompanied by a crow. But Apollo also has a dark side in which he runs with the wolves and shoots plague arrows with his silver bow. He and Odin are not the same god, but I suspect that they sometimes hang out in the same bar.

Another deity who is sometimes linked with Odin is the Irish battle and crow-goddess, the Morrigan. According to author Morgan Daimler, who has worked with the Morrigan for many years, they have a lot in common.

> Although it's fairly popular to equate the Morrigan to the Valkyries, I find that a bit of an unequal comparison myself and feel that it makes more sense to compare her to the Valfather than to those who are known to serve him. The two deities have a variety of things in common including a tendency in mythology to interfere directly in human affairs and a reputation in modern paganism

to be active among their followers. Both the Morrigan and Odin are known to sway the outcome of battles in favor of those they want to win and are associated with the dead. Both are also associated with prophecy and strategy, and both are known for appearing in disguise or presenting themselves to people in stories as someone else. And of course Odin and the Morrigan are both strongly associated with magic of various kinds. They are not, however, identical, as the Morrigan is not known to wander as Odin does nor is she striving to gain wisdom or to prevent any battles, such as Ragnarok. I've always thought the two Gods would probably get along well enough and enjoy sharing a drink, when they weren't enjoying fighting and trying to outwit each other.

By the time the migrating Germanic tribes encountered the Romans, Wodan was well established. In his *Annales* (13:57), Tacitus, writing in the first century, tells of a war fought between the Hermunduri and the Chatti for possession of a sacred salt river. The victorious Hermunduri then sacrificed the entire beaten side, with all their arms and possessions, to "Mars and Mercury' that is, Tiwaz and Wodanaz. This suggests that Odin and Tyr played complementary roles in warfare. The origin story of the Lombards, recounted by Jordanes in the 6th century, portrays Godan (Wodan) in a more kingly role, tricked by his wife into giving the tribe both victory and a name.

The God of Skjalds and Kings

Whatever his origins, by the Viking Age, Odin appears as the leader of the Æsir, patron of poets and kings. Until the conversion to Christianity was complete and the task of reporting history taken over by monkish chroniclers, it was the poets who recorded the deeds of the kings and heroes. The livelihood of the skjalds and the fame of the king were equally dependent on that relationship. We should not be surprised by the number of battle names recorded for Odin—the kings made offerings to him for victory, but there are only so many ways to describe a battle—the poets were probably asking the god for more words.

In the Younger Edda, Snorri Sturlusson introduces Odin as All-father. Nonetheless, a few paragraphs later, we are given a list of additional names for the god, indicating that, despite the propaganda, his other aspects were still known. Bynames such as *Vidrir* ("Weather god") and *Thund* ("Thunder") link him to the wind and storms; names such as *Hagvirk* ("Skillful Worker") and *Thrór* ("Thrive") give him an even broader sphere. Even though Odin received sacrifice mostly from Norse nobility and kings, he is not a sovereign in the medieval sense of the word. Indeed, our image of Odin as "king of the Norse gods" seems to owe more to later writers brought up on classical mythology than it does to the Eddas.

Odin Goes Underground

Iceland was the last of the Scandinavian countries to convert to Christianity. Odin was remembered in the sagas set in earlier times, but he was no longer worshipped. He did survive in folklore, especially in stories of the Wild Hunt, about which we see more in chapter 8. Grimm records some tantalizing traditions from Germany, in which the last sheaf in the wheat harvest might be left out for Odin's horse. There is also the curious appearance in the 13th century of *Wunsch*, or "Wish" (about whom there is more in chapter 5), personified as a powerful creative being who sounds a lot like Wodan (Grimm 1966, I:138).

Was Odin gone? My belief is that for a time he went underground, wandering the world in disguise throughout the Renaissance and Enlightenment, inspiring new ways of thought and invention.

The Return of the Wanderer

In England, the publication in 1770 of Thomas Percy's *Five Pieces of Runic Poetry* and *Northern Antiquities* reintroduced Odin to a changing world. As the 18th century gave way to the 19th, the rationalism derived from the philosophy of classical Greece was replaced by a new romantic nationalism that drew on European folklore. The Brothers Grimm collected fairy tales, and Jacob Grimm produced his monumental collection of German folklore, *Teutonic Mythology*. For inspiration, writers, artists, and musicians mined the legends of their lands. Interest spread even to the United States, where Henry Wadsworth Longfellow wrote several poems based on incidents in *Heimskringla*.

In England, the men who founded the British Empire sought inspiration in the North. In *The Vikings and the Victorians,* Andrew Wawn suggests that it was the Victorian interpretation of the old lore that shaped the way we see the Vikings today. A bookshelf full of works on Odin debated wheather he was

> a mighty Scythian leader who had once challenged the tyranny of Rome, and who could now act as a role model for upwardly mobile Victorian young achievers? Or was he a uniquely gifted member of a primitive society invested by his awestruck fellows with supernatural authority? Or was he part of a primeval nature myth transmitted by oral tradition? Or could his presence be found in contemporary folklore in rural Britain? (Wawn 2000, 5)

They may have found support for the first theory in a classical story that a "tribe from the Sea of Azov, allied with Mithradates, carried on his dream of one day invading Italy. Led by their chieftain Odin, this tribe was said to have escaped Roman rule after Pompey's victory by migrating to northern Europe and Scandinavia" (Mayer 2010, 360).

At first, like Snorri Sturlusson, the scholars followed the Greek philosopher Euhemerus in interpreting gods as deified men. In "The Hero as Divinity," a lecture given in 1840, Thomas Carlyle, who saw mythology as personification of the workings of nature, focused on Odin as a man remembered as a god:

> Wheresoever a thinker appeared, there in the thing he thought was a contribution, accession, a change or revolution made. Alas, the grandest "revolution" of all, the one made by the man Odin himself, is not this, too, sunk for us like the rest! Of Odin what history? Strange rather to reflect that he *had* a history! That this Odin, in his wild Norse vesture, with his wild beard and eyes, his rude Norse speech and ways, was a man like us, with our sorrows, joys, with our limbs, features—intrinsically all one as we, and did such a work! But the work, much of it, has perished; the worker, all to the name. "Wednesday", men will say tomorrow, Odin's day! Of Odin there exists no history, no document of it, no guess about it worth repeating. (Carlyle 1840)

Northern mythology was new and exciting, but the people who read it had been educated in the classical tradition, and it was natural for them to see Odin, or Wotan, as a northern equivalent of Zeus. It was Richard Wagner, abandoning the Italian models that dominated the opera of his day, who repopularized German mythology on an international scale with *The Ring of the Nibelungs*, an epic four-part retelling of the legend of Siegfried and Brunhild, creating, or perhaps discovering, a new incarnation of the god.

In *Das Rheingold*, the first opera in the *Ring* cycle, Wotan is a young warrior/king, already fond of women and wandering but driven most by a lust for knowledge, which leads him first to capture the Ring of Power and then to give it up. In *Die Walküre*, the second opera, he is the All-father, trapped in the conflict between Will and Love and seeking a way around the laws that he himself has made. In *Siegfried*, the third opera, and the one with the most explicit borrowings from the Eddas, he appears as "the Wanderer," who tempts and manipulates the other characters rather than intervening directly. By

Götterdammerung, the last opera in the cycle (in which he does not directly appear), Wotan is bound by the fate he has laid down and can only wait, hoping that his offspring will end the old world so that a new one can be born.

Myths have a wonderful capacity to adapt to changing cultures. Wagner, sensing the potential hazards of the forces unleashed by the Industrial Revolution, made the "ring" a key to boundless wealth and power and Wotan a tragic figure struggling with the problem of how to use it. Wagner's operas occupy a unique position in music today, and some of Odin's divine nature still shines through. In a radio interview, I have heard a Wagnerian singer describing performing the *Ring* as a "religious experience."

This romantic nationalism continued into the early 20th century, especially in Germany, where, as Jung observes in his essay, "Wotan," "What is more than curious—indeed, piquant to a degree—is that an ancient god of storm and frenzy, the long quiescent Wotan, should awake, like an extinct volcano, to new activity, in a civilized country that had long been supposed to have outgrown the Middle Ages" (Jung 1936).

In the early 20th century, young people wandered through the forests and revived Pagan ceremonies. By the 1930s, however, they were marching for the Nazis. Jung saw Wotan as the Wild Huntsman, a fury that was sweeping the Christian culture of Germany away. Writing before World War II, he could not imagine the horrors to which the *furor teutonicus* would lead; however, he clearly identified the power of those aspects of the god that bring madness and destruction, about which I have more to say in chapters 8 and 9.

Who Was That Masked Man? Odin Today

During and after the First and Second World Wars, many German-Americans anglicized their names, and Scandinavian newspapers and cultural organizations closed. After the Second World War, it was decades before Wagner's *Ring* operas became acceptable once more.

Even today, the swastika, an ancient sun symbol found all over the world, cannot be used.

Ralph Metzner, who grew up in Germany during the Second World War, "had an almost visceral revulsion against any belief system even remotely associated with the Nazis' genocidal ideology" (Metzner 1994, 4). In *The Well of Remembrance,* he describes his struggle to reconnect with Germanic mythology. As he began to explore, it seemed to him that

> the entire trajectory of European culture, with its relentless pursuit of knowledge in many forms, seems in some way related to the figure of this wandering god, his Greek counterpart Hermes, and such legendary wizard figures as Faust and Merlin. Strangely, the Odin myth seemed to describe many aspects of my own life-path, my continuing interest in exploring nonordinary realms of consciousness, triggered by my first psychedelic experience in 1961, as well as my continuing fascination with cross-cultural studies of religion, mythology and shamanism. (Metzner 1994, 10)

For many, *The Lord of the Rings* by J. R. R. Tolkien, a Rawlinson and Bosworth Professor of Anglo-Saxon at Oxford University, was their first exposure to Germanic culture. Originally appearing during the mid-fifties, the trilogy became a worldwide sensation in 1965, when Don Wollheim published the first paperback editions. I first encountered the books in 1963 when they were recommended to me by my mentor Dr. Elizabeth Pope, head of the Mills College English department. At that time, fans were dedicated but few, and having read the books admitted you to a select society, populated by medievalists and science fiction/ fantasy fans. But by the end of the 1960s, posters advertising Middle Earth were on dorm room walls, and high school students were learning to write in runes.

By the time *The Lord of the Rings* had become a cultural icon and Metzner was beginning to explore consciousness, old memories were fading. Change was, one might say, in the wind, and one of the things that suddenly seemed possible was worshipping the old gods once more. A "church of Odin" had been founded in Australia before World War II. It was reestablished in England in the early '70s, and in 1980, it was renamed the "Odinic Rite."

Else Christiansen started the Odinist Fellowship in 1969. A lot of her work was done with people in prison, which I discuss at more length in chapters 7 and 9. In 1973, Sveinbjörn Beinteinsson petitioned the Icelandic Parliament for recognition of Ásatru as a legitimate religion. Since then, it has flourished in Iceland, where, as of 2015, the Ásatruarfelagid had 2,700 members (in a population of 370,000) and is now building a national temple.

In the United States, an early group was the Asatru Free Assembly (AFA), founded by Steve McNallen. It foundered for lack of support, though it has since reorganized as the Asatru Folk Assembly and is now specifically limited to people of European ancestry. In 1987, former members of the AFA started two new groups, the Asatru Alliance (a federation of kindreds for people of European ancestry) and the Troth (which is open to all who are called by the Germanic gods). For a more complete account of all these developments, see chapter 7 of *Our Troth: History and Lore*. The Troth is the organization to which I have belonged since 1992, and I am understandably prejudiced in its favor. If you are looking for an inclusive organization that values both scholarship and inspiration, I recommend it. For information, see *www.thetroth.org*.

So what role is Odin playing in the 21st century? In the chapters that follow, in addition to the testimony of the lore, you will find comments and accounts from people who are encountering him today.

Practice

1. Build an Altar

If you are hoping to develop a relationship with someone, a good first step is to find a place to meet. When the "someone" is a god, begin with an altar. In time, your altar for Odin may become quite elaborate, but start simply. A dark blue cloth, a candle, and a shot glass for offerings are enough to serve as a focus for meditation. If you want to do more, you can make a backdrop from a cardboard box in the form of a triptych, painted or covered with cloth. Find three images of the god online, print them, and attach. This will also be useful as a traveling altar. However, be prepared to expand the space—if you continue to work with Odin, you will collect additional items, and your altar will grow.

Fig 3. Portable altar for Odin

2. Collect a library

Odin may be a god of inspiration, but he is also a master of lore. Your altar should be balanced by a bookshelf. If followers of the Abrahamic religions are the "people of the Book," Heathens are "the people of the Library." For starters, I suggest:

H. R. Ellis Davidson, *Gods and Myths of Northern Europe,* Penguin, 1965 (reissued as *Gods and Myths of the Viking Age,* Crown, 1982). This is a classic work that provides a good general introduction to Old Norse culture and mythology. Used copies are readily available.

Neil Gaiman, *Norse Mythology,* Barnes & Noble, 2017. A new and sometimes irreverent retelling of the basic myths.

John Lindow, *Norse Mythology,* Oxford University Press, 2001. An accessible, dependable source to help you keep track of who's who.

Andy Orchard (trans.), *The Elder Edda: A Book of Viking Lore,* Penguin Classics, 2011. These are the great poems that are the basis of Norse mythology.

Snorri Sturlusson (Anthony Faulkes, trans.), *Edda,* J. M. Dent & Sons, 1987. This is a complete, relatively recent translation of the *Younger,* or *Prose Edda,* a 13th-century compendium of stories about the gods intended as a sourcebook for poets.

If you want to find out more about Heathen religion, try *Our Troth: History and Lore* and *Our Troth: Living the Troth,* by Kveldulf Gundarsson (available from *Lulu.com* or Amazon) or, for a more introductory account, my own *Essential Asatru* (Citadel, 2009).

Contemporary writers are telling new Odin stories of their own. For tales of how the gods may appear today, see:

Steve Abell, *Days in Midgard: A Thousand Years On,* Outskirts Press, 2008.

Laure Gunlod Lynch, *Odhroerir, Nine Devotional Tales of Odin's Journeys,* Wild Hunt Press, 2005.

John T. Mainer, *They Walk with Us,* The Troth (*Lulu.com*), 2015.

"WANDERER"

Who is this who walks the roads,
An old man, tall and grey?
One of his eyes is gone,
The other looks far away.
He's leaning on a walking-stick,
It's very long, it's very thick,
His steps are slow, his eye is quick,
On this cold, foggy day.

Always be kind to travelers,
Wandering near and far,
Always be kind to travelers,
You don't know who they are . . .

The old man knocking at the door
Asks if you'll be kind,
Two crows in the sky,
Circle close behind.
Give him a cup of what you've got,
Beer that's cold or coffee hot,
A bowl of stew if you've a pot,
Whatever you can find.

Always be kind to travelers,

Wandering near and far,

Always be kind to travelers,

You don't know who they are . . .

Patterns always weaving

More than you can see,

The courage, wit and kindness,

Strength and honesty,

Can weave the pattern round you

Better than you know,

Take the old man's blessing

That he'll give before he'll go.

Who was that gone down the road?

You never got his name.

He never said where he's bound

Or said from where he came.

What comes after, who can tell?

Earthly heaven, earthly hell?

But did ye treat him ill or well

Then you will reap the same.

Always be kind to travelers,

Wandering near and far,

Always be kind to travelers,

You don't know who they are . . .

—Leslie Fish, *Avalon Is Risen* (Prometheus Music,
2012)

Fig. 4, "Vegtam"

chapter two

The Wanderer

Wide have I wandered, dared many deeds,

Striven in strength against Powers . . .

—Vafþrúpnismál 3

Most names have been given to him as a result of the fact that with all the branches of languages in the world, each nation finds it necessary to adapt his name to their language for invocation and prayers for themselves, but some events giving rise to these names have taken place in his travels and have been made the subject of stories . . .

—Gylfaginning 22

As we've seen, Odin is a god of many names, and the hero, or sometimes the villain, of many tales. Books on Norse mythology usually identify him as the ruler of Asgard, but when you look at the lore, it's clear that if Odin were a full-time executive, he would never have time for all the traveling he does. Sometimes we encounter him on the road, sometimes he comes to our door. Whether we seek his guidance on our own journeys or welcome him to our hearts and our halls, we need to understand where he wanders—and why.

Many of Odin's journeys are recorded in the Eddas. When he exchanges insults with his son Thor in *Hárbardsljódh,* he says he has been in distant lands seducing witch women. In *Baldrsdraumr,* Odin saddles Sleipnir and fares down to the underworld to consult the Völva, whose burial mound stands by the eastern gate to Hel. With songs and spells he summons her, and despite her complaints, he compels her to tell him why his son Baldr is having bad dreams. When she asks his name, he calls himself *Vegtam* ("Way tamer"), son of *Valtam* ("Tamer of the slain") (*Baldrsdraumr* 6), simultaneously claiming power over travel and over the dead. His final question is apparently one too many. The seeress recognizes him as "Odin, oldest of gods" and predicts that the next time he sees her will be at Ragnarók.

In *Vafthrúthnismál,* he journeys to wager his head in a contest of wits and wisdom with the giant said to be the wisest of all, giving his name as *Gagnradh,* "Giver of good counsel." The giant, understanding the rules of hospitality, offers him a good seat and proposes a contest of riddles, but Odin insists on standing until he has answered the questions and thus won the first round. The god then questions Vafthrúthnir. When the giant has given twelve correct replies, the god continues with questions until he stumps the giant by asking what Odin whispered in the ear of his dead son as Baldr lay on the pyre. This—the great question of the lore—reveals his identity. The answer, however, is not revealed.

In the *Hervararsaga,* a man called *Gestumblindi* ("blind guest") sacrifices to Odin for help in a riddle game with King Heithrek. In answer, a man who looks exactly like him and also calls himself Gestumblindi takes his place in the contest. He wins by asking King Heithrek the same question that won against Vafthrúthnir. When the king tries to strike Odin with the cursed sword Tyrfing, Odin turns into a falcon and flies away.

When the last of the Germanic lands turned Christian, the god's statues were pulled down, his worship suppressed. But if Odin became a wanderer upon the roads of the world, it was not a defeat but an opportunity. Wotan appears as "the Wanderer" in the opera *Siegfried*. Despite the fact that Gandalf also has many names, it is as the wandering wizard that we best remember him.

Neil Gaiman's novel, *American Gods*, is the story of a road trip. In the book, Mr. Wednesday offers to Shadow, whom he has recruited as a sidekick, his own explanation of how gods get around.

> When the people came to America they brought us with them. They brought me, and Loki and Thor, Anansi and the Lion-God, Leprechauns and cluricans and Banshees, Kubera and Frau Holle and Ashtaroth, and they brought you. We rode here in their minds; and we took root. We traveled with the settlers to the new lands across the ocean. (Gaiman 2001, 123)

Although Mr. Wednesday's belief that the gods have been forgotten may have been true for a time, I do not believe it is so today. Wagner's operas kept Wotan in the public consciousness through the 20th century, and Gaiman's book and the TV series are contributing to Odin's resurgence today. Gods do change from time to time and place to place, but the more people study the lore, the more likely the god is to look like the Odin whom Shadow meets in the epilogue rather than like Mr. Wednesday.

Some years ago, I was interviewed by an Icelander whose first question was how we could practice a Scandinavian religion in California. I replied that we do it the same way the Norwegians did when they settled Iceland. We honor the spirits of the land where we live now, and we look at the lore to learn about the gods.

But they do not exist only in the lore. The gods travel in our minds, and not only when we are consciously thinking about them. I've met too many people who have encountered Odin quite spontaneously not to believe that gods also exist in another dimension of being, call it the Collective Unconscious or what you will, from which they can emerge to confront us when the time is right. As my friend Becky puts it:

> In that first year, the All-father showed me only a few of his faces—the Wanderer, the Wisdom-Seeker, the Trickster, and the benevolent All-father. Those faces spoke to parts deep inside that were safe and fascinating and that I wanted to be closer to. The Wanderer was the first to knock, and it was no accident that he felt like Gandalf of the stories. Gandalf could be terrible but never to his friends. Odin who wore Gandalf's hat at my door got around my fear and was invited in. Odin, Wanderer, matched so many of the figures from my well-loved stories, and so I answered the knock of the stranger with bed and board and stories exchanged. I knew well that courtesy was needed for the one who knocks and that he honors the gifts freely given, no matter how humble, so I could give hospitality safely.

> The Trickster has always whispered in my heart, and I have always smiled. Now when the trickster whispers, it is sometimes my voice. The All-father was much like the God of my childhood—all powerful, all knowing, all loving, and I never, ever feared him. He loved me and wanted the best for me. Starting there, I was able to pick apart what was Odin, what was Yahweh, and a child's dream of climbing into the lap of "god," held in perfect love and safety and interest and joy.

Journeying

Odin journeys to gain wisdom. When we ourselves travel, what are we looking for, and what can we learn? Life itself is a journey, and our travels from place to place no more than stops on the way. Odin can be a good guide to both physical and spiritual journeying.

This poem by James Moore-Hodur expresses one way in which we can participate in Odin's journeys.

> Óðinn is breath, The All-Father is the very air that fills
> your lungs. He is the wind. He is everywhere wandering
> like the breeze through the new autumn leaves.
>
> Óðinn wanders on . . .
>
> He is in the roaring scream! He is in the Galdr Chant.
> He is the speech among kinsmen. He walks among us as
> we are reflections of Yggdrasil itself.
>
> Óðinn wanders on . . .
>
> Breath connects all life. Breath makes peace. Breath
> makes love. Breath makes war. Breath sings a Rune's
> true song. Breath tells lies. Breath whispers secrets. The
> absence of breath brings death and destruction. Breath
> brings poetry to life. Breath connects us all.
>
> Óðinn wanders on . . .

When I begin a trip, I call on Odin as *Vegtam* the Way tamer, *Gagnradh* the giver of good counsel, and *Farmögnudhr* "Journey Power." If I'm traveling by car, I ask him to show the way, along with Heimdall to watch my back, and Thor and Tyr to guard the car on either side. Odin gets called again when I am trying to figure out the best way to get somewhere. He is also my best ally when communicating with the people I meet along the way.

We can learn also from the way Odin travels. Rather than appearing in full armored glory, he usually journeys in disguise. If we keep a low profile when on the road, we'll learn more. Nobody likes the tourist who complains his way across the world, refusing to adapt to local customs and cuisine. If you weren't ready to listen, why did you leave home?

And you may meet Odin on the road. There have been a number of sightings. My friend Amy "saw him driving down the interstate in a jeep one day. The wheel cover was wolves. I know it was him; he looked very much like I picture him." In a bar, another friend encountered a tall lanky man with a white beard and long hair, wearing a navy suit and a wide-brimmed hat. He had a long nose and clear eyes. The bar was loud and crowded. My friend bought the man a drink. He says the fellow thought he was crazy.

Julia wrote to tell me that

> I had an encounter with an Odin-like wanderer in January. I had just arrived in New Zealand and was visiting an island named Waiheke off the coast of Auckland. We were at the beach, and my husband was reading a book about Marx. A man with long white hair, a beard, and wearing a tie-dyed shirt and no shoes appeared out of nowhere, sat down, and started a conversation with us. He was extremely intelligent, and we had a fascinating conversation with him about globalism, Marxism, and environmentalism for about a half hour. Before he left he told us . . . that he was just staying on the beach for the night before moving on. He told us he had no home and was just a traveler who had recently lost his boat.
>
> After he left, I turned to my husband and told him that I thought we had just met a god. I had the sense that it was Odin, and my husband agreed with me. We were on the island for about another week and never saw him again. A very strange experience indeed. It almost seemed like he was welcoming us into the way of the wanderer.

Was that *really* Odin? Sometimes the encounter results in a life-changing realization. But other meetings are more in the nature of an omen—something you see or hear that is ordinary in itself but meaningful because of the significance you attach to it. When you travel, a word to Odin at the beginning of each day will sensitize you to events and images that deepen your understanding of the world.

Wandering through Midgard teaches us many things, but some of our most productive travels are those that lead within. In my book *Trance-Portation,* I wrote about the skills needed for inner journeying, in which one detaches the mind from the outer world to take the road east of the sun and west of the moon. One goal for such travel is for us, like Gylfi, to seek the High One in his own hall.

Close Encounters of the Thridhi Kind

Artists may be particularly open to Odinic influence, but sometimes the god appears in person. In addition to the chance encounters quoted above, there have been times when someone who looked like the god acted like him as well.

For instance, a friend of mine told me that some years before, she had been forced to leave Arizona and take a job as a receptionist in a Midwestern city. She had promised to come back, but somehow it never seemed to be the right time. One afternoon, a tall man with grizzled hair and beard came to see her boss. As he was leaving, he turned to her and asked, "Why are you still here?" in a tone that made it clear he was not referring to quitting time. In that moment, she saw him as Odin, and realized that she had been delaying too long. After that, things fell into place for her to go back to Arizona.

Another friend, on her way to check on the progress of a legal case, passed a well-dressed gentleman with an eye patch on the steps of the courthouse who gave her an approving smile. Inside, she learned that the decision on the case had been what she'd hoped for.

Odin is not the only god who appears in this way. When my husband has had car trouble, several times Hermes, in the form of a young red-haired man, has turned up in answer to his prayers. When such things happen, what is actually going on? In Homer's epics, the gods often take the forms of humans to give advice or otherwise move the plot along. It is only after the god or goddess disappears that the mortal realizes to whom he was talking. There are several possibilities. The human may have imagined it, the god may have actually taken human form, or—my favorite theory—the god has dropped in on an appropriate human and spoken through him.

The Greeks were not the only people to recognize the presence of a god only after he had gone. Take this example from the *History of Olav Trygvason* 71:

> It is related that once on a time King Olaf was at a feast at this Ogvaldsnes, and one eventide there came to him an old man very gifted in words, and with a broad-brimmed hat upon his head. He was one-eyed, and had something to tell of every land. He entered into conversation with the king; and as the king found much pleasure in the guest's speech, he asked him concerning many things, to which the guest gave good answers: and the king sat up late in the evening. Among other things, the king asked him if he knew who the Ogvald had been who had given his name both to the ness and to the house. The guest replied, that this Ogvald was a king, and a very valiant man, and that he made great sacrifices to a cow which he had with him wherever he went, and considered it good for his health to drink her milk. This same King Ogvald had a battle with a king called Varin, in which battle Ogvald fell. He was buried under a mound close to the house; "and there stands his stone over him, and close to it his cow also is laid." Such and many other things, and ancient events, the king inquired after. Now, when the king had sat late into the night, the bishop reminded him that it was time to go to bed, and the king did so. But after the king was undressed, and had

laid himself in bed, the guest sat upon the foot-stool before the bed, and still spoke long with the king; for after one tale was ended, he still wanted a new one. Then the bishop observed to the king, it was time to go to sleep, and the king did so; and the guest went out. Soon after the king awoke, asked for the guest, and ordered him to be called, but the guest was not to be found. The morning after, the king ordered his cook and cellar-master to be called, and asked if any strange person had been with them. They said, that as they were making ready the meat a man came to them, and observed that they were cooking very poor meat for the king's table; whereupon he gave them two thick and fat pieces of beef, which they boiled with the rest of the meat. Then the king ordered that all the meat should be thrown away, and said this man can be no other than the Odin whom the heathens have so long worshipped; and added, "but Odin shall not deceive us." (Sturluson 1844)

Welcoming the Wanderer

How do you know who's knocking at your door? This is the problem faced by the dwarf-smith Mime—not to be confused with Mimir who owns the mythic well that is discussed in later chapters—in the first act of Richard Wagner's opera *Siegfried*.

As the opera opens, Mime and the young and brash Siegfried are arguing because the dwarf has not been able to forge a sword that Siegfried cannot break. There is one sword that might serve—Nothung—but only if it can be repaired. This is the point at which a stranger in a ragged cloak and a broad hat appears at the door, leaning on a staff whose shrouded tip hides the fact that it is really a spear. He proclaims himself a way-weary guest seeking shelter and names himself "Wanderer."

Much I've sought for, and much I've learned.

I have made men wise and knowing,

Saving many from their sorrows,

Healing their wounded hearts.

Many believe that wisdom is theirs,

Yet most of all they lack what they most need.

When they ask me, seeking for knowledge,

Then I teach them my lore.

—Richard Wagner, *Siegfried*

Mime, however, insists that he knows all he needs, and, failing in hospitality, tries to send the Wanderer away. At this point, Wotan shifts to another of his identities, Gizurr (the Riddler). He wagers his head on a battle of wits. Following the pattern in *Vafthrúthnismál*, each player then asks three questions. Mime's questions are about the world and its inhabitants, which of course the Wanderer answers easily. Winning, he can now require Mime to wager his own head on another three. Mime is able to answer two of the Wanderer's questions, but the third fixes on the one problem he has been wrestling with since the beginning of the opera—how to reforge Nothung. Wotan points out that if he had used his opportunity to ask that question of his guest, he would know what he needed. He now owes his head to the Wanderer, who passes the forfeit to the person who will forge the sword, the man who has never known fear.

For most of us, however, the first image for a wandering wizard that comes to mind is that of Gandalf in *The Lord of the Rings.* Not too surprisingly, given that Tolkien was a professor of Anglo-Saxon literature at Oxford, the book, like the earlier *Hobbit,* is studded with gems from Germanic culture, especially in the portrayal of Gandalf, who "…wore a tall pointed blue hat, a long grey cloak, and a silver scarf. He had a long white beard and bushy eyebrows that stuck out beyond the brim of his hat." (Tolkien, 1954, 33). It reads like a portrait of Odin the Wanderer.

The name *Gand-alf* (Wand-elf) comes from the catalogue of dwarves in *Völuspá,* which also provided many of the dwarf names in *The Hobbit.* In the *Lord of the Rings,* the wizard grows in both physical and spiritual stature. To the elves, he is Mithrandir, the Pilgrim Grey. Among the other kindreds, he has still different names. After Gandalf is lost in Moria, Frodo's song of mourning lists his wanderings but also his ability to communicate with all beings and his skills as a warrior and healer. He is a lord of wisdom, a deadly fighter, and "an old man in a battered hat" who leans on a staff. Gandalf is not a name of Odin, but it's only a half-step from *Göndlir* (Wand-bearer), which is, and his characterization is unmistakably Odinic. If one has any doubt, having Gandalf arrive on a Wednesday and drink only red wine (like Odin in *Grimnismál* 19) at the dwarves' dinner should be a giveaway. When Bilbo opened the door to admit Gandalf to Bag End, for many readers he also admitted a reflection of the god.

In 1983, before I ever encountered Odin personally, I had already written about him in a book called *Brisingamen* in which he periodically possesses a biker-poet who lost an eye in Vietnam. Not too surprisingly, after I began to work with him, Odin began to turn up in my other novels as well. He is, of course, a major figure in the *Wodan's Children* trilogy, my own retelling of the story of Siegfried, Brunhild, and Gudrun, and a major force in *The Book of the Spear,* book two of my Arthurian tetrology, in which Merlin (whom Nikolai Tolstoy also considers a somewhat Odinic figure) ends up with Odin's spear.

Hosts and Guests

As Leslie Fish's song points out, you may not always recognize Odin when he comes to your door. When a traveler knocks, it is not enough to let him in. You must know how to offer hospitality. The first section of the Old Norse poem called the *Hávamál*—the sayings of the High One—is a manual of etiquette for both guest and host.

To the givers, hail! A guest has come.

Where shall he sit?

Anxious is he who by the fire

Must test his luck.

—*Hávamál* 2

This is followed by several stanzas detailing the heat, food, dry clothing, and wash water that will be needed by the newly arrived guest and thirty stanzas of instructions to the newcomer on how to behave while he is there, beginning with "Wits are needed by the one who travels far" (*Hávamál* 5) and ending with a warning not to outstay your welcome.

One of Odin's bynames is *Fjolnir*, variously translated as "Many Shaped," "Much Knowing," or "Concealer." *Grimnir*, the "Masked One," is another name Odin uses when traveling. The old lore offers examples of what can happen when you get hospitality wrong. The Eddic poem *Grimnismál* opens with an argument between Odin and his wife Frigg regarding which of the two brothers each of them favors as the better man. Frigg claims that Odin's protégé, King Geirrod, "is mean with food, and abuses his guests if he thinks too many have come." She challenges Odin to go see for himself, then warns the king that a dangerous sorcerer is around, who can be identified because no dog will attack him.

When Odin arrives, he gives his name as Grimnir and refuses to say another word, even when the king has him tied to a post between two roaring fires. Whether this was the first celebrity roast, I do not know. When this has gone on for nine days and nine nights, the king's son cannot stand the abuse of hospitality any longer. He unbinds the toasted guest and offers him a horn of ale. Grimnir's first response is to predict that the young man will be king. He then proclaims seventeen stanzas of lore, including a list of his names. By the time he is done, King Geirrod has managed to figure out who he is. The king leaps to his feet, trips, and falls on his sword, thus fulfilling the god's prophecy.

In "Völsa Þattr," a story found in the *Flateyjarbók*, "Grim" is the name given by King Olaf Digre and his companions when they come in disguise and more or less invite themselves to dinner at the home of a farmer in a remote district of Norway. As it happens, the family always begins the evening meal by passing around the room the phallus of a horse that has been preserved in herbs, invoking its fertile power. When the thing comes to King Olaf, he throws it to the dog, adding bad manners to the impiety of impersonating the god. He then throws off his gray cloak, reveals himself as the king, and requires that the family immediately become Christian. In the story, the king was the victor, but he eventually ticked off enough of his subjects for them to ally against him, and he was killed at the Battle of Stiklastader in 1030.

The relationship between host and guest is a complex one. According to the *Online Etymological Dictionary*, both words are descended from an original Indo-European term, **ghos-ti-*, meaning "someone with whom one has reciprocal duties of hospitality," representing "a mutual exchange relationship highly important to ancient Indo-European society."

As with so many things in Germanic culture, successful hospitality depends on an equality of exchange. Both host and guest are sacred. Once you have claimed the shelter of the hearth, your host is honor bound to defend you, even if you later prove to be an enemy. For either to turn against the other is a betrayal. Drawing on this tradition, in *Die Walküre*, Sigmund, having been welcomed at Hunding's hearth, is safe even when his host discovers that Sigmund has killed some of his kin.

The rune *Gebo*—X—means "Gift." Its equal lines express the importance of keeping the balance in an exchange. In *Hávamál* 42, we find the advice that a man should give gift for gift, laughter for laughter, and lies for lies. Even the generous appreciate gifts (39), but it is good to give gladly (48). Later (145) we are told, "A gift always looks for a gift." This also applies to hospitality and to our relationships with the gods.

We offer the gods praise and welcome them to our feasts. What do we get in return? Two more names of Odin—*Fjölsvidh*, "Wide of Wisdom," and *Svithur*, "Wise"—suggest one answer. For Odin, especially, the greatest reward is the exchange of knowledge. Casting that exchange in the form of questions adds the excitement of a contest. What can Odin learn from us? Our human experience, the things we have learned from living in a fleshly body in a physical world. What can we learn from him? To find an answer we must learn more of his names.

> Nine worlds there are upon the Tree,
>
> BEHOLD THE RAVENS FLY,
>
> Who knows the secrets of them all?
>
> THE WANDERER DRAWS NIGH.
>
> He knows the darkness and the light,
>
> The heavens and the sea,
>
> A HORN WE RAISE IN WELCOME TO
>
> THE GOD OF ECSTASY!
>
> —Diana L. Paxson, "God of Ecstasy"
>
> (for the rest of this song and the music, see appendix 2)

Practice

1. Reread the riddle game scene between Bilbo and Gollum from *The Hobbit*, or watch it in the Peter Jackson film. Bilbo is playing for his life. What is Gollum getting out of the game?

2. Make dinner for the god. Fill one plate for yourself and set the other before your Odin altar. There is general agreement that rare roast beef or ribs please him, or smoked salmon. I often cook asparagus spears with garlic—"spear-leek." If you have a dog, ask it to act as priest of Odin's wolves and clean the god's plate afterward. For drink, pour mead, whisky, or red wine.

3. As you walk downtown, pay attention to the homeless. Look out for people, signs, etc., that seem significant. Take nine quarters, or, if you can afford it, nine dollars, and give them to someone who asks for a handout.

4. Make a car charm and bless your car before going on a trip. The illustration shows the one I use. This charm is a bind rune in which three runes have been combined:

ᛗ – EHWAZ, the horse who carries you

ᚱ – RAIDHO, riding, the act of travel

ᛉ – ELHAZ, the Elk rune of protection

These god runes have been sketched on the back:

ᚠ – for Odin, to guide your wanderings

ᛗ – for Heimdall, father of men, to watch your back

ᛏ and ᚦ – Tyr and Thor on the sides to ward you from harm

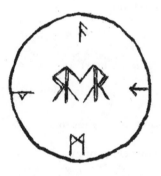

Fig. 5. A car charm

5. Write the story of your life as a journey.

6. Learn to spirit journey using the exercises in my book, *Trance-Portation*.

7. Do the First Night of the Nine Nights meditation.

You can do these meditations, inspired by the structure of a meditation for Loki in Dag Loptson's *Playing with Fire,* as you finish each chapter or on nine consecutive nights after you have completed the book.

Set up your Odin altar and make sure the room is secure. Light a grey candle and pour a little mead or whisky into a glass as an offering. Then say:

> Odin by these names I call you:
>
> *Gangrádh* (Journey Advisor)
>
> *Gangleri* (Wanderer)
>
> *Vegtam* (Way Tamer)
>
> *Farmögnudh* (Journey Power)
>
> *Farmatyr* (Cargo God)
>
> *Gestr* (Guest)
>
> *Gestumblindi* (Blind Guest)
>
>
> Grant me wisdom for my journeys,
>
> Wanderer, in your cloak of gray,
>
> Tame the obstacles before me,
>
> Give me strength by night and day.
>
> And when, returning from my travels
>
> I try to listen for your call,
>
> Help me see you in the stranger,
>
> A welcome guest within my hall.

Think about journeys you have made. Remember people and places and what you have learned. Let the wind off the moors sweep through you. Scent the forest and the sea. See the white road unrolling before you and leading at last to the home you love. Then sit in silence, opening your heart, and when you hear the knock at the door of your spirit, welcome in the god.

The Second Merseberg Charm

Phol ende uuodan uuorun zi holza.

du uuart demo balderes uolon sin uuoz birenkit.

thu biguol en sinthgunt, sunna era suister;

thu biguol en friia, uolla era suister;

thu biguol en uuodan, so he uuola conda:

sose benrenki, sose bluotrenki, sose lidirenki:

ben zi bena, bluot si bluoda,

lid zi geliden, sose gelimida sin!

Phol and Wodan were riding to the woods,

and the foot of Balder's foal was sprained

Then spake Sinthgunt, Sunna's sister,

Then spake Frija, Volla's sister,

Then spake Wodan, as well he knew:

So bone-sprain, so blood-sprain, so joint-sprain:

Bone to bone, blood to blood,

joints to joints, so may they be glued.

Fig. 6. Göndlir

chapter three

Master of Magic

Ljóð ek þau kann er kannat þjóðans kona

ok mannskis mögr . . .

Magic songs I know, not known by queens,

or any human . . .

—*Hávamál* 146

The second poem in the Elder Edda is called the *Hávamál*, the sayings of the "high one," a byname of Odin. It is a tantalizing mix of advice on manners and references to Odin's magic, but to learn what that magic is like, we must go elsewhere.

In *Ynglingasaga* 7, Snorri Sturlusson tells us that

> Odin could transform his shape: his body would lie as if dead, or asleep; but then he would be in the shape of

a fish, or worm, or bird, or beast, and be off in a twin-kling to distant lands upon his own or other people's business. With words alone he could quench fire, still the ocean in tempest, and turn the wind to any quarter he pleased. . . . Sometimes even he called the dead out of the earth, or set himself beside the burial-mounds; whence he was called the ghost-sovereign, and lord of the mounds. He had two ravens, to whom he had taught the speech of man; and they flew far and wide through the land, and brought him the news. In all such things he was pre-eminently wise. He taught all these *íþrótt* [arts] in Runes, and songs which are called galdrar. . . . Odin understood also the *íþrótt* [art] in which the great-est power is lodged, and which he himself practised; namely, what is called *seið* [magic]. By means of this he could know beforehand the predestined fate of men, or their not yet completed lot; and also bring on the death, ill-luck, or bad health of people, and take the strength or wit from one person and give it to another. But after such *fjolkynngi* [witchcraft], followed such *ergi* [weakness and anxiety], that it was not thought respectable for men to practise it; and therefore the *gydhjunum* [priestesses] were brought up in this art. (Sturluson 1844)

What are these "crafts" of which Odin is the master? One of his bynames is *Þhrótt*, usually translated as "strength" or "might." Here, the term *íþrótt* is translated as "art." I suggest that in this case, a more appropriate translation might be "powers." In the passage above, the magical terms are given in Old Norse, followed by the translation. As you can see, Old Norse had a much larger vocabulary for magical prac-tices than we do.

Odin's Magic Powers

Galdr

Galdr, which covers roughly the same kinds of skills as modern English words derived from the Latin root *cantare* (such as "enchantment" and "incantation"), is the type of magic most associated with Odin. This should be no surprise, given Odin's importance as a god of communication. He is the god who gave the gift of önd, the breath that is life, to the first humans, Ask and Embla (*Völuspá* 18). In the Anglo-Saxon Rune poem, the verse for the rune that survived in Scandinavia as the word *ás*, a god (especially Odin), became óss, sometimes translated as "mouth." I think we can assume that whatever kinds of magic Odin is performing, it will include sung or chanted spells.

The last part of *Hávamál* contains a list of these spells. I say a "list" because although Hár tells us what the charms *do*, he does not actually give us the spells. Of the eighteen, two refer to healing, four to battle, two to control of the elements, one to mind control, three are for protection, one for talking to the dead, and two for gaining knowledge. The last three are love spells.

There is a special poetic meter for spells, called *Galdralag* (Incantation Meter). To see what this looks like in English, go to the translation of the Elder Edda by Lee M. Hollander.

An example of galdralag from *Hattatal* (102) in the Younger Edda goes,

> *Sóttak fremd, sótta ek fund kinungs,*
>
> *Sóttak ítran iarl,*
>
> *Thá er ek reist—thá er ek renna gat—*
>
> *Kaldan straum kili—*
>
> *Kaldan siá kili.*

Honor I sought, sought to meet with a king,

Sought out a splendid jarl,

There where I cut there where I ran,

Through cold current with keel

Over the cold sea.

A major part of Odin's verbal magic involves the runes, which we'll look at in greater detail in chapter 4.

Healing

We may find the lack of actual spells in *Hávamál* frustrating, but even though one's first thought of Odin is not usually in connection with healing, we do have two spells in which he does just that. The Second Merseberg Spell is a charm for healing a horse, and it is the only surviving example in Old High German of a Heathen spell. It consists of a mythological setting and an incantation.

Christian versions, in which Wodan's role is played by Jesus, are found in later Scandinavian folklore, but the essence of the incantation is far older. A. G. Storms traces it to a Vedic charm dated to around 500 BCE (Storms 1949, 111). I have given the original and a fairly literal translation of the Second Merseberg Spell. A video of the spell sung in Old High German by Birgit Knorr may be found on YouTube at *https://www.youtube. com/watch?v=NjVRLcOjOGc.*

Here is another version that I have translated more freely.

Phol and Wodan rode to the wood,

Balder's foal has sprained its foot.

Sinthgunt, Sunna's sister, spoke

Frija, Volla's sister, invoked.

Then spoke Wodan as well he knew,

Bone sprain, blood sprain, joint sprain, too:

Bone to bone, blood to blood,

joints to joints, may they be glued.

I have used the spell myself for friends with broken bones, sprains, or wounds from surgery, focusing on the incantation and adding "flesh to flesh," "skin to skin," and any other body parts required.

One of the most interesting of the surviving Anglo-Saxon charms is called the "Nine Herbs Galdor," which lists the powers of mugwort, plantain, lambs-cress, cock's-spur-grass, chamomile, nettle, apple, chervil, and fennel to resist poison and infection. It is also the only spell in Storms's collection to mention a god. The spell concludes, "These nine have power against nine poisons. A worm [personified disease spirit] came crawling, it killed nothing, for Woden took nine glory-twigs. He smote then the adder that it flew apart into nine parts" (Storms 1949, #9). When the entire spell has been pronounced, the healer makes the herbs into a salve that is applied to the infected wound.

Seidh

Galdr, while important, is only one of the terms we encounter in discussions of Viking Age magic. As a more inclusive label, Neil Price of Uppsala University chooses *seidh* (pronounced "saythe"), which is the other category given in *Ynglingasaga* for Odin's magic.

> Again and again in the sources . . . we seem to find *seiðr* used *simultaneously* as a precise term and also as a generalization for "sorcery" in our modern sense of the word. In using seidr as a primary category, in a manner that implicitly includes the other magics, we would therefore seem to be following the fashion in which the Norse themselves understood the concept. (Price 2002, 66)

Seidh is a term that has attracted considerable attention in recent years, particularly as a label for knowing "of man's fate and of the future," via the oracular *spá* ritual described in the *Saga of Eric the Red* 4 and elsewhere in the sagas. This was the skill I was seeking to learn when I first got interested in Norse magic (described in my book *The Way of the Oracle*), although for a better understanding of the culture, I first studied the runes.

What *Völuspá* calls "sporting with souls" is essentially the same idea we find in Aleister Crowley's definition of magic—the art of causing changes in consciousness in conformity with will. References to seidh in the sagas may describe magic performed to achieve a positive end, such as attracting fish or foretelling the future, as well as for negative purposes. To perform operant magic (actions that are intended to affect the physical world), the magician must change his or her consciousness, and one of the most effective ways to do this is actually *galdr*, the use of songs or spells. Thus, it makes sense that Snorri should attribute both classes of magic to Odin, although (not too surprisingly, given that he was writing two hundred years after the Christian conversion) he seems to be a little unclear on the distinction between them.

Spá—the work of the seer or seeress—is only one of the kinds of magic Price includes under the heading of seidh. In his book, *The Viking Way*, he states, "More than anything else, *seið* seems to have been an extension of the mind and its faculties" (Price 2002, 64). In the story of the war between the Æsir and the Vanir, a mysterious figure called Heidh appears. In addition to her other skills, "by seið, she sported", or "played around with souls" (*Völuspá* 22). Not only does this stanza tell us something about the different kinds of Norse magic, it indicates that seidh was considered to be primarily a female practice and highly suspect, which makes it surprising that it should be ascribed to Odin. For more about this, see chapter 6, in which I discuss Odin's relations with women.

There are certainly many stories in the sagas about men who practice witchcraft, but as time went on, it became restricted to women, probably because men were expected to take physical rather than magical action against their foes. During the period when kings were attempting to force Norway to become a feudal Christian kingdom, it was the *men* who practiced magic who were persecuted, not the women. In the *History of Harald Hairfair 36* (Sturlason 1990, 70), a seidhmadhr (man who practices seidh) called Vitgeir objects when the king outlaws seidh, on the grounds that the king's own son, Ragnvald Rettlebone, is practicing magic in Hadeland with eighty companions. The king solves the problem by sending another son, Eric Blood-Axe, to deal with the situation, which Eric does by burning his brother and the other seidhmadhrs in their hall. Eric, by the way, was married to a woman called Gunnhild who had herself learned seidh from two Finns (probably Saami) and made trouble with her spells in the sagas of Njal and of Egil. Apparently it was all right for queens to know magic.

Males were still practicing seidh a generation or two later when the first King Olav tried to do the same thing to the seidhmadhrs in Tunsberg, including a grandson of Ragnvald called Eyvind Kelda (Sturluson 1990, *History of Olav Trygvason* 62–63, 165–166). Eyvind escaped and tried to overcome the king by magic, but was eventually captured and drowned. This pattern persisted into the witch-burning phase of the late Middle Ages, when, unlike the situation in the rest of Europe, in Scandinavia it was men rather than women who were usually accused.

In the sagas, Seidh practiced by men is more likely to be negative. In *Gislisaga* 18, a seidhmadhr is hired to work seidh "that there should be no help for the man who had killed Thorgrim, however much men might want to give it to him, and there should be no rest for him in the country." In *Laxdaelasaga* 35, Kotkel and his sons build a seidh scaffold and work weather magic against Thorold. A storm comes up and he is drowned.

At the end of the description of Odin's magic in *Ynglingasaga*, Snorri explains that at one time, this kind of magic was practiced by both genders, but it eventually was considered so *ergi*, or "unmanly," that it was restricted to women. The term *ergi* is a complex one, with meanings ranging from "sexually receptive" to "cowardly" or "sneaky," all of which seem to have evolved as Norse gender roles became increasingly polarized. Some years ago, I attempted to analyze the relationship in an essay published in *Idunna* 31 called "Sex, Status and Seið: Homosexuality and Germanic Religion" (available online at *www.seidh.org*).

In her article, "Regardless of Sex: Men, Women and Power in Early Northern Europe," Carol J. Clover demonstrates that when there is a conflict situation in the sagas, the important distinction is not between the male and female sexes but between the roles of *hvatr*, someone who takes physical action, and *blaudr*, which may refer to a woman or an old man or a person of any gender who cannot take up a sword and deal with the matter directly (Clover 1993, 2). As you shall see when we look at Odin as a battle god, his role in a military situation usually involves strategy or magic rather than combat.

Gand

Seið and Galdr are not the only kinds of magic mentioned in the passage from *Ynglingasaga*. In Old Norse, the term *gand* refers to anything enchanted, in particular magical items used by sorcerers, and by extension to magic. In the Old Norse dictionary, Cleasby and Vigfusson define a *gandr* as an object that has been bewitched. It occurs in a variety of compound terms, such as the *gand-reid*, or witches' ride. It can also mean a spirit-being and can take the form of a wolf. Price sees it as "a general kind of sorcerous energy from which all power was drawn" (2002, 66). It is probably in this sense that the word is used in the *Völuspá* 22 description of Gullveig/Heidh. Orchard translates *"vitti hon ganda"* as "the skill of wands."

By the later Middle Ages, the word "gand" had come to mean a magical wand or staff. Price (2002, 87) cites a study by Clive Tolley, who points out that a derivative of *gandr* is the word *göndull*, which seems to refer to a staff, possibly used to summon or direct the *gand* spirits. As it happens, another of Odin's names is *Göndlir*, which by this reasoning would mean "staff-bearer." Another byname, *Sveigðir* means "cane (or wand?)-bringer." Price also quotes a spell collected during a 14th century Norwegian witch trial—"I ride [or 'thrust'] from me *göndull's* breaths, one to bite you in the back, another to bite you in the breast, a third to turn harm and evil upon you" (Price 2002, 178).

The evidence is inconclusive, but the image that comes to me is of Odin using his staff and his önd to send his wolves Geri and Freki forth to attack his foes. This certainly gives them a more worthy purpose than recycling the god's uneaten offerings.

Shamanism

Coming fresh from my study of the shamanic literature, the *Ynglingasaga's* negative description of Odin's magical powers struck me as very like the way a Christian missionary encountering a Pagan tribe might summarize the local shaman's skills. But can we call Odin a shaman? Shamanism, a term that originated among the tribes of Siberia, has been widely used, or misused. In his exploration of shamanic practices around the world, Mircea Eliade defines it as

> a technique of religious ecstasy. Shamanism encompasses the premise that shamans are intermediaries or messengers between the human world and the spirit worlds. Shamans are said to treat ailments/illness by mending the soul. Alleviating traumas affecting the soul/spirit restores the physical body of the individual to balance and wholeness. The shaman also enters supernatural realms or dimensions to obtain solutions to problems afflicting the community. Shamans may visit other worlds/dimensions to bring guidance to misguided souls and to ameliorate illnesses of the human soul caused by foreign elements. The shaman operates primarily within the spiritual world, which in turn affects the human world. The restoration of balance results in the elimination of the ailment. (Eliade 1972, 3–7)

The shaman is a spiritual practitioner who serves a tribe or rural community. He or she may be called to the work after having a near-death or visionary experience in which he or she is destroyed and reconstituted by the spirits. The new shaman is trained by the spirits or by an older shaman. Shamanic skills include trance journeys to gain knowledge or information, to heal the sick by retrieving their spirits, or to access otherworldly power with the help of spirit allies. Like many other spiritual traditions, the context and details of shamanic practices in different places are shaped by the culture and the influences of other religions in the area in which they occur. Properly speaking, in each culture, the local name for such spiritual specialists should be used, but it is also clear that a very similar pattern of experiences and skills is found in cultures from Siberia to Tierra del Fuego. If shamanic practice has indeed survived from a very early stage of human evolution, it seems reasonable to expect that traces of it would be found in Europe as well.

In 1980, Michael Harner, who had done ethnographic work among the Jivaro people of the Ecuadorian Amazon, published *The Way of the Shaman,* the seminal work in contemporary neo-shamanism, and established the Foundation for Shamanic Studies. His work does not claim to be "authentic" shamanic practice but is rather a synthesis and adaptation that can be effectively used by modern Americans and Europeans in a very different culture. People trained in his system are doing good work as "shamanic" therapists in many countries today.

At the time Harner's book came out, my own studies had already taken me through Women's Spirituality, eclectic Wicca, and Western Esoteric Kabbalah, and I felt a need to balance my ceremonial training with more intuitive skills. By then I had enough experience with trance journeying to take Harner's book and put into practice many of the skills covered there. It was not until 1987 that I had an opportunity to actually participate in the introductory workshop. This is the workshop where, as described in the introduction, I met Odin. This book is one of the results of that encounter.

While I understand the reactions of those scholars who stoutly maintain that Odin is not a shaman, the fact that he chose to tag me at a neo-shamanic workshop where I was most certainly not expecting to encounter him requires that I look at the reasons writers like Mircea Eliade, who devotes several pages to the evidence for shamanic practices in Scandinavian culture, think that he *is*.

In part 1 of *Shamanism*, Eliade identifies the following features of shamanism, which can be compared to the list in *Ynglingasaga* as follows:

1. Shamanism—The shaman is the most prestigious spiritual worker in his region, although he may coexist with other kinds of priests or even other religions, because his spirit leaves his body and travels between the worlds.

   Norse myth—Odin and Freyja are the Norse gods most famed for their mastery of magic. Both wander the world or worlds.

2. Shamanism—The shaman has one or more spirit allies, taking the form of animals, ancestors, or other beings, that are called and controlled by magical songs.

   Norse myth—Odin gets information from his ravens, Huginn and Muninn, and rides his magical horse, Sleipnir, between the worlds. His wolves may also be allies. He is famed for his mastery of magic songs.

3. Shamanism—The shaman can perceive souls and soul parts and retrieve them to heal or guide a soul to the afterlife.

   Norse Myth—Odin can talk to the dead, on earth or in the Underworld. His valkyries escort those whom he chooses from the battlefield to his hall.

4. Shamanism—The shaman experiences an illness or near-death crisis in which he may experience death and reconstruction, learns from the spirits through dreams and visions, and is trained in his people's magical tradition.

   Norse Myth—Odin "dies," self-sacrificed, by being stabbed and hanging on the Worldtree. In the process, he acquires the runes and learns their mysteries.

5. Shamanism—The Otherworld has levels and a detailed cosmology

that can be mapped.

Norse Myth—The Norse Otherworld has nine worlds, including our own. Odin wanders through them all.

Of these elements, the one that has perhaps attracted the most attention from the shamanic scholars is Odin's ordeal on the Worldtree. We will be discussing that in more detail in the next chapter, which looks at Odin as the giver of the runes.

One objection to identifying Odin's magic as shamanism is the absence of one of the most powerful shamanic tools for altering consciousness and raising power—the drum. Certainly the Saami, who have shared a great deal of magic with their Norse neighbors, use drums; however, the lack of references in the sagas (or, I must admit, of archaeological evidence) has led most scholars to doubt that drums were used by the Vikings. There is, however, one example that is, if not conclusive, at least suggestive.

One of the few humorous poems in the Elder Edda (given Old Norse definitions of humor) is the *Lokasenna,* a story in which Loki crashes a party at Aegir's place and proceeds to systematically insult all the gods and goddesses. Unfortunately, all the evidence we have from other sources suggests that everything he says, however scurrilous, is true. When Odin attempts to defend Gefjon, Loki responds,

> But you worked Seidh, they say, on Samsey Isle
>
> Beat on the drum(?) like the *völur;*
>
> Like unto a *vitki,* fared among men:
>
> I think that those were *ergi* ways.
>
> —*Lokasenna* 24

Völva (singular of *völur*) and *Vitki* are terms for a female and male worker of magic, respectively—witch and wizard, you might say. *Draptu á vétt*—"Beat on the drum"—is my attempt to translate a much-debated phrase, since the closest we can come to a translation of *vétt* is something like "box lid." Chisholm gives the phrase as "plied magic"; Hollander, "wove magic"; and Orchard, "beat the drum." I conclude that when Odin was working magic like a Völva, a term usually translated as "witch," he was using some kind of rhythm as an aid to altering consciousness.

In the years since I started working with Odin, I have created and collected a variety of magical tools, including a seidh staff, a rune wand, and a drum.

Fig. 7. Seidh staff, wand, and drum

The drum is made of elk hide and shows creatures from the Norse tradition placed in the Upper, Middle, and Lower worlds. Although this drum is too sensitive to moisture to be of much use outdoors, in a controlled environment, striking the images showing different levels or animals is a useful way to guide myself through a trance journey.

Practice

The path that drew me to Odin was magic. The skills to which it led me required years of exploration—presented in my books, *Trance-Portation, The Way of the Oracle,* and *Possession, Depossession, and Divine Relationships*—and what I know now is only a beginning. The first step on this path is self-knowledge.

1. Self-evaluation before studying magic

What magical practices have you tried?

What knowledge/abilities do you already have?

___ concentration and focus

___ memory

___ poetry/song

___ visualization

___ sigils and charms

___ energy sensing

___ trance work

___ connection with spirits

2. Use the Galdralag verse form to write a spell.

For an example of a verse in Galdralag, see the prayer on page 59.

3. Second of the Nine Nights Meditations:

Set up your altar and prepare the space as before. Light a blue candle and invoke Odin as Vitki. Then say:

Odin, by these names I call you:

Göndlir (Staff Wielder)

Jolnir (Yule Being)

Sváfnir (Sleep Bringer)

Thrótt (Magical Power),

Fjölsvidh (Much Wise)

Sanngetal (Truth Guesser)

Jalk (Gelding)

Grímnir (Masked One)

Magic's Master, Wand Wielder, hear me,

Mighty Singer of spells,

Word power I want, wisdom I wish for

To work my will in the world,

To work my will.

Seidh madhr show me, spirit inspiring

How to soar between the worlds.

Drum with the witches, whisper open my heart,

Till it pulses with power,

To receive the power.

Meditate on the meaning of power. What power do you have and how do you use it? Do you want "Power over" or "Power to"? Sit quietly and count your breathing, letting the words bubble up into your awareness and then float away until your spirit is still. Continue to breathe and open your awareness to the currents of energy around you. Open your heart to the god. If words come to you, write them down. When the time feels right, breathe more quickly and move your limbs to return to ordinary consciousness.

RUNE SONG

Odin old one-eye

hanging nine nights on a tree

waiting for wisdom.

You hung till the tree

grew into you

branching red tree of life

bare white bone tree of death.

The first night fear fastened your lids;

the second fog formed in vague clusters,

at eye corner blooming and buzzing;

the third night world came into focus

trees, mountains, meander of rivers,

sharp as new-made;

the fourth night was motion:

boar, cave bear and flea;

the fifth night came Huginn to sit on your head

you brought into being the four thinkers,

your one eye struggling for their shapes.

The sixth night you stretched down,

drank Mimir's water,

recalled and called them by name;

the seventh Muninn, black clot of feathers,

settled on your shoulder.

Nothing, you could forget nothing now.

The eighth night your black mind

saw, inner eye saw

all was nothing:

nothing within, nothing without

nothing now, nothing then, nothing to come.

On the ninth night hanging

on the tree of yourself

you saw

how you held it all within you,

everything and nothing within you,

and you lifted your voice, singing.

Holding yourself together,

inner and outer together,

blood tree and bone tree and world tree together,

beginning and ending together,

holding all things together,

you sang.

—Elizabeth Harrod (1999, 10)

Fig. 8. Odin on the Tree

CHAPTER FOUR

Rider of the Tree

It is time to speak at the seat of Thul

At the Well of Wyrd.

I saw and stayed silent, I saw and thought:

I heard men speak;

Of runes they spoke, nor were they silent at council,

At the hall of Hár, in the hall of Hár:

I heard them say these things.

—Havamál 111

As we have seen, Odin appears in many tales, but three of them in particular have a weight that transcends mere story—how he got the mead of poetry, how he gave one of his eyes for a drink from the Well of Mimir, and the deed for which he may be most famed: his self-sacrifice on the Worldtree to gain the runes.

Once my own wanderings had brought me to that unexpected encounter with Odin, I had to learn how to work with him. Trance journeys were useful, but I feared that when my life got busy (an outcome virtually guaranteed), I would let my spiritual practice slide as I had so many times before. I also realized that to understand Odin, I needed to know a lot more about the culture from which he came. It occurred to me that a good way to get that background would be to study the runes. And to make sure I didn't abandon *that* project, I resolved to start a class so that every month I would have to research another rune.

It is my good fortune to live in a community that includes a lot of extremely talented people. When I announced the class, I got an enthusiastic response, and in January 1988, a few months after my initial encounter with Odin, the class began. The fifteen people who turned up for the first meeting included several poets, a graduate student in Scandinavian studies, and another student whose study of Anglo Saxon was more recent than my own. In 1988, Heathenry as an organized spiritual path was just beginning to emerge. Everyone in the class was Pagan or Pagan-friendly, but only a few had worked with the Norse gods.

My plan for the class was to study the Elder Futhark two runes at a time, collecting and comparing information from the old rune poems and the lore and looking for ways to apply the concepts to our own lives. Ralph Blum had popularized his own unique interpretation of the runes, and Ed Fitch had written the Wicca-based *Rites of Odin,* but Edred Thorsson (1984) was the only writer with a scholarly background who approached the runes as a spiritual system.

My class worked together to find information and share ideas on how the runes, or the forces behind them, manifest in the world. To internalize what we were learning, we did rituals. And every month, as I wondered what I should do for the next class, I would open my mind to Odin; one word would lead on to another word, one insight to another, giving me a periodic download of information.

Like the letters in the Hebrew alphabet, the runestaves work simultaneously with vision, sound, and memory. We found that each rune served as a doorway to some aspect of Germanic culture. By the time we reached the last rune in the Elder Futhark, Othala, we had encountered all the major gods and goddesses, the most important myths, and a great deal of the history and values behind them. The material generated for this class, expanded and refined by additional rounds in the years that followed, eventually became my first nonfiction book, *Taking up the Runes*. What follows is based on the introduction to the runes that I give at festivals and conferences. For a more inclusive and detailed account, see the books on runes listed at the end of this chapter.

Mysteries and Alphabets

Most people today would call "Y" a "rune." Properly speaking, it is a rune *stave* (a runic "letter"). *Rune* is actually a term that has been applied to many things considered magical, such as the Saami rune drum (which has no rune staves on it). It is usually translated as "secret" or "mystery." A spell or formula can be called a "rune." Furthermore, the staves most often seen in contemporary magical and religious contexts are only one version of the *futhark,* a word made from the sounds of the first six staves of the rune row, the equivalent of the Latin letter alphabet.

There are two ways to explain the origin of the runes. One is the story of how Odin hanged himself on the Worldtree to win them, about which we shall see more later. The other is based on archaeology. The earliest runic inscriptions date from the second century CE. Many of the rune staves resemble letters in northern Italian alphabets being used at the time. They could have been brought to Germany by Germans who had served with the Roman army, or they might have been introduced by traders. Most of the early runic texts come from what is now northern Germany and Denmark, suggesting that wherever the Elder Futhark was actually developed, it is in that area that it came into use.

Pollington concludes that "the runes are not a wholesale cultural import but a Germanic creation inspired by knowledge of at least one other, contemporary writing system (Spurklund 2010, 661). The invention of the futhark was born out of a desire to own a means of writing, and the need for such system to *not* be a transparent copy of the dominant (Roman) model" (Pollington 2016, 79).

There are, in fact, three futharks. The Elder Futhark, which we know from inscriptions made in Migrations Period Germany, contains twenty-four rune staves and is the version used most often in Heathen religious and magical practice today. The Anglo-Saxons carried the Continental Germanic runes to England and added nine more to bring the total to thirty-three. On the other hand, in the Viking Age the futhark was reduced to sixteen staves. Some sounds were no longer needed because the language had changed, and some runes, like Bjarkan, did double duty for two related sounds ("B" and "P"). The most common forms and order for these three futharks are given in figure 9, but in inscriptions, variations of all of them may appear. Interpretation of runic inscriptions is also complicated by the fact that spelling was not regularized, and staves or inscriptions were sometimes written right to left as well as left to right, reversed, or even upside down.

The Principal Futharks

#	Elder Futhark form/s	name	Younger Futhark form/s	name	Anglo-Saxon Futhorc form/s	name	sound
1.	ᚠ	fehu	ᚠ	fé	ᚠ	feoh	F
2.	ᚢ	uruz	ᚢ	úr	ᚢ	úr	U
3.	ᚦ	thurisax	ᚦ	thurs	ᚦ	thorn	th
4.	ᚨ	ansuz	ᚨ	áss	ᚩ	ós	A
5.	ᚱ	raidho	ᚱ	reidh	ᚱ	rad	R
6	ᚲ	kenaz	ᚴ	kaun	ᚳ	ken	C/K
7.	ᚷ	gebo	–	–	ᚷ	gyfu	G
8.	ᚹ	wunjo	–	–	ᚹ	wynn	W
9.	ᚺ	hagalaz	ᚼ	hagall	ᚺ	haegl	H
10.	ᚾ	naudhiz	ᚾ	naudhr	ᚾ	nyd	N
11.	ᛁ	isa	ᛁ	iss	ᛁ	is	I
12.	ᛃ	jera	ᛅ	ár	ᛄ	gér	Yuh
13.	ᛇ	eihwaz	–	–	ᛇ	éoh	ei
14.	ᛈ	perthro	–	–	ᛈ	peordh	p
15.	ᛉ	elhaz	–	–	ᛉ	eolhx	zh
16.	ᛋ	sowilo	ᛋ	sol	ᛋ	sigil	S
17.	ᛏ	tiwaz	ᛏ	týr	ᛏ	tír	T
18.	ᛒ	Berkano	ᛒ	bjarkan	ᛒ	beorc	B
19.	ᛖ	ehwaz	–	–	ᛖ	eh	eh
20.	ᛗ	mannaz	ᛘ	madhr	ᛗ	mann	M
21.	ᛚ	laguz	ᛚ	lögr	ᛚ	lagu	L
22.	ᛜ	ingwaz	–	–	ᛝ	ing	ng
23.	ᛞ	dagaz	–	–	ᛞ	daeg	D
24.	ᛟ	othala	–	–	ᛟ	éthel	O
25.					ᚪ	ac	a
26.					ᚫ	aesc	aah
27.					ᚣ	yr	u
28.					ᛡ	ior	io
29.					ᛠ	éar	ea
30.					ᛢ	cweorp	qu
31.					ᛣ	calc	k
32.					ᛥ	stán	st
33.					ᚸ	gár	g

Fig. 9. The Elder, Younger, and Anglo-Saxon Futharks

The earliest runic inscriptions are on objects—to identify the owner or maker or to empower the objects, like the bind rune of ᚷᚠ, ᚷᚠ, ᚷᚠ inscribed on a spearshaft from the Anglian homeland, possibly meaning "I give good luck" (Pollington 2016, 174). During the Viking period, runes were widely used for communication and sometimes for graffiti. Archaeologists found a large number of runic messages inscribed on pieces of wood in the remains of a medieval trading center beneath the modern Norwegian city of Bergen (Liestol 1966). Later, runic memorials were inscribed on stones. Today they are used primarily for magical, religious, and decorative or culture-related purposes (such as the bind rune of Bjarkan and Hagall that forms the logo for the Swedish company Bluetooth).

From time to time, someone comes along who loves Northern mythology but cannot cope with Odin or what she believes Odin to be. Usually it's because, until recently, retellings of the myths based on the 19th century version of the Norse pantheon were pretty patriarchal, and Odin, as king of the gods, was portrayed as the worst of the lot. I have even seen claims that the runes were invented by Freyja or some other goddess or god who taught them to Odin. Freyja is indeed a mistress of magic, but her specialty is *seidh,* not the runes. If any Power other than Odin might claim them, I would suggest the three Norns, especially if Odin "took up" the runes from the Well of Wyrd.

In her book *The Norse Goddess,* the Swedish artist and feminist Monica Sjöo identified aspects of Norse mythology of which she approved as ancient and authentic, while branding anything she disliked a patriarchal interpolation. Ingrid Kincaid writes on the back cover of her book on the runes that "*The Runes Revealed* will challenge you to remove the tainted, distorted, lens of patriarchal interpretation and start seeing the runes with clearer vision. Long before Odin, the Vikings or Christianity, the runes were." Given that each rune is the key to an aspect of reality, I would agree, but I continue to hold that it was Odin who obtained and gave them to the world. Kincaid's book is intended to share her personal interpretations and responses to the runes, and her conclusions about their *meanings* are in fact not too different from my own. My feeling is that Odin doesn't care who gets the credit for finding the runes so long as you use them well.

The Tree and the Well

So where does the story about how Odin gained the runes come from? In *Hávamál* 138 (the Speaking of the High One), we find the following: "I know that I hung on the wind-tossed tree, nine full nights . . ." The "wind-tossed tree" is the Worldtree, *Yggdrasil*, "the horse of Ygg" (the Terrible One), another name for Odin. The god is therefore the Rider of the Tree.

In *Völuspá* 19, the seeress states,

> An ash I know, named Yggdrasil,
>
> a high tree, moistened with white mud,
>
> from thence dews drip down into the dales.
>
> ever green it stands over Urdh's well.

Since the Well of Urdh (Wyrd) is located at the base of the Tree, if Odin took up the runes after looking down, it may be in that Well, in which all that has been is preserved and all that is becoming is continually being "laid down," that he found them. Or he may have encountered them in another dimension of consciousness.

In *Völuspá*, Yggdrasil is called an ash tree. However, according to Simek, F. R. Schröder has speculated that the name might mean "yew pillar," based on a link between the Proto-Indo-European words for yew tree and support (Simek 2007, 375). Furthermore, in Old Norse, *barraskr*, the needle-ash, is another name for the yew. The Worldtree is also referred to as "ever green," which would support its identification as a yew rather than the deciduous ash. For these reasons, although the ash is noble and beautiful, I rather favor the identification of Yggdrasil as a yew, which is the longest lived of European trees, with the age of some specimens estimated at 2,000 years old or more.

The yew was often planted in churchyards and held to be a link to the land of the dead. The flesh of the red berries of the yew can be eaten, but every other part of the tree, including the seed, is poisonous. I have been told that some people have developed headaches and hallucinations from sitting under a yew tree on a warm day. The wood of the yew is prized for making bows and also for magical staffs and wands. However, you should only work with it where there is good ventilation, especially when you are sanding it.

That said, in the trance journey that led to my first meeting with Odin, the tree up which Raven led me was the redwood, which to my Californian eyes seems more beautiful and impressive (as well as taller and older) than either the ash or the yew. Yggdrasil is the *axis mundi* that grows at the center of the spiritual dimension that lies within Midgard. In Siberia, the Worldtree is represented by the birch, by a saguaro among the Tohono O'odham of the American Southwest, and in Central America by the kapok. I think that in the world of the spirit, we see the Worldtree as the most impressive tree that grows in the forests of our home.

In the Norse cosmology, Midgard, our world, is in the center; the world of the gods above and the ancestors in Hel below. The configuration of the other worlds around them has been variously described. References in the lore put Niflheim in the north, slightly lower than Midgard. Jotunheim is in the east and Muspelheim in the south, which leaves the west for Vanaheim. Presumably the light elves live closer to Asgard and the *svartalfar* below.

From *Völuspá*, we know that three roots reach into the depths. Beneath one of them lies the Well of Urdh where the three Norns (figures analogous to the three fates of classical myth, though not exactly the same) dip up water to nourish the Tree. This is also the site where the gods sit in council. In his fascinating study of world and time in Germanic culture, Paul Bauschatz proposes that all the Otherworld wells described in the lore are connected. From the Well rises the Tree, containing all the worlds, whose events fall into the well in "seething, active strata" (Bauschatz 1982, 122). This creates a source of power that is drawn up through the tree to be released to the worlds.

To quote *Völuspá* (20) once more,

> From there come maidens, knowing much lore.
>
> Three, from the lake that's under the tree.
>
> One is called Urd, the other Verdandi,
>
> the third is Skuld. On wood they carved signs,
>
> laws they laid down, lives they chose.
>
> They worked ørlög for the sons of men.

Far from being a simple representation of past, present, and future, the Norns—Urd, Verdandi, and Skuld—represent a complex concept of time. My understanding of the discussion presented by Bauschatz (1982, 153–187) in *The Well and the Tree* is that the names of the first two Norns derive from tenses of the verb *wairthan*, "to be." A simple preterite form of the verb gives us *Urd*, governing those actions from the primordial to a minute ago that have already been "laid down" in the Well. The word *Verdandi* is not only a present tense, but a participle that emerges from the past. The future, however, can only be expressed with the aid of a helping verb. *Skuld*, from a different verb, *skulan*, is added to another verb to indicate what shall or should happen as a result of what has gone before.

"They stress the proximity or real presence of the following action without specifically predicating it" (Bauschatz 1982, 183). I interpret this to mean that the past is fixed, and the present, the perpetual "becoming" in which we experience the world, is shaped not only by the past but also by the choices we make right now. Therefore, until those decisions become part of the past, the future can only be a probability.

The lore does not tell us on which branch of the Worldtree Odin was hanged, but it makes sense to me to place the event near the Well, where the inalterable past, the protean present, and the ever-mutating future coexist in the swirl of the cosmic cauldron that is the Well.

The Sacrifice

Here we enter the dimension of myth, where logic is transcended by meaning. In *Hávamál* 138, the High One speaks in both the first person and the third, observing his ordeal even as he experiences it.

> By spear wounded, given to Odin,
>
> myself to myself,
>
> On that tree of which no man knows
>
> the roots from which it rises.

The speaker is "given to Odin," *sjalfur sjalfum mér*. To understand what a sacrifice to Odin entailed, let us consider the death of King Vikar in the complicated history of the hero Starkad, which provides much of the plot for *Gautrek's saga*. As the story goes, King Vikar's ship is becalmed, and divination tells them that Odin requires a human sacrifice to provide a favorable wind. Each time they cast lots, the choice falls on the king. Of course, no one wants to kill him, especially Starkad, who has been his friend and right-hand man since they were boys.

That night Starkad goes (or perhaps dreams he goes) with his foster father to a meeting in which all the participants are called by the names of (or are possessed by) the gods. "Odin" tells Starkad that he must "send the king to me." In the morning, the men decide to perform a mock sacrifice of the king. "At that, Starkad let loose the branch. The reed-stalk turned into a spear which pierced the king, the tree stump slipped from under his feet, the calf guts turned into a strong withy, the branch shot up with the king into the foliage, and there he died." (Pálsson and Edwards 1985, 157).

To hang a man and then to stab him would seem to be overkill, but the use of multiple methods for a single execution goes back a long way. Some bodies found preserved in northern peat bogs appear to have been bound, clubbed, *and* stabbed before being sunk in the marsh. A young man killed sometime in the first century CE and found in Lindow Moss near Cheshire had been strangled and hit on the head before his throat was cut (Joy 2009, 45). This triple form of execution has reso-nances with "triple deaths" found in the stories of the Irish Suibhne, the Scots Lailoken, and Merlin, whose deaths included piercing, stoning, and drowning or burning.

In *The Quest for Merlin*, Nikolai Tolstoy proposes that the death of Llew Llaw Gyffes, the Welsh version of Lug whom Tolstoy believes to be cognate to Odin, is an example of the triple sacrifice. In the *Mabinogion*, Llew says he can only be killed if several impossible conditions are met and makes the mistake of telling his wife what they are. She tells her lover, who stabs Llew with a ritually fashioned spear while he is standing with one foot on the back of a goat and the other on the edge of a bathing tub. Llew turns into an eagle (an ability shared with Odin) and flies to a tree, where he sits, rotting, until he is found and healed by his uncle, the wizard Gwydion.

The men and animals sacrificed at Uppsala were hanged on trees. We do not know if they were also stunned and stabbed. The Odinic sacrifices feature only two methods of killing, which may have been the Germanic version of the custom. Some have proposed that the descrip-tion of Odin's death on the tree was inspired by the death of Jesus. But the story of King Vikar suggests that it was a pre-Christian tradition in the north.

Certainly when the Germanic peoples encountered the story of the execution of Jesus, they saw in it a parallel to the ordeal of Odin. Although Jesus was crucified, not hanged, both were suspended on a gallows and speared. For a sense of how Germanic peoples viewed the Christian story, see *The Heliand*, a fascinating version of the gospels in Germanic terms written in Old Saxon in the 9th century. In this version, Jesus is portrayed as a warrior chieftain with his war band around him. The section on the crucifixion includes the driving of the nails, but thereafter Jesus is described as hanging from ropes on the gallows. "The Protector of the Land died on the rope" (Murphy 1992, 173).

Although some have portrayed Odin suspended by one foot like the hanged man in the Tarot cards, the evidence in the lore supports hanging by the neck. Certainly strangulation, which stops the breath, would be appropriate for a god of communication who, as we see in chapter 5, gave the gift of breath to humankind. However he was hanged, it is also important that Odin is *suspended*, a liminal state that allows him to move between the worlds.

As the rope uplifts the body, the spear opens it to receive the power. When a king cast a spear over an enemy army, he dedicated them to Odin and took no prisoners. The god's special weapon is the spear Gungnir, with which he dedicates his offerings. I believe that Odin is pierced by his own spear, though no one seems to know who dealt the blow.

> They gave me no bread nor drinking horn,
>
> I looked down below.
>
> I took up the runes, screaming, I took them,
>
> fell back after.
>
> —*Hávamál* 139

Why does Odin go to the Tree? What exactly happens to him, and what does he learn? For nine days and nights the god endures, half starved, half choked, weakened by blood loss, and hanging between the worlds in a state of detached and altered consciousness. Conversations with friends whose allergies have nearly killed them have made me vividly aware of what happens when the throat is closed by anaphylactic shock. Interestingly enough, the adrenaline released by pain can slow the process, leading to interesting speculations on the balance that might be achieved by the simultaneous action of the noose and the spear.

Odin is effectively dead, but in that moment of ultimate awareness, he is able to perceive and "grasp" the runes, comprehending their essence and internalizing it. Writers like Mircea Eliade see in this story an analogue to an initiation in which the new shaman has a visionary experience of death and disintegration after which he is given a new, magical body by the ancestors or spirits. If Odin rides the Worldtree to his death, it is in quest of transformation.

These stanzas from a poem by Jennifer Tifft express the experience.

Wrist, waist, neck hemp-wound, taut on the tree

stricken through and intersecting worlds

Pierced and piercing, my throat rune-raw with screams

Words hammer in my heart, lie on my tongue,

Shape my breath

Double and single-sighted eyes look out, see in

Oldest and youngest

Perish never the desire: will to live

Dying to know

Fleeting wing-beats, demanding hardness:

The words are real

Untame warmth, unbridled strength:

The seeing is true

Phantom rope-wounds, remembered pain:

The knowing is all

Odin has no Gwydion to rescue him. It is not the spirits who resurrect the god but that other Self to whom he has been offered. One glimpses a higher self or an expanded consciousness that can only manifest when the less evolved portion has been cast away. In mythic time, all events take place simultaneously; therefore, Odin is always hanging on the Worldtree and always taking up the runes.

When we finish a round of my rune class, those who have fully absorbed their meaning may choose to experience an initiatory ritual that includes being tied to a tree for most of a night, during which, every ten minutes, those conducting the rite bless you with a new rune. The script and directions are included at the end of *Taking up the Runes*.

When it was my turn, I found that being fully supported by the ropes allowed me to relax into a trance state, while the delivery of a new rune at regular intervals kept trance from turning into sleep. The result was an altered state of consciousness that lasted for six hours, in which it was possible to contemplate all the runes simultaneously and thus to perceive the relationships and connections between them.

Odin, of course, went further. He offered himself to himself—but what does that mean? In Edred Thorsson's magical text, *The Nine Doors of Midgard,* the student is asked to emulate Odin, becoming not the god but "himSelf or herSelf. This is the true nature of the cult of Odhinn. The Odian does not seek union with Odhinn, but rather with his or her own unique self, a mirror of Odhinn's own godly task" (Thorsson 1991, xx).

This is essentially self-realization, a worthy goal, but I cannot help wondering how the student can understand which aspects of himself to reject until he has gained enough wisdom to glimpse what that true self, not to mention Odin's actual goals, might be. One has visions of young men blithely trying to transform themselves into the gung-ho warriors of the *mannerbund* (about whom we learn more in chapter 7), forfeiting the opportunity to encounter the other dimensions that Odin's sacrifice revealed.

My experience has been that most people who work with Odin did not set out to find him. When Odin calls, the question they ask is "Why me?" not "How can I gain your power?"

Working the Runes

Once you have the runes, what do you do with them? In *Hávamál* 142 and 144, respectively, the description of Odin's ordeal is followed by several stanzas discussing how to fashion the physical rune staves and use them.

Runes must you find, and meaningful staves,

Very mighty staves,

Very strong staves,

Which *Fimbulthul* ["Mighty Sage" or "Speaker," a name
of Odin] stained,

And the *Ginnregin* ["Great Powers"] fashioned,

And *Hropt* ["Tumult" or "Speaker," a name of Odin]

carved from among the powers:

Do you know how to rist [cut/carve]? Do you know how
to read?

Do you know how to stain [color]? Do you know how to
test [or wield, or pray]

Do you know how to invoke? Do you know how to *blót*
[sacrifice]?

Do you know how to dispatch [offer, send]? Do you
know how to slaughter [literally, "stop the breath"]?

These questions are followed by eighteen spells for healing, battle,
protection from powers human and supernatural, and talking to the
dead. Their purpose and effects are described, but the spells themselves
do not appear. Are these rune spells? If so, apparently the rune master
is expected to know which runes to use. What we are given is a description of carving and painting runes on wood or stone. We find the same
pattern elsewhere in the lore. When Skirnir tries to scare the giant-
maiden Gerd into agreeing to marry Freyr, he describes what the runes
will do to her but not, perhaps fortunately, which ones he will use.

When Sigurd awakens the Valkyrie from her charmed sleep in
the Icelandic version of the story (*Sigrdrífumál*), she rewards him with
several pages describing how to inscribe the runes for various kinds of

magic—Tiwaz for victory, Naudhiz to protect one's drink. The runes for the other purposes listed are not named. One stanza describes inscribing runes on wood, then scraping them off and mixing the shavings with mead. They may also be inscribed on weapons or gear, or worn on jewelry or on an amulet.

> These are the book-runes
>
> These are the protection-runes,
>
> Also all the ale-runes,
>
> And the splendid power-runes,
>
> For those who can, unblemished and unspoiled,
>
> Have them on their amulets.
>
> Use them, if you've learnt them,
>
> Until the Powers are destroyed.
>
> —*Sigrdrífumál* 19

In the saga about the noted poet and warrior Egil Skallagrimsson, we see him inscribing runes on a drinking horn to reveal the poison within (chapter 44). In another episode (chapter 72), he notes that the daughter of a farmer with whom he is staying is ill. He is told that a neighbor's son inscribed some runes on a sheep's shoulder bone to help her, yet she is no better. Egil, observing that people who don't understand the runes shouldn't mess with them, scrapes off the runes and burns the bone to destroy the first spell and replaces it with a spell of his own.

Sound and Sense

The sounds and meanings that go with each rune stave are derived from three rune poems: the Anglo-Saxon, the Icelandic, and the Old Norse. You can find the texts and translations online at a number of sources, including *https://en.wikisource.org/wiki/Rune_poems*.

For example, let us look at the rune most often associated with Odin. This is the fourth rune, whose reconstructed old Germanic name is Ansuz. The Old English Rune Poem gives it as:

ᚩ   *[Os] byth ordfruma*   ælcre spræce,

    Mouth (or "the god") is the chieftain of all speech

wisdomes wrathu   *ond witena frofur,*

    mainstay of wisdom,   comfort to wise ones

and eorla gehwam   *eadnys ond tohiht.*

    for every noble warrior   hope and happiness.

This rune poem was composed in the 8th or 9th century, when the English had already been converted to Christianity but were still using runes or sometimes a combination of rune staves and Latin letters. In a somewhat glorified manner, the stanza for Os celebrates communication.

The Norwegian rune poem covers the runes of the Younger Futhark, which were in use by the 9th century. The earliest manuscript that records it was written in the 13th century, also after the conversion. It translates the rune name as "mouth" and explains it as the mouth of a fjord.

ᚬ   *[óss] er fiestra færa*   River mouth is the way of
    most journeys:

for, en skalpr er sværa   but a scabbard of swords.

The Icelandic poem may not be any older than the Norwegian, but Iceland was the last Scandinavian country to convert to Christianity (in the 11th century). Even in the 13th century, when Snorri Sturlusson was writing, the old mythology was the foundation of poetry and culture. It specifically identifies óss, with "ás," a god, Odin.

ᚬ   *[óss] er aldingautr*   Ase is the olden-father [Odin],

    ok asgardhs jofurr   Asgard's chieftain,

    ok valhallar visi.   and the leader of Valholl.

We do not know whether the rune originally meant "mouth" or the god Odin, but given that he was the patron of poets as well as being the giver of the runes, if you take the Anglo-Saxon and Icelandic poems together, you get Odin as a god of speech and communication. My own rune poem describes the rune as, "ANSUZ, ÓSS, is Odin's wisdom, communicating ecstasy."

When we salute Odin as Master of the Runes, we also hail him as Rider of the Tree, recognizing the price he paid for that power. But he did not seek the runes for himself alone. Some he shared with the other gods, some he gave to leaders among the elves and the dwarves, and some he wrought for "earth-born men" (*Hávamál* 143). We do not know if all beings received the same runes, but if we take up the ones that Odin gave to humankind, it is our responsibility to use them wisely.

Odin's identity as a god of communication might also explain why a number of people who work with him find that he speaks through and to them through trance dictation, in which you open your mind to the god and simply take down the words he puts there. This technique is discussed more fully in my book *Possession.* Examples of these transmissions from several different mediums are available on the Odinspeaks website (*www.odinspeaks.com*).

Given that anything passing through the filter of a human mind may be subject to bias and error, the fact that material transmitted through different individuals may still show a remarkable consistency in style and tone suggests a single source. But whether the comments come from the minds of the writers or from the god, they offer insight into the experience of working with Odin today.

Practice

If you have not yet studied the runes, now is a good time to begin. My own book *Taking up the Runes* is only one of the useful resources now available. Here are some others:

Edred Thorsson, *Futhark* (Weiser, 1984)

———, *Runelore* (Weiser, 1987)

————, *At the Well of Wyrd* (Weiser, 1989)

These books, written at the beginning of the "Runic Awakening," were the first to develop working with the runes as a contemporary magical and spiritual system.

Freya Aswynn, *Leaves of Yggdrasil* (Llewellyn, 1993). Interpretations by a longterm priestess of Odin with a background in British magical traditions.

Kveldulf Gundarsson, *Teutonic Magic,* (Llewellyn, 1993). More magical technology with particularly good pathworkings.

R. I. Page, *Reading the Past: Runes* (British Museum, 1987).Historical background on the runes from a mundane and scholarly perspective.

Stephen Pollington, *Rudiments of Runelore* (Anglo-Saxon Books, 1995). A useful introduction to Elder, Anglo-Saxon, and Norse runes.

————, *Runes, Literacy in the Germanic Iron Age* (Anglo-Saxon Books, 2017). An in-depth examination of everything archaeology and scholarship have been finding out about the origins and use of the Elder Futhark and its later development in England.

Ann Gróa Sheffield, *Long-Branches* (*Lulu.com,* 2015). An excellent study of the Younger Futhark.

Many have found it useful to make their own rune sets from wood, river stones, or even Sculpi. Meditate on the meaning of each rune as you make it, and keep your runes on your Odin altar. When/if you have a complete set, try drawing one or three runes when you have a question. This is one way to talk to the god.

Meditation for the Third Night: The Rider of the Tree

Set up your altar and prepare the space as before. Light a green candle. Or you may choose to do this meditation sitting with your back against a tree. Then say:

Odin, by these names I call you:

Váfuth ("Dangler")

Hangi ("Hanging One")

Svidrir ("Spear God")

Ómi ("Crier")

Fimbulthul ("Mighty Speaker")

Rider of the Tree

If you have already memorized and studied the runes, galdor (intone) them one by one, feeling the vibrations roll through your body and taking a few moments to meditate on the meaning of each. If not, read the rune poem that follows or another of your choice, taking time to contemplate each meaning.

ᚠ   Fehu (FAY-hoo) is herds and fertile fields,
      Freely, Freyr finds wealth for friends.

ᚢ   Uruz (OO-rooz), Aurochs, urges earthward
      Spirit strength to shape creation.

ᚦ   Thurisaz (THUR-ee-sahz) the thorn of Thor,
      Is force that frees, or fights a foe.

ᚨ   Ansuz (AHN-suz), Ós, is Odin's wisdom,
      Communicating ecstasy.

ᚱ   Upon Raidho (RIDE-oh) the road is ridden
      To work and world around together.

< Kenaz (KEN-az) kens creation's fire;

With torch transforming hearth and hall.

X Gebo (GAY-bo) unites the gift and giver

In equal exchange of energy.

ᛈ Wunjo (WOON-yo) wins Wishfather's blessing,

Joy joins folk in family freedom.

ᚺ Hagalaz (HAH-gah-laz) hails ice seeds hither,

Harm is melted into healing.

ᚾ Naudhiz (NOW-theez) is Necessity,

Norn-rune forcing Fate from Need.

| Isa (EE-sah) is the Ice, inertia,

Stasis and serenity . . .

ᛃ Jera's (YARE-ah) Year-Wheel yields good harvest,

Right reward as seasons ripen.

ᛇ Eihwaz (AY-wahz), yew of Yggdrasil,

Bow of Life and Death, worlds binding.

ᛈ Perthro (PEAR-throw) pours its play from rune cup,

Chance or change for man or child.

ᛉ Elhaz (EL-haz), Elk is sharp-tined sedge,

Totem power provides protection.

ᛋ   Sowilo (So-WEE-low) sets the sun wheel soaring,
    Guiding light by land or sea.

ᛏ   Tiwaz (TEE-waz) is the rune of Tyr,
    Victorious victim, enjoining justice.

ᛒ   Berkano (BEAR-kah-no), Birch tree, Bride, and Mother,
    Brings us Earth-power for rebirthing.

ᛗ   Ehwaz (EH-waz), Eoh, extending energy,
    The Holy Horse links god and human.

ᛗ   In Mannaz (MAH-naz) every man is master,
    All Ríg's children are relations.

ᛚ   From Laguz (LAH-guz) Lake life ever-flowing
    Wells from Mother-depths of darkness.

ᛜ   Ingwaz (ING-waz) wanders the world in his wagon,
    And dying, leaves life in the land.

ᛞ   Dagaz (DAH-gaz) is a bright day's dawning,
    Life and growth and light for all.

ᛟ   Othala (OH-thah-lah) is holy heart-home
    For clan and kin of mind and body.

The Building of Bifrost

Long ago, in the dreaming time that begins all stories of origin, the gods of the north came forth from the mists where the primal ice met Muspel's flames. Odin was first among them, first to know himself, to see and understand that he saw, to speak the words of power that named all things. So it was in those days, when the jotnar—the primal powers of wind and weather, the giants of the frost and the cliffs and the mountains, of the sky and sea—walked the world.

Odin took thought for the future, for a vision had come to him of Middle Earth and how it would be tilled and settled by humankind. But for that to happen, the newly made humans must have protection; for in those days, those who would become humankind still sheltered in caves and hollows, gathering roots and berries and chipping tools from stone.

Odin, who is a great wanderer, sought the spirit of Earth, Jordh, Mother Earth in woman shape, a giantess of the most ancient kin. He reminded her that humankind was also her offspring, and they needed a protector. And they lay together, and from that union came Thor, who strides the skies, striking the clouds to bring the lightning and laughing in the thunder. To Thor was given the task of battling the wild powers, to defeat just enough of them so that there would be room for humankind to flourish on the land. And so it is that even now he does not kill all the giants—just a few, when it is needful. But these days, humans themselves destroy many of the elder kin.

But even Thor's strength was not enough. A center was needed, a refuge from which the gods might fare forth to shape the worlds. Odin contracted with one of the mightiest of the jotnar to build him a place of power. If he should finish it in the time set, he would have Freyja, lady of love and beauty, for his bride. Odin dared to make this promise because Loki had assured him that he would find a way out of the bargain. But the giant harnessed up his giant horse, and together they worked too well, and Loki could find nothing the giant would take in exchange for the goddess. One day was left on the contract, and the walls were almost completed. What to do?

Loki, in desperation, changed himself into a mare, sleek and rounded—and in season. He, or rather she, trotted past the giant's horse, waving her tail seductively, and the stallion, unable to resist, broke his harness and went after her. The giant raged, but without his horse to pull the stones he could not finish the wall. Eventually, the horse came back, but the deadline was passed, and Freyja was saved.

There was one other consequence—when the time was accomplished, Loki, still in the shape of the mare, gave birth to an eight-legged steed who could outrun the wind. He was called Sleipnir, and Odin raised him up and taught him to run between the worlds.

And so the fortress the gods had envisioned was finished, fair and mighty, a castle in the clouds. And there were the gods on Middle Earth, gazing up at it. Odin could enter, for it was his mind that had shaped it, and he had Sleipnir to bear him. But he did not wish to dwell there alone.

That castle was not entirely in the world. Sometimes the walls seemed as transparent as mist; sometimes they were solid stone. At all times they were curiously hard to gaze at, for the eye somehow kept slipping away. No one of mortal race could come there, and it was not easy even for the holy gods. A bridge was needed, and not just a link between one world and the other, but a bridge that would itself be a transformation, so that those who walked it would be able to move between the worlds.

Odin called on Thor to summon the mists and swing his hammer, and clouds curdled in the sky. Odin called a gentle wind to hold them and summoned Sunna from the east to bless the sky with her rays. And as she rose, all the assembled gods saw a shimmer in the air.

"What is it?" they asked. "What are you doing to the sky?"

But Odin only smiled. "Behold," he said then, "Sunna's disc rising in the dawning, the brightness of Idunna's apples, the blood that gives you life. Set your feet firmly upon Middle Earth and see as men see. . . ." and he uttered a rune of power—URUZ. . . .

And the gods blinked, for the vibration in the air had a color. They saw red, they saw crimson, an arc of color arching across the sky. And the bow arched downward until that ruddy light bathed all of them, and they saw one another as red, children of earth one and all.

"That is wonderful, but what is it good for?" they asked.

"Wait," said Odin. And they could tell that the air beside the red arch was moving, but that was all. "Cannot you see," he asked, "the blaze of sunset on the sea? The warm skin of lovers in close embrace? Look at Freyja with the sunlight on her hair. Feel desire pulse within you and *see*. . . ." and he uttered a second rune—FEHU. . . .

And suddenly they realized that the red was shading into an arc of blazing orange, glowing in the heavens. And the band arched down and they felt desire, and Freyja moved among them, blessing them with her love.

But now it was clear that the air next to the orange band was vibrating, too.

"What is this?" they asked. "Show us how to see—"

"It is you who must will this," said the god. "Draw the fire of the sun and the radiance of the growing grain into your centers, and see!" Once more he chanted a rune—SOWILO. And the gods stared at the shimmer and willed it to enfold them, and as it did so, fire flared through them, and they were bathed in golden light.

A fiery arch now spanned the sky; it was like a road, but not yet broad enough to bear them, and the air still shook with colors they could not see.

"The next band will be harder," said Odin, "for you must open your hearts to all the world. See the waving grass, see the glossy leaves of the Worldtree, and become those things." And he uttered the rune JERA, and they touched the green grass that grows everywhere and the green leaves of the tree Yggdrasil, which bears the worlds, and they loved them all.

As each band of color was added, they could feel themselves changing; now they shook with excitement as well.

"Can you tell me what you are seeing?" Odin asked then. And they shook their heads in silence, for they knew only a wonder for which they had no words. "Until you can speak of what you see, you have no power over it," he said. "Look up into the sky, and breathe deeply, and let the wind fill you with words."

And he spoke the rune that is one of his own names: ANSUZ. . . .

And a great blue wind rushed about them, and suddenly they were babbling. "Turquoise, cerulean, ultramarine, sky, sea . . ." they cried, and a shimmering band of blue flared out from the green and arched across the sky.

"The bridge is broad now," they said. "Let us go across."

"No," answered Odin. "You think you see, but you do not, for you are only seeing with the eyes of the body. Move into the vibration that comes now, and let it shake you until you *truly* see. . . ."

And the rune he uttered then was PERTHRO, which signifies the Well in which the eye he gave for Wisdom is hid.

And what they saw then was the deepening color of the sky as it passes from sunset to midnight lit by the moon; they saw all other colors in this new light more luminous and radiant than before. They saw with the eye that is hidden behind the brow. They saw indigo. . . .

The gods looked upon one another and saw each transformed, and Odin whispered the last rune, which is the rune of his spirit, and is named JOY . . . WUNJO. . . .

And the gods saw color beyond color, a radiant violet, and they saw the rainbow complete, arching like a bridge before them, linking the heights of Odin's sanctuary to the lands below.

"Behold Bifrost, the shaking bridge, that vibrates with all the colors there are. Now the substance of which you have formed your essence is all light, and you, shimmering with all vibrations, can see all things. Follow me now, my children, and we will enter our new home."

And Odin stepped onto the bridge, and his body shook with all of its colors, and shimmered like a rainbow. First to follow was Heimdall, Odin's son by the nine waves, the god who can see farther and hear better than any other being in the worlds; for that, Odin made him Bifrost's guardian. And after him, one by one, all the holy gods and goddesses stepped onto the bridge and ascended into the realm that is called Asgard, the sanctuary of the gods.

And we know that this is so, for after the storm the sun returns, and Bifrost shimmers in her holy light. And those who learn to shimmer with the colors of the rainbow, seeing and understanding all things, may journey to dwell with the gods.

I wrote this tale in 1996 for a conference at Asilomar near Monterey that had been focusing on a new chakra each year. Think of it as a fantasy on the origin of the Rainbow Bridge, inspired by, though not based on, the lore. When I was at the conference, they had reached Ajna, the chakra of Vision located in the Third Eye. The conference hall was draped in indigo and had some of the biggest quartz crystals I have ever seen. While I didn't agree with everything they were saying, for me it was a very Odinic weekend.

Fig. 10. All-father

chapter five

All-father

Gylfi: *"Who is the highest and most ancient of all gods?"*

High: *"He is called All-father in our language, but in Old Asgard, he had twelve names."*

—*Gylfaginning* 3

Actually, as we have already seen, for Odin, twelve names is barely a beginning. But among his bynames and epithets, "All-father" is one of the most popular.

We may have met Odin first as the wanderer or the wizard, but a search of his images will show that he is most often portrayed as the ruler of Asgard, greatest and most glorious of the gods. When Odin is not wandering the world, he watches over it from Asgard. In the old days, the chieftains were as fathers to their people. The title "All-father" expresses Odin's protective relationship to men and gods.

Kings and Skalds

Names like *Fimbultyr* (Mighty or Awesome God), *Godjadharr* (God Protector), *Ítrekr* (Splendid Ruler), *Jörmunr* (Mighty One), *Fjölsvidhr* (Much Wise), *Forn-Ölvir"* (Ancient Holy One), and *Haptagudh* (God of the Gods) convey an image of might and majesty.

As Snorri says, "When he sat with his friends he was so fair and noble in looks that all were joyful" (*Ynglingasaga* 6). When to this you add the descriptive names that refer to his long, grey beard and bushy eyebrows, you get a figure reminiscent of the Emperor from a Tarot deck, the archetype of the Wise Old Man. Tyr may have been the original monarch, but over the centuries, Odin has grown into the role.

Pictures from the 19th century, especially, show him presiding over the feast in Valhalla from his richly carved throne, often wearing the inaccurate but picturesque winged helmet, with his spear leaning against the chair. An eye patch may cover one eye, but the glance of the other is eagle keen. He is cloaked in the deep luminous blue of the evening sky just after sunset. As the torches flicker, light flares from his armor. His ravens perch on the high back of the great chair, and at his feet two great gray wolves gnaw on the bones of the offerings.

In the opening to the Younger Edda, Snorri portrays Odin as a monarch of supreme wealth and power who rules the world because of his might and because of the part he played in creating it. The Younger Edda was written as a handbook for poets, who were supported by the great lords and the kings. It was a mutually advantageous arrangement. Until conversion to Christianity had provided men who could chronicle the deeds of the kings in Latin, the only way for a ruler to win undying fame was to have his deeds recorded for posterity in elegant poetry.

> One particular service which Icelanders performed was that of court poet (skjald) whose task was to compose poems in praise of his lord. . . . This poetry was therefore a very important element in Icelandic culture and greatly influenced the Icelanders' ideas about their past,

powerfully reinforcing their interest in kings, especially the kings of Norway. (Sawyer 1982, 14)

Snorri himself had traveled to Norway in the hope of serving the young King Hákon in this way. The *Hattatal,* later incorporated into the Younger Edda, consists of 102 stanzas analyzing different poetic meters. The examples are taken from praise poems written by Snorri for King Hákon and his regent, Earl Skuli. Many of the stanzas celebrate the military prowess of the king and his army, but a number paint a picture of the king in peace and prosperity.

> The leader is eager to distribute fen's fire [gold]—
>
> the hand tends to act in accordance with custom.
>
> The punisher of plundering gives Rhine's amber [gold]—
>
> princes become famous among men.
>
> The ruler greatly trusts his men's experience—
>
> a gift looks to its recompense.
>
> The king has power over men for the future—
>
> each man gains from companionship.

> —*Hattatal* 26

The words in brackets give the meanings of the "kennings," which are phrases that describe what something is like or does, rather than giving the actual name. For instance, a king is a "hater of gold" because he gives away the gold he wins to reward his followers. In *Beowulf,* written five centuries earlier, the people praise the valor with which the king protected them, and cry "that he was ever of the kings of earth of men most generous and to men most gracious, to his people most tender and for praise most eager" (Tolkien 2014, 2663–5).

In addition to the Younger Edda, Snorri compiled the *Heimskringla, The Lives of the Norse Kings.* This begins with the legendary history of how

Odin led his people from old Troy to establish his kingdom in the north, and recounts the biographies of those who ruled Scandinavia all the way to the reign of Magnus Erlingson, who died in 1184, shortly after Snorri was born. The focus is on battles and victories, but even for a Christian king, the greatest praise is that "the land was prosperous during his rule, for there were both good seasons and peace" (Sturlason 1932, "History of Sigurd the Crusader," 41).

However, a reading of *Heimskringla* shows that there were limitations on the power of Norse kings. Even after conversion to Christianity had given the Scandinavian kings a claim to Divine Right and a literate civil service in the form of monastery-trained clerks, their subjects clung to a sturdy independence. The people who settled Iceland were fleeing royal power and resisted Norwegian attempts to reclaim them until social and environmental pressures overwhelmed them in the 13th century.

The fundamental Germanic political structure, as seen not only in Scandinavia but also on the Continent and in Anglo-Saxon England, seems to have been to have a king chosen from among the men within the eight degrees of royal kinship, who was supported by his sworn warriors and advised by a council of the leading men of the community.

Was Odin actually the kind of king that Snorri praised? In the Eddas, he does not seem to exercise even that much authority. During the war between the Æsir and Vanir, the most holy gods meet to discuss their response at their *rökstóla* (seats of destiny), the judgment seats that are by the Well of Wyrd (*Völuspá* 6, 23, and 25). This is a phrase we find in several places in the Eddas when a decision has to be made. Odin casts his spear above the foe to begin the battle, but going to war is a joint decision.

I see his role more as that of a CEO with a board of directors than as that of the president of a company. This makes sense, since if his job were to run the world, he would hardly have time to wander through it. As we see in chapter 7, in the literature of the saga period, the area in which Odin does exercise sole leadership is in preparing for Ragnarök; and when the last battle takes place, he is the one who will lead the gods and heroes to the field.

By the time Richard Wagner was writing the *Ring* operas, Europe had had an additional seven centuries to develop the concept of absolute monarchy, and scholars reinterpreted Odin's role as leader of the Germanic gods. In *Das Rheingold*, Wagner portrays the god as one of the young hero kings beloved of the skalds, hungry for wisdom but even more eager for glory. The "Entry of the Gods into Valhalla," with which that opera ends, is a musical portrait of the fortress that will be the physical manifestation of his power. In *Die Walküre*, we see Wotan as a reigning king, his power constricted by the laws he himself has made. In *Siegfried*, he abandons his role as king to become the Wanderer, manipulating events but not controlling them, and in *Götterdammerung*, he has given up even trying and retreats to his fortress to wait for his mortal children to bring the old world to an end.

In the 20th century, Odin's character continued to evolve. As we saw in chapter 2, Tolkien's Gandalf bears a striking resemblance to Odin as the Wanderer. As the writing of *The Lord of the Rings* progressed, the figure of Gandalf, like many other elements in Tolkien's story, evolved. Eventually, the wandering wizard is revealed as one of the Maiar, a lesser god who is a servant of Manwë, in whom we find a figure evocative of Odin as Sovereign of Asgard.

In Tolkien's *Silmarillion*, Manwë is chief of the Ainur, the godly beings who have created Middle Earth. He reigns from the top of a heavenly mountain. Robed in blue, he is the Elder King and Lord of the Winds, and the great eagles are his servants.

The most recent version of Odin as king of the gods comes from Marvel Comics. In 1962, Odin appeared in *Journey into Mystery* #86 and became a regular character in the comics as the ruler of Asgard and father of Thor. After evolving through a convoluted series of story lines in comic book form, in the current Marvel film series, he has had a new incarnation, played by Anthony Hopkins. Of course the Marvel version of Norse mythology only follows the actual lore when convenient, but Odin, in his aspect as All-father and sovereign of Asgard, is a commanding figure there.

Maker of Midgard

Odin's role in Asgard is not his only claim to the title of All-father. Whatever stories might have been told about the creation of the world in earlier times, by the time the Eddas were being written, the role of primary mover and shaker had been given to Odin.

He is not, however, the ultimate source. In *Völuspá* 3–4 and *Gylfaginning* 4–8, we are told that the universe was born from the collision of the elements of ice and fire, a Norse equivalent of the "Big Bang" theory. They met in *Ginnungagap*, the Abyss, and from the resulting yeasty ferment came a primal being, Ymir, whose limbs, rubbing together, generated the frost giants. Ymir was nourished by the supernatural cow, Audhumla, who licked away the salty rime to reveal a being called Buri, the first of the gods. Buri's son was Bor, who married Bestla, daughter of the frost giant Bolthorn. Their sons were Odin, Vili, and Vé.

How are we to interpret this story? My feeling is that this triad, born of the union of the god essence with one of the beings generated by the manifestation of matter, represents the beginnings of consciousness. The Proto-Indo-European forms of these names would have been *Wodhanaz, *Weljon,* and *Weixan* (Orel 2003, 453). As I interpret them, *Wod* (the root of "Odin") is the ecstatic passion of creation. *Vili* is "will," or focused intention. *Vé* is the name for a holy place or sanctuary and thus can stand for holiness manifest in the material world. If the earlier phases of the creation story record the interactions of barely personified forces, with the appearance of Odin and his brothers, Mind begins to act on Matter.

Its first act is to dismember the primal being, and from Ymir's parts to construct the world. "They took Ymir and transported him to the middle of Ginnungagap, and out of him made the earth, out of his blood the sea and the lakes. The earth was made of the flesh and the rocks of the bones, stone and scree they made out of the teeth and molars and of the bones that had been broken" (*Gylfaginning* 8).

Ymir's other bits and pieces were used for the rest of the world, including a palisade to protect Midgard that was made from his eyelashes. Similar stories are found in a number of mythologies. The fact that the Hindu version, in which the primordial being Purusha is sacrificed to create life, comes from the oldest Vedic scriptures suggests that the motif was already present in Proto-Indo-European religion.

When I contemplate this process, I see the Power that we now know as Odin focusing what had been a diffused cosmic consciousness in separate modes more powerfully and precisely, because "he" is aware of them. One of the primary ways of differentiating elements so that one can work with them is to give them names. Thus, I propose that Odin's association with communication developed during the process of creation. The visual image that comes to me is of the god ranging through this evolving environment, fixing and shaping the emerging entities through words.

But he does not do this alone. He works with his brothers to build the world and cooperates with the *Ginn-heilög Godh*, the highest, most holy gods, to organize the workings of the heavens and the wheel of the year. We do not know the names of these other gods. Perhaps they are other children of Bor and Bestla, an earlier generation of deities, or the evolving forms of the gods whom we find in the mythology. What they do, however, is establish a template for civilization with temples, technology, and entertainment.

This poem by Fjolnirsvin expresses one perspective on Odin's role as creator.

1. OÐINN

Before I made the world from Ymir's body

with my brothers, Villi and Ve,

who may or may not be me

(that's the trouble with hypostases),

the first giants said:

"There is only ice and fire and the place they meet.

That's all there is,

the only conceivable order."

Now the earth flowers in all its complexity.

So, know. When dead Yggdrasil grows new shoots

and Baldur returns,

in whose ear I whispered

(no, I won't tell you what),

and from the riven trunk,

the parents of future descendants emerge,

blinking at the new sun,

there will be not just reiteration

but transformation

and an unfolding order, unimagined.

The Tree People

After the story of creation, the next section of Völuspá (9–16) lists the names of the dwarves. Creating them seems to have been a group effort. In stanzas 17–18, we come to the story of the creation of humankind. Here we find another opportunity for Odin to be considered as All-father.

One day, as they are walking along the shore, three gods find two logs of wood. In the Younger Edda (*Gyrlfaginning* 9), Snorri simply calls them the sons of Bor, but in *Völuspá*, we are told that the three who found the logs were Odin, Hoenir, and Lódhur.

One log is of *ask*, ash wood. The other, *embla*, is interpreted as elm, or sometimes as a vine (Lindow 2001, 63). Other spiritual traditions say that humans were created from mud, but I have always enjoyed the idea that we are actually related to the trees. This does, however, give us a special responsibility to take care of our relatives.

The first thing we know about Ask and Embla is that they were *örløg-lausa*, "without *örløg*" or "unfated." Not only were they not yet human, but they were also not even living. They were pure potential, ready to be shaped. To understand what the gods did to them, we need to look at who they were and what each of them gave.

We know Odin (or think we do). Hoenir turns up several times in the mythology. In addition to his role in the creation of humans, at the beginning of *Skaldskaparmál*, he appears as the companion of Odin and Loki in the journey that leads to the kidnapping of Idunna.

There may have been other stories in which these three traveled together; as in the poem *Haustlong*, Loki is referred to as Hoenir's friend. In *Ynglingasaga* 4, Hoenir is one of the hostages sent by the Æsir to Vanaheim after the war between the Æsir and Vanir. He looks good but refers all opinions to his fellow hostage, Mimir. The disappointed Vanir behead Mimir (about whom we hear more when we discuss the Well of Mimir in chapter 10) and kick Hoenir out of Vanaheim. Hoenir is also one of the few first-generation gods who is destined to survive Ragnarök (*Völuspá* 63), after which he will perform divination with the "wooden lots."

The third deity, Lódhur, is even more enigmatic. One kenning for Odin is "Lódhur's friend." John Lindow (2001, 212) points out that another Odin kenning is "Lopt's friend." Lopt is a name for Loki, and some have identified Lódhur with him.

Perhaps we can get a better sense of what is going on by comparing the versions in the Elder and Younger Eddas.

	Völuspá	Gylfaginning
1. Deity	Odin	Odin
Gift	Önd	Önd ok líf
	(breath/spirit)	(breath/spirit and life)
2. Deity	Hoenir	Vili(?)
Gift	Ódh	hvit ok hræring
	(mind, inspiration, passion)	(wit and motion)
3. Deity	Lódhur	Vé(?)
Gift	lá ok litu goda	ásjónu, mál ok heyrn, ok sjón
	(life and good looks)	(face, speech and hearing, and sight; i.e., the senses)

In both versions, Odin provides önd, the breath of life, the spirit that is taken in with the first breath and released with the last. It is a term that has much the same weight as the Hebrew *ruach* and the Greek *pneuma*. Breath brings us the oxygen that catalyzes all other bodily processes. Without it, the other gifts would be useless. Breathing is a process, just as the combustion of breath in our blood is a process. Odin is a process, which is why he is so hard to pin down.

Meditating on this brings an understanding of Odin as a dynamic force, source of the breath that carries communication and the wind that is the breath of the world. This poem by Paul Edwin Zimmer (1979) expresses some of its meanings.

> With breastbone and brain, breathe the sky!
>
> Allow your lungs long to fill:
>
> Weighted with wisdom, wind in the lungs
>
> Reddens blood with rust, that rushes through the body
>
> And the brain, bearing breath everywhere;
>
> Blowing in the blood, blithely stirring life,
>
> Let wind awake wisdom in your mind!

Ódh is the gift of Hoenir, which seems odd, given that it is the root of Odin's name. It is also one of the most difficult Norse words to translate. In their monumental dictionary, Cleasby and Vigfusson (1874) offer a translation for it as an adjective meaning "mad," "violent," "frantic," which fits with Adam of Bremen's 11th century definition of "*Wodan id est furor.*" However, Cleasby and Vigfusson follow this with an entry for ódh as a noun, in which its meaning is given as "wit" or "mind" with a secondary meaning of "song" or "poetry." Most translators of this passage prefer to interpret it as the noun. For a deeper exploration of the meanings, see chapter 10.

In the Younger Edda, however, the gift is listed as "wit and motion," which could be said to incorporate both senses of ódh. Today we tend to think of mental activity as detached and controlled, but my own understanding of ódh is something like "creative fervor," the act of thinking agitated into passion. This does not fit particularly well with what we know of Hoenir, but it might work for Vili if we view it as "fervor focused by the will."

The third gift is a collection of qualities that enable the human being, already possessed of the ability to move and think and feel, to live in the world. The senses enable us to give and receive information. I take the gift of a face as the equivalent of "good looks," the final sculpting that gave Ask and Embla the forms that humans wear today.

The identity of the Power who gives this third gift is even more puzzling than that of the second. In a fourteenth century poem, the *Thrymlur* (a retelling in Icelandic *rimur* form of the Eddic *Thrymskvidha*), *Lódhur* appears as another name for Loki. This, when combined with the inclusion of Loki as a traveling companion for Hoenir and Odin in the Younger Edda story in which the trio encounter the giant Thiazi, inclines me to favor Loki/Lódhur as the third deity involved in the activation of Ask and Embla.

The gift of the third god, whoever he may be, is external—the shape of the body and the senses. As such, it fits well as a gift of Vé, transforming a thing of the physical world into something holy. Speculating further, I could make a case for Loki, source of so many tools and devices, as the giver of the means by which our bodies interact with the world.

At this point, perhaps I should say a few words about Odin and Loki, who is not Odin's son but with whom he has a complex connection. As I see it, between the boundaries of the creation of Midgard and the final battle of Ragnarök that will end the world we know, the gods exist in an eternal present from which they move in and out of our chronological time. Thus all the myths, including Odin's sacrifice at the Well and his ordeal upon the Tree, are simultaneously occurring. Although a time will come when Loki is the enemy, in the Younger Edda he is always listed among the gods. In *Lokasenna* 9, Loki reminds Odin that they are "blood brothers," and that Odin promised that if he had a drink, he would share it. The story of how this happened is lost, but the relationship is clearly an important one. For this reason, even in kindreds where Loki is not explicitly recognized, some Heathens will sprinkle a little of whatever is being offered to Odin on the candle or into the hearth.

When we contemplate Odin as All-father, we need to realize that his role in creation was not that of a clockmaker who sets up his machinery and leaves it to run. He is an active force in our development, inviting us to participate in the coevolution of the world. Michaela Macha's poem "Who Started It All?" (2004) expresses the relationship.

> So who
>
> started it all
>
> did you begin
>
> with Ask and Embla
>
> or did *we* shape *you*, Shape-Shifter?
>
> a mirror reflecting a mirror
>
> anyone's guess
>
> but do we need you? Or you us?
>
> To survive
>
> love isn't needed,

nor laughter, friendship nor gods

but to live

dearly we need them.

Did you call me, or did I

visit you uninvited?

Do I follow, or do you

watch *me* from behind?

It is no matter

as I bring you my sacrifice

I don't know who started it all, but

let's finish it

together.

Father of Gods and Kings

In *Gyrlfaginning* 19, Snorri (1987) tells us, "Odin is highest and most ancient of the Æsir. He rules all things, and mighty though the other gods are, yet they all submit to him like children to their father." Personally, I tend to doubt that the other gods are always that submissive—I can imagine some pretty heated discussions at those judgment seats by the Well.

Whether the relationships are part of the original stories or were assumed as gods from different Heathen tribes were amalgamated into the mythology, at various points in the lore, Thor, Heimdall, Tyr, Baldr, Hermod, Höd, Váli, and Vidar are all said to be Odin's sons.

Thor

Thor, god of storm and thunder, is Odin's son by Jordh, a giantess whose name means "earth." Her importance is indicated by the fact that Thor is often identified as "Son of Earth" rather than as "Son of Odin." We have no story about how this happened, but to me, the fact that *Bjorn,* "Bear," is given as a byname both for Thor and for Odin is suggestive. Decorated bear skulls found in Paleolithic burials indicate an ancient reverence, and the bear was held to be sacred to the goddess of the earth in a number of cultures. I imagine the two of them meeting in the form of bears.

Odin's byname of *Raudgrani,* "red moustache," explains how Thor came by his red hair, but by the time they meet in *Hárbardsljodh,* the only story describing their interaction, Odin is *Hárbard* ("Hoar beard").

There is yet another way in which we can view the birth of Thor. In general I avoid interpreting the myths as explanations of natural phenomena, but when I was doing some research on Thor, I found a fascinating meteorological analysis of the cause of lightning and thunder. Translating it back into mythic terms produced the following description of Jordh's encounter with Odin from *her* point of view.

> Well, you have to understand—it was a long time ago,
> and we were different then. Talking to you humans, we've
> learned to see ourselves in different ways. But back then
> . . . we were forces, we were feelings. And the worlds were
> in flux—we acted and reacted as the situation changed.
>
> In those days, I did not have a name. I knew that I *was.* I
> felt the impact of stones from the sky that vaporized my
> rock and released the water that had been locked within.
> I felt the explosions of heat from within. Heat and Cold
> . . . Fire and Ice . . . and as they warred, the first teasing
> touch of the wind . . .
>
> Oh . . . that wind . . . and the Voice that called my name . . .
>
> The wind touched me, courted me, coaxing the moisture
> from my cracks and hollows until the droplets of water

swirled upward and became clouds. As the wind shaped them, I could sense a tension growing between the warmer foundations of the clouds and the chill towers that reached for the sky. The energy in those lower areas repelled me. I felt my own tension growing. I wanted . . . something . . . and I could feel that something was changing in the upper air.

The clouds were moving, creating a channel of energy. Once more I heard that Voice, calling, compelling, crying out my name.

And I reached out, up, with all my might. My Power touched His and completed the connection. And then . . . human words cannot convey the glory, the ecstasy as I received the discharge of His Power in an explosion of incandescent air.

The shockwave that was the joining of our voices reverberated in the first clap of thunder, as Thunder, the Son of Earth, was born. And as the echoes faded, I felt the cool kiss of falling rain.

Heimdall

Heimdall, whom we know primarily as the god whose supernatural sight and hearing enable him to guard Asgard, is the son of nine mothers. They are giantesses, and according to Snorri, the nine waves are the daughters of the giant Aegir, who rules the deeps of the ocean. However, their names are unfortunately not the same as the names listed for Heimdall's mothers in the *Shorter Seeress's Prophec* (Orchard 2011).

It is, however, possible to speculate on how Heimdall might have been begotten. In *Harbardsljodh,* Odin boasts that he slept with seven witchy sisters in a distant land. To connect with Aegir's daughters, however, he would have had to give himself to the waves, which seems to me just the kind of expansion of experience Odin would have sought in his wanderings.

In the poem *Rígsthula,* Heimdall, under the name of Rig, is also said to have sired the three social classes: *thrall* (serf or slave), *carl* (farmer), and *eorl* (ruler). Presumably, this was during a period of wandering before he settled down as watchman of Asgard. It is a story that in general seems more typical of Odin, especially when we see that *Kon* (king) the youngest son of Eorl, turns out to be a master of rune lore, rivaling Ríg himself. Kon is either the grandson or the great-grandson of Odin. As he is out hunting, a crow counsels him to seek the warrior path, and according to a note in Hollander's translation of *Rígsthula* (1986), he eventually becomes the founder of the royal line of Denmark.

Tyr

As with Heimdall, the claim of Tyr to be a son of Odin rests on a simple statement by Snorri in the Younger Edda. The only surviving story that mentions Tyr's parentage is *Hymiskvidha,* in which Tyr and Thor journey to the hall of Hymir, who is either Tyr's father or grandfather, to obtain a cauldron big enough for Aegir to brew sufficient ale for all the gods. Tyr's mother is a "golden girl," perhaps a goddess, who is not named.

Although only two stories about him survive in the Eddas, unlike Heimdall, Tyr is a god who has been known since Roman times. His name, coming from the same root that gave us the names of Zeus and Jupiter, suggests that he may have been the original sky god. Given that Odin himself is the son of a giantess, the *jotun* parentage ascribed to Tyr in *Hymiskvidha* may itself be evidence of his antiquity.

Baldr and Hermod

Other than Thor, Baldr is the best known son of Odin. In *Gylfaginning* 22, Baldr, Odin's only offspring by his wife Frigg, is portrayed by Snorri as "so fair in appearance and so bright that light shines from him. . . . He is the wisest of the Æsir and most beautifully spoken and most merciful, but it is one of his characteristics that none of his decisions can be fulfilled."

Fortunately, Baldr's own son, Forseti, is much more successful as a mediator. To balance this rather Christ-like portrait of Baldr, it should be noted that in the *Gesta Danorum* of Saxo Grammaticus (1905), Balderus and Hotherus are rivals for the hand of Nanna (Baldr's wife in the Younger Edda), and Hotherus slays him in battle.

The Icelandic version of the story, pieces of which appear in several places in the Elder Edda and in full in the Younger, begins when Baldr starts having bad dreams. Odin responds by riding to the gate of Hel, where he uses his necromantic spells to summon up the ancient Völva who is buried there and ask her what's going on. Complaining, she rises, and proceeds to tell him not only that Hella is brewing the beer and decorating the hall to welcome Baldr, but also that Baldr's killer will be his own half-brother, Höd, and his avenger another son of Odin, Váli, who has not yet even been begotten.

The great mystery is why Odin, returning with this information, does nothing to stop the tragedy. Frigg does better, wandering the world to take the oaths of all beings not to hurt her son, but for some reason she tells the first person who asks that there is one being that did not swear, the insignificant mistletoe. When the gods, in a fine display of Viking humor, test Baldr's protection by throwing things at him, Loki attaches a dart of mistletoe to an arrow and guides the aim of the blind god Höd.

Baldr drops dead, and everyone gathers for a magnificent funeral. Frigg promises to reward Hermod if he will ride to Hel and beg Hella to release her son. Baldr greets him as a brother, but it is unclear whether Hermod is a son of Odin or a human hero in the service of the gods. Hella's condition for releasing Baldr is that all things must weep for him. One giantess refuses, so until Ragnarök, Baldr must stay where he is.

The story goes that as Baldr lay on his funeral pyre, Odin bent over the body to whisper in his ear. The nature of that message becomes the most famous trivia question in Norse literature, revealing Odin's identity and giving him victory in more than one riddle contest, since he is the only one who knows the answer.

This has not stopped people from speculating. One popular interpretation is that Odin's farewell to his son is a promise that Baldr will be safe in Hel until Ragnarök releases its inhabitants, when he will return to reign over a world that has been reborn.

But the price both of them must pay is that unless they pass on the road to Hel, Baldr—among all of Odin's offspring—is the one child All-father will never see again.

Höd, Váli, and Vidar

Saxo's Hotherus is a mighty human warrior with a magic sword who kills his rival Balderus in battle. In his Eddic incarnation as Höd, he is a son of Odin and he is blind. We are not told the identity of his mother. He, too, ends up in Hel, and after Ragnarök is destined to return with Baldr to rule over the new world.

The god who avenges Baldr is called Váli, specifically begotten for that purpose by Odin on the goddess or princess Rind, possibly against her will but in accordance with the Völva's prophecy. We will take another look at this incident in the chapter on Bölverk. The newborn, Váli, is transformed in one night into a warrior who goes unshorn and uncombed until he has killed Höd.

Vidar, often paired with Váli for purposes of alliteration, is Odin's son by the giantess Grid. Kennings for him given in *Skaldskaparmál* include "silent god," "owner of the iron shoe," "enemy and killer of the Fenris wolf," and "vengeance-god of the gods." His destiny is to avenge his father after Odin has been killed by Fenris, either by killing the wolf with a sword or by ripping apart its jaws. Along with Höd and Váli, he will survive Ragnarök.

Brünnhilde

The most powerful portrayal of Odin as a father is not in the Eddas, but in Wagner's opera *Die Walküre*. Brünnhilde, leader of the valkyrie daughters borne to Wotan by the earth goddess Erda, is his favorite, his confidant, the mirror of his soul to whom he can open his heart as a lifetime of marital warfare prevents him from doing with his wife Fricka.

Brünnhilde, caught in the middle of their sparring, defends Wotan's mortal son Sigmund, which is what she knows Wotan *wants*, rather than protecting Hunding, whom Wotan's own laws force him to support.

Furious at himself as much as at her, Wotan pursues and condemns Brünnhilde with a godly wrath. The end of act 3, in which she begs him to give her to a hero instead of leaving her the prey of a common man, is one of the most soul-wrenching scenes in opera, more profoundly moving than most operatic love scenes I have seen. As Wotan and Brünnhilde sing their pain and their love, the tension mounts, until at last he breaks and becomes the loving father once more. The past cannot be undone, but Wotan has forgiven her and leaves her surrounded by a wall of flame that only the greatest of heroes can cross.

Humans

In her famous analysis of Wagner's *Ring* operas, musical comedienne Anna Russell observes that Wotan fathered the twins Sigmund and Sieglinde "under the singularly appropriate name of Wolf!" Apparently, Odin's encounters were not limited to giantesses.

However it was accomplished, in the Germanic countries, Odin, or Woden, appears at the top of a remarkable number of royal family trees. In Scandinavia, his offspring include Sigi, ancestor of the Volsungs (*Volsungasaga*); Scyld Scefing, ancestor of the Danish royal line (*Ynglingasaga*); the Geats and the Amelung Goths (Jordanes' *Getica*); and Sigrlami, king of Gardariki (*Hervararsaga*). In *Ynglingasaga* 8, we learn that after separating from Njord, Skadi took up with Odin and bore him several sons, including Saeming, ancestor of Jarl Hákon.

In volume 1 of his *Teutonic Mythology,* Grimm (1966, 165) includes the genealogies of the Anglo-Saxon kings. In England, Woden was listed in genealogies compiled during the 7th to 9th centuries in Bede's *Historia Ecclesiastica,* the *Historia Brittonum,* and the *Anglo-Saxon Chronicle.*

Anglo-Saxon kings claiming descent from Woden who are mentioned in both the prologue to the Younger Edda and the *Anglo-Saxon Chronicle* include Wecta, ancestor of Hengest and the kings of Kent; Beldeg, ancestor of the kings of Wessex; Wihtlæg and Casere in Anglia; Winta, in Lindisfarne; and Seaxneat in Essex. All of these give Odin a good claim to another of his names, *Veratýr* ("God of Men").

In "An Eye for Odin? Divine Role-Playing in the Age of Sutton Hoo," Neil Price and Paul Mortimer discuss a number of archaeological finds, starting with the famous Sutton Hoo helmet, in which the left eye of an image, mask, or helmet has been crafted or altered so that it appears to be missing. Experiments with a replica of the Sutton-Hoo helmet have shown that "seen indoors by the flickering light of the fire, the wearer of the Sutton Hoo helmet was one-eyed" (Price and Mortimer 2014, 522). They conclude that a resemblance to Odin was intended to support the mystique of kingship.

Fig. 11. Reproduction of the Sutton Hoo Helmet

Odin's Godchildren

Identifying oneself as a child of Odin is not the sole prerogative of kings. Many of those who are drawn to work with him today characterize their relationship as that of a child to a parent,, although not necessarily an obedient one, as we see in this poem by Laurel Mendes.

All father, my father, old friend new found.

The chosen now chooses to be daughter once more.

Not obedient, but most obstinate,

Shared among many, not singular, not solemn.

Such will my dedication be to you.

Yet I will do what I can for your children's aid.

When am I able I will walk with you.

Thor give me the strength in my limbs to move forward,

Freya give me grace and truth in my heart

Sif give me kindly words for my lips to utter

Frigga lend my will your steely resolve

This is the service that is now mine to offer

So, tell me, old man, do we have a deal?

James Hodur describes his relationship with Odin thus:

I thought I'd share how I view Óðinn, the All-Father. To me, Óðinn is a grandfather figure. He's a grandfather who has a past. He has seen war, tragedy and has those scars in him. He doesn't let those scars rule him. Like any grandfather or family member, he can be kind and loving. But he can also be cruel and uncaring. It's a part of life and any familial relationship. I also see Óðinn as a teacher. He inspires and rewards me with many ideas and thoughts. But he can be a challenging taskmaster and present me with problems to solve. And I must show my work.

To say my relationship with Óðinn is an easy one is far from the truth. To say I haven't experienced other aspects of Óðinn in my life is an understatement. Our relationship is as varied and complex as he is. It takes on many facets and probably will continue to as we grow together.

When a Power has as many names and as many masks as Odin, there are obviously going to be many ways of working with him. The relationship of child to parent is one of the most positive. Many Heathens refer to the gods as our Elder Kin. To call ourselves children of Odin is not a claim to divinity but rather a recognition that we have a lot to learn. Being willing to accept the god's lessons can be another matter.

A person may have a number of reasons to relate to Odin as his child. Those who had good relationships with their fathers might seek in him a spiritual parent who will continue and extend the support and instruction they remember from childhood. Those whose fathers failed them may be seeking the love they never knew. However, one responsibility of a father is to encourage and, if necessary, to force his children to grow. Odin never asks of us more than he demands of himself—of course what he asks of himself is a great deal. If what we get at first is "tough love," we have to believe that beneath it is a boundless compassion. All-father may not take the hard tasks and choices from us, but he will share the pain.

Practice

1. Breathe

Breathe in to a count of four, hold for four, breathe out to a count of four, and hold again. Continue that rhythm, returning to the count if you become distracted. Fill your lungs, let air expand your chest, fill every part of your body, and then, still counting, let it go. As you continue to breathe, feel the oxygen you draw in energizing every cell. As you breathe out, intone the syllable "ond." Repeat this practice regularly as a preparation for meditation.

2. Engage in cocreation

Choose an environmental project and support it with money or, better still, with physical action. Join in a local creek-cleanup day, or a tree-planting project, or take a trash bag on your next hike and clean up the trail as you go along.

3. Adopt a tree

This may be a tree in your own yard or in a park. Choose one that is well grown, vigorous, and healthy. Hail it as your kin. Pour out offerings of water. Put your arms around it and send your awareness inward to sense the life flowing upward and downward through the trunk. Then sit down with your back against the trunk.

Now close your eyes and visualize that day when the gods came walking along the shore. See Odin standing before you. Sit up straight and breathe slowly in and out, paying attention to the movement of air through your lungs. Feel the oxygen in your blood, singing through your veins. Let that energy awaken the awareness of your own spirit. Verbalize the syllables of your own name. Who are you? What does that mean? Then let awareness flow outward into your limbs. Feel the limits of your body, touch your face to relearn its contours. Listen to the sounds around you. Then open your eyes and rejoice in the world.

4. Fourth Night Meditation: All-Father

Set up your altar as usual and light a gold candle. You may also want to set out a glass of red wine. Then say:

Odin, by these names I call you:

Alfadhr (All-father)

Fimbultyr (Mighty or Awesome God)

Godjadharr (God Protector)

Ítrekr (Splendid Ruler)

Jörmunr (Mighty One)

Fjölsvidhr (Much Wise)

Forn-Ölvir (Ancient Holy One)

Haptagudh (God of the Gods)

Veratyr (God of Men)

In the word of the king is wisdom,

In the eye of the king is inspiration,

From his high seat comes protection,

and holiness from his hall.

In the mood of the king is might,

In the hand of the king is healing,

At his table abundance,

And bright blessings for all.

Odin is our king, who rules over Asgard,

Odin, our father who made for us this world,

Odin's gift, the way to glory

If we will but heed his call.

Visualize yourself standing at the door to Valaskjalf, Odin's hall. It is roofed with silver that blazes in the sun and glitters beneath the stars. Inside, torches burn in their sockets on the carved pillars, casting a flickering light on the weapons and jewelry of the men and women within. As you start forward, you feel a breath of air and a great raven swoops above you and onward.

Your gaze follows it to the high seat at the end of the hall. Another raven calls a greeting from the post that supports the chair back, all its wood carved in an interlace of figures that seem to move. Two wolves lie before it, gnawing on bones.

But your attention is fixed on the figure sitting in the high seat, a drinking horn in his hand. A deep blue cloak, edged with silver, drapes his shoulders. Silver also are the clasps and fittings of the dark tunic below, and silver threads glint in the brindled beard and the hair that flows from a silver band around his brow.

He sits straight, keen eye fixed on something beyond the walls of the hall, and you know he is watching Midgard. The other eye is shadowed. You do not know what that eye sees. As you gaze, the light grows brighter, catching on each point of metal, surrounding him in a golden glow.

Will you bow before him or try to withstand that piercing gaze? Act as your heart bids, and honor him. Perhaps he will turn and speak to you.

When the time seems right, return to the door. Breathe deeply, return to awareness of the here and now and open your eyes to the place from which you came.

In Gunnlöðh's Bed

Who are you?

Who dares this darkness,

slithering like a serpent, seeking my bed?

Long have I waited at Worldheart, warding my secret.

Who dares draw near to me now?

You hiss in the shadows, or is it laughter?

It has been lonely here; I would be glad to laugh . . .

Ah, I see you now, one eye of light and one of darkness,

and a breath of air follows,

a breath of life from the world beyond these walls.

Well, I am sick of secrets and shadows.

Speak to me, serpent, what have you to say?

Tell me a tale; how you traveled in man form,

tricked the thralls, won Baugi's help with your labor,

and as Bolverk made him bore a hole through the belly
of the world.

You were strong then, and cunning.

Do you mean to trick *me?*

Serpent coils spiral runes around me,

and serpent tongue whispers a spell.

Do you think thus to trance me?

Now it is my turn for laughter.

Indeed, I admire your transformations,

but if you would win me,

you must make another magic.

What, I wonder, would you have here?

An hour in my bed, or two, or three?

Do you draw back from that suggestion?

Perhaps my appearance is not quite what you expected . . .

You will have to be cunning indeed to cozen me.

I am as old as the rocks or the running water.

I am of the race of Ymir,

more ancient than any woman you have known—

Now I see you smiling.

So . . . you know a way to win me after all.

Come closer. Please me . . .

Show me that your lips know more than spells.

Will you put at hazard even your manhood,

surrendering your power?

If you plan to possess me, you are wrong—I will engulf *you*,

but you cannot stop now, can you?

You must give everything, having thus begun.

I wind you in my arms, all your wisdom lies within me.

My lips are like honey . . .

Drink deeply, wanderer.

Ecstasy fountains upward, filling me, filling you . . .

Then rest, for you have pleased me well.

For a night of the world, you may sleep in my arms.

What, are you not yet ready to leave me?

Perhaps you are learning—

I begin to see beauty mirrored in your eye.

This time, Desired One, it will be easy.

Come once more to my bed

while a second night strides across the world.

Kiss my breasts, and taste honey;

for you I am all golden.

Devour me! Consume me entirely,

drink deeply from the cauldron at the heart of my life.

All that I am I will give to you,

for your love has made me lovely.

Embrace me, my beloved,

as we build the world anew.

Now, in my arms you lie exhausted.

You would sleep for an age of the world.

But the third night approaches, and there is more,

you know there is more.

Do you want it, Old Man?

Have you the will to seek it

even when your flesh is weary and your spirit quails?

You have no lust for it now, have you?

You look at me and wonder how you could have desired
me;

it would be so easy now to withdraw

and slink homeward with what you have won.

But you will never rest if you leave me now . . .

Come then, and I will call you Wise.

Though spirit quails and flesh is unwilling,

let us seek together through the shadows.

Sink into my arms, not knowing if death awaits you.

Now . . . now you are come where Need compels you.

This vessel is filled with a dark mead,

bitter to the tongue, but in the belly, sweetest of all. . . .

The third night is past.

Wanderer, Beloved, Wise One, I release you,

for you possess me now entirely,

and wherever you go, I am there as well.

Swiftly then, let love grow wings.

Suttung roars, reaching out for the eagle—

The jealous ones pursue and attack you.

Let them lap up the drops spilled by your passing,

not knowing that what you have won from me

is a prize they never dreamed.

Will they say you have stolen my virtue?

It is not so, for I remain hidden in the heart of the mountain,

and my cauldrons are always full.

Those who will give what you have given,

those who can pursue the path you traveled,

shall find through your gift, Galdorfather,

the way to my arms.

—Diana L. Paxson

Fig. 12. Oski

chapter six

Desired One

Speak fairly and be free with wealth

If you will win a woman's love.

Praise the looks of the lovely lass.

Win by wooing.

—*Hávamál* 92

Though Odin always returns to Frigg, he is often involved with female figures in his wanderings. In books about Norse mythology, descriptions of Odin stress his role as the ruler of Asgard and leader of the warriors who will fight at Ragnarök. As we shall see in chapter 7, all this is true, but a look at the lore will show that more often than any other Germanic god, Odin interacts with women. His interest is not limited to sex. He is even more likely to go to them in search of wisdom. He connects with humans, goddesses, and giant-kin, and he is the primary god for many Heathen women today.

Under "pleasure names," Price lists *Oski* (god of wishes, fulfiller of desire), *Sadh* or *Sann* (the true one), *Thekk* (pleasant, much liked, clever),

Unn or *Udh* (lover, beloved), *Njótr* (user, enjoyer), and *Glapsvidhr* (seducer) (Price 2002, 105). Although "Harbard" is a misleading choice from among Odin's names, in the *Vikings* TV series, the character who goes by that name certainly takes Oski's role in fulfilling women's desires.

Here we might also place *Jolnir* (Yule being) and *Wunsch* (wish), a 13th-century medieval personification, possibly derived from the same root as *Wunjo,* the rune for joy. As described by Grimm, "The sum total of well-being and blessedness, the fullness of all graces, seems in our ancient language to have been expressed by a single word, whose meaning has since been narrowed down; it was named *wunsch* (wish)" (Grimm 1966, I:138). In the poetry, God gives "Wish" the power to create perfection. Every Yule, my kindred sings to this composite figure as the German *Weihnachtsmann*, "Man of the Holy Night." For the music, see appendix 2.

Since I live in Berkeley, I am always amused when I encounter references to "Oski," the Golden Bear who is the mascot for the University of California. The name seems to have come from the "Oski Yell." At football games, the mascot is fond of making mischief and flirting with girls. Given that *Bjorn*, "Bear," and *Bjarki*, "Little Bear," are listed by Price among Odin shape-shifter names, my friends and I tend to view him as an aspect of Odin. Flowers are sometimes left in front of his statue before an especially important game.

*Fig. 13. "Oski," the University of California totem bear, with name
embroidered on jacket (from the UC Alumni display)*

In the course of his adventures, Odin is linked with goddesses, giantesses, and mortal women. This may or may not involve "knowing" them in
the biblical sense. I think that what really drives him is a lust for knowledge.
Whether the connection includes sex or not, in the relationships that we
know about, he usually has a purpose that goes beyond simply getting laid.

When I first started working with Odin, one of the first things he
did was to put me in touch with his wife and his old girlfriends. Here are
some of the things I learned.

Frigg

Those who have only encountered Odin's wife as the ball-busting Fricka in the first two *Ring* operas may wonder what he sees in her. Wagner portrays her as an even bitchier version of the Greek Hera—the archetypal jealous wife, forever scheming to keep her long-suffering husband from wandering. It is said that the characterization was modeled on Wagner's relationship with his first wife, Minna, who had good reason to complain.

As we encounter Frigg in the lore, we find a very different figure. Her name comes from the old word for love. (c.f. Old English, *frigu*, love. "Frigga" spelled with an "a" is an incorrect, though very common, version.) The relationship between Odin and his wife is one of mutual respect, and their only recorded quarrels are political.

If Frigg is not to be viewed as a jealous bitch, how should we see her? The references that are made to her in the surviving literature, though not copious, provide some interesting insights. In *Lokasenna,* we are told that Frigg is the daughter of a giant, Fjorgynn. The feminine name Fjorgyn is also given to Jordh, Earth. Either way, Frigg comes of giant-kin. By ancestry she is therefore an earth goddess, appropriate mate, and counterpart to a god who rides the skies. Many of Frigg's qualities, such as her rooted stability and deep wisdom, seem to derive from this earthy origin.

Loki accuses Frigg of having lived with Odin's brothers (Vili and Vé) while he was away (an episode that also appears in the Younger Edda and Saxo's history of the Danes). Since Frigg is otherwise thought of as a model of fidelity, some speculate that the "brothers" are really aspects of Odin. I would offer another possibility: If Frigg is an earth goddess, the territory to which she is linked is that of the Æsir, and she carries its sovereignty. In that case, her polyandrous association with Vili and Vé would give them the legal and spiritual right to reign without interrupting Odin's sovereignty. "Vé," the holiness of place or spiritual focus, and "Vili," the Will that rules, remain with the goddess in Asgard while the ecstatic "Wod" wanders the worlds.

Though Frigg may stay quietly at home, she has been known to take an interest in the affairs of humankind. In the 8th-century history of the

Lombards written by Paul the Deacon, we are told that for some reason Odin was against that tribe. Frigg instructed the women to come out with their hair bound beneath their chins. When Odin asked, "Who are these long-beards?" she declared that since he had named them, he was obliged to gift their army with victory.

Even better known is the story told in *Grimnismál*. Odin and Frigg had taken under their protection two brothers, Agnar, protected by Frigg, and Geirrod, who was favored by Odin. Through Odin's counsel, Geirrod cheated Agnar out of his heritage and became king, while Agnar ended up in the wilderness. To even the score, Frigg accuses Geirrod of lacking in the primary Germanic virtue of hospitality, and dares Odin to prove it by showing up incognito. She then sends her handmaiden Fulla to warn the king that a dangerous sorcerer is wandering about, who can be recognized because no dog will attack him. Naturally, when Odin shows up at Geirrod's door, the dogs cower before the Lord of Wolves, and the king, determined to find out what is going on, seizes the stranger and orders him to explain himself.

Odin will say no more than that his name is Grimnir, the Hidden One, so Geirrod has him bound to a stake between two fires. When he has roasted there for eight nights, the king's young son can no longer stand the crime against hospitality, brings the stranger a horn of mead, and sets him free. Odin's first response is to declare that the sovereignty has passed from the king to his son. Then, as if to make up for his silence, the god gives us forty-seven stanzas of lore. Geirrod, finally realizing just who he has been tormenting, jumps up, trips, and stabs himself with his own sword.

In his poem "Sonatorrek," Egil Skallagrimsson refers to the dwellers in Asgard as "Frigg's descendants." But though she may be regarded as "All-mother," we know of only one child born of her body—Baldr the Beautiful. The story of his untimely end is also the myth in which Frigg plays the most active role.

When Odin has returned from Hel with the Völva's interpretation of Baldr's dreams, Frigg acts to save her son by exacting oaths from all things to do him no harm—or rather, almost all. Unfortunately, after completing this labor, she undermines her own action by confessing to an old hag that she has neglected to take an oath from the lowly mistletoe. Of Frigg it is said that she knows all fates, though she does not tell what she knows (*Lokasenna* 29). One cannot help but wonder why, in that case, she does not realize that her efforts to save her son will be fruitless, or that the "hag" is really Loki, or that telling him about the mistletoe will bring about the very tragedy she is trying to prevent. Her failure to save Baldr is Frigg's first great sorrow, as the claims of motherhood give way to those of wyrd. Her second sorrow, of course, will be her inability to save her husband at Ragnarök (*Völuspá* 52).

Frigg is called first among the ásynjur (the goddesses). The sense I have of her is that she is the still center to which Odin, in all his wanderings, can always return. She has been called All-mother, an appellation which seems especially appropriate when we consider that the twelve "handmaidens" whom Snorri associates with her can, in fact, be viewed either as separate figures or as hypostases or aspects of the goddess herself—personae that she adopts to play a more active role.

Sága

One of these aspects, or handmaidens, is Sága, who in the Younger Edda is listed second after Frigg herself. Sága lives in *Sokkvabek* (Sunken Hall), "a very big place." In *Grimnismál* 7 we are told,

> Sokkvabekk the fourth is called,
>
> where waters cool roll round about;
>
> there Odin and Sága drink every day,
>
> glad from golden cups.

I suspect that while Odin and Sága are drinking together, they are trading stories. According to the *Icelandic-English Dictionary*, the name Sága is

> akin to *segja* (to say) and *saga*, which is a story, tale,

legend, history. The very word owes its origin to the fact that the first historical writings were founded on tradition only; the written record was a "saga" or legend committed to writing; the story thus written was not even new, but had already taken shape and had been told to many generations under the same name. (Cleasby and Vigfusson 1874)

One can picture them matching beers and competing to see who can outlast the other in capacity both for booze and for stories. We are familiar with Odin's role as a patron of poetry, but his friendship with Sága gives him a connection to prose narrative as well.

Freyja

Odin's relations with his wife are well documented. Except for the "endless battle" story in the *Flateyjarbók,* his relationship with Freyja can only be inferred, but the idea that an involvement existed is accepted by many Heathens today. For evidence, we look at *Völuspá* and *Lokasenna* in the Elder Edda and Snorri's account of the early history of the Æsir in *Ynglingasaga.*

In stanza 21 of *Völuspá,* the seeress who is recounting the ancient tales for Odin tells of the "first war of the world." Oddly enough, it begins not with a challenge by men but with the arrival of a mysterious female called *Gullveig* ("Gold drunk" or "Gold power"), who walks into the Hall of Hár. The response is not hospitable:

Gullveig with spears they stabbed

And in the hall of Hár burned her.

Thrice she was burned, thrice reborn,

Often, over, and yet she lives.

The following stanza suggests why:

Heidh she is called when she comes to houses,

Völva and spae-woman. Gand she knew,

Seið she understood, messed with minds by Seið,

Ever was she dear to ill-working women.

In other words, she was a witch, wielding a kind of magic the Æsir did not understand. Gullveig and Heidh may be seen as separate figures, but Lindow (2001, 155) and a number of other scholars conclude that at least in this passage they are names or titles of Freyja. After she leaves, the gods meet to discuss whether they should pay tribute, and decide to fight the first war in the world. Odin casts his spear over the enemy, but the Vanir are clearly winning.

For what happens next we must turn to *Ynglingasaga* 4, where we learn that after some inconclusive fighting, they held negotiations in which they exchanged hostages to guarantee the peace. The hostages sent by the Vanir were Njordh and Frey. With them came Frey's sister Freyja. "She was a priestess and she first taught the Asaland people seidh, which was in use with the Vanir." Since a page or two later we are told that Odin practiced seidh, he must have learned it from Freyja.

That this relationship also included sex can be concluded from Loki's assertion at Aegir's famous party that Freyja has slept with every male in the room. This may or may not have been a problem. As her father Njordh points out in her defense, "It is no crime that a woman have both husband and lover" (*Lokasenna* 33).

In the *Sörla Tháttr*, an episode included in the *Flateyjarbók*, which was written down in the 14th century, Freyja is a mortal woman, the concubine of "King Odin." To win the wonderful necklace Brisingamen, she spends a night with each of the dwarves who forged it. Following Odin's orders, Loki steals it. To win it back, Freyja must cause two kings and their men to engage in endless battle. The poem *Húsdrápa* offers another version in which Heimdall and Loki fight in the form of seals, and Heimdall recovers the necklace.

This is not the only association of Freyja with battle. In the survey of the homes of the gods with which Odin begins his download of the lore in *Grimnismál* 14, we learn that

> Fólkvangr (the field full of folk) is the ninth, where Freyja decides
>
> Who shall sit where in the hall.
>
> Half of the slain she chooses each day,
>
> And half Odin has.

Today, most people seem to think that Freyja chooses first. In the words of Lorrie Wood's Freyja song,

> Weeping gold, you walk the world now,
>
> Falcon-winged, ply windy ways.
>
> Ygg's men fight, but none can say how
>
> Freyja's first-picked spend their days.

But what does she want them *for?* Again, we can only speculate. The lore does not say what happens to the goddesses after Ragnarök. Perhaps the warriors who drink in Sessrumnir (Freyja's "many-seated" hall) will guard her as she helps to rebuild the world.

The final question about Freyja's relationship with Odin has to do with her mysterious husband, Ódh. The only thing we know about their marriage is that he gave her two daughters and then disappeared. Eventually she went after him. In *Gylfaginning* 35, Snorri explains that she (like Odin) has so many bynames because she "adopted many names when she was travelling among strange peoples looking for Ódh."

The fact that the name of Freyja's husband is the first syllable of Odin's name does make one wonder. As Patty Lafayllve puts it in her book about Freyja:

Important in this case are two concepts, the first a question: are Od and Odin one and the same? There is no real answer to this, but as shall be seen, Odin and Freyja have quite a lot in common . . . it is interesting to consider that Freyja traveled many worlds seeking her spiritual arousal (or, to stretch the metaphor, an ecstatic state of inspiration). This author often wonders if all these realms were in the mundane world. (Lafayllve 2006, 50)

Given the kind of magic Freyja was teaching him, the relationship between her and Odin must have transcended physical sexuality. If Frigg provides an enduring stability, I think that Freyja is the one who challenges Odin and pushes him beyond his boundaries, and perhaps he does the same for her. When we are doing trance work with both Freyja and Odin, the priestess of Freyja has been known to take charge and calm the mediums carrying Odin when they get too boisterous—in one case, threatening to "take back every bit of magic I taught you" if the god did not return the medium to normal consciousness once more.

In modern Heathenry, Freyja seems to be second only to Odin as a recruiter. I know of at least as many people who have dedicated themselves to her as to him. Some of those who follow her are hostile to Odin, but sometimes the god and the goddess work together, as in the case of a dream a male friend on the Troth members' list, who is just getting into Heathenry, sent to me.

So, not very long ago I was into Germanic Mythology as an interest, not a belief. One night I had this dream. I was running through a village, which looked like it could be in England, New England, or Europe. As I was running I looked down, and my deceased dogs materialized beside me. They led me inside a house which had a rich golden light and beautiful hardwood floors. The walls were a glimmering ivory.

I felt the warm presence of family and friends, but I didn't get a chance to look at anyone, because I was distracted by my pet cat (who I had to put down earlier that year); he kept rubbing on me and getting underfoot. He also kept climbing into a pine tree which was indoors and set up like a Yule tree or a Christmas tree, while a woman was trying to tie ribbons on its branches.

She giggled as he was climbing inside the tree. Her hair was braided which led to a bun on the back of her head. Her hair was a golden-reddish yellow color that emitted the same color light. Her face looked like the face of every beautiful woman I've ever seen. She seemed very sweet and loving, but also had this intense sexual energy about her; the kind in which a guy would have to tell himself to not be too enamored by her, because she'd unintentionally break his heart. Better to know her as just a friend and nothing more. Not even a lover in the most casual sense.

I woke up from that dream, and I asked myself who that woman was, and something told me it was Freya. It made sense, of course that my cat would go to her, as her sleigh is pulled by cats. Then I realized that she was putting ribbons on a Yule tree. The following day, just for fun I did a Google image search of "Yule," and I came across an image: It was a picture of a cat curled up in front of a roaring fire with the words "May your Yule and Winter Solstice be warm and bright," signed, "Odin."

I'm aware of the intended humor in the image. But the cat in this picture could've very well been mine, and the picture looks like it could've been a scene from my dream. I know a person made this image, and it wasn't Odin himself. And I think Odin means it in an ironic sort of way, to confuse me, as I've always thought of him as a tough love kind of guy. Maybe he has that type of humor in which you don't know if he's being serious or pulling your leg.

I think the way signs work is that they are things which are to be found by someone in a kind of sequence, after or before an event; in my case the dream. For me it's significant, because I've always felt closer to my pets than to most of my family. I've always been the oddball. I know, I know, my mysterious heathen dream is about my cat. Yes, I'm very aware how crazy this makes me sound. I know it's not an awesome dream in which Odin handed me a rune, or a dream about Thor slaying a giant with Mjolnir. I've never been the guy who puts on a macho front, I don't try to be anyone I'm not. To tell you the truth, I really miss that little guy and my other animal family, and I am very grateful that they have taken refuge with Freya.

Gunnlödh

Odin's affairs with goddesses seem to have been conducted on equal terms. Some of his relations with other females are problematic, although in at least one case—his attempt to seduce the daughter of Billing, a lady who "had sport of me with all manner of mockery, and I had not my way with her"—he failed(*Hávamál* 102). Odin is also acquainted with giantesses. When he trades insults with Thor in *Harbardsliodh* 18, he tells of his visit to the island Algroen (All-green), where, unlike Thor, he has been seducing giantesses instead of slaying them. He alone is able to win their lust and their love.

It is tempting to cherry-pick the lore and skip those episodes that show Odin's darker side. We will be considering his reputation as a seducer in more detail when I discuss Odin as Bölverk in chapter 8. Here, however, I want to examine the motivation behind his visit to Gunnlödh and see if it can be, if not excused, at least viewed in a more positive light. The poem that precedes this chapter is my attempt to understand how Odin came to lie with her and what each of them got out of the exchange.

Among the deeds of Odin, three are especially famed because they result in gifts to humankind. One of them, as we have already seen, was acquiring the runes. In chapter 10, I tell you the story of how Odin gave his eye to gain wisdom. The third achievement is the winning of the mead of poetry. Part of the tale is told rather allusively in *Hávamál* 104–110. In parts 57–8 of *Skaldskaparmál*, we find the full story.

The mead of poetry is the product of a complicated series of events that occur during the conclusion of the war between the Æsir and the Vanir. It eventually comes into the possession of the giant Suttung, who stores it in three cauldrons, called *Odhroerir, Bodn*, and *Son* (in Norse mythology, *everything* has a name), hidden in a cave inside a mountain and guarded by his daughter Gunnlödh. Odin enters the mountain in the form of a serpent, using the name Bölverk.

> Bölverk went to where Gunnlödh was and slept with her for three nights, and she granted him three drinks of the mead. In the first he drank everything in Odhroerir, in the second everything in Bodn, in the third everything in Son, and so he had all the mead. Then he changed himself into an eagle and flew off as quickly as he could, but when Suttung saw the eagle flying, he changed himself into an eagle and flew after him. But when the Æsir saw where Odin was flying, they put their barrel out front, and when Odin came over Asgard, he spat up the mead into the barrel. But Suttung was so close to catching him that he sent some mead out the back, and this was not saved. Everyone who wished had some of that, and it is called the bad poets' share. But Odin gave the mead to the Æsir and to those humans who could compose verse. (Lindow 2001, 225)

Two points occur to me when I read this tale. The first is that Gunnlödh is a *giantess*. The fact that Thor fights more female than male giants would suggest that they are well able to defend themselves, so what happened in that cave was certainly not a rape, though it might be a seduction. In *Hávamál* 106, Odin admits that he dealt her an evil reward for her good will and left her with a heavy heart, and later (110), that he broke a promise made on an oath-ring. "To Gunnlödh he brought sorrow." Clearly what happened between them was something more than simple physical pleasure. The tone suggests that he felt love for her, as well, and regretted having to leave her.

Which brings us to a second point. For Odin, pain is not a deterrent. Again and again we see him risking and enduring it to achieve some greater goal. In this case, it was bringing to the world the gift of poetry, a fundamental part of Norse culture, and an art that has the power to teach the deepest truths. If leaving Gunnlödh hurt him as well as her, it was the price of doing business. Those who work with Odin today recognize that he cannot always spare them, but our experience is that he will share their pain.

Women of Wisdom

Freyja is not the only woman from whom Odin learns magic. In chapter 3, there was the passage from *Lokasenna* in which Loki accuses Odin of not only working with women but also of being *like* a woman as he worked seidh on Samsey Isle. Viewed from the deck of a boat, Samsø (off the east coast of Jutland) is an unimpressive gray blur on the horizon, but it had quite a reputation in Viking times as the burial place of Angantyr and his brother berserkers, the setting for the wonderful scene in *Hervararsaga* in which Hervor wakes her father from sleep in his grave-mound and demands his magic sword.

When Odin came there, he learned ecstatic practices, possibly trance induced by drumming and dancing, "like the völur" (plural of *völva*). One imagines a sisterhood of witches living on the isle. When Odin had learned their magic, he fared forth among men in the form of a *vitki*, a term that could mean a man of wisdom or a sorcerer, either a Gandalf or a Saruman. The stanza conjures images of an old earth magic, women's magic that was even less acceptable for a male than Odin's own galdor.

So Loki calls Odin "*args adal*," having the quality of being effeminate, which is rather a laugh coming from the mother of Sleipnir, as Frigg implies in the next stanza when she tells the two of them to stop talking about their past. *Argr*, or *ergi*, is a complicated concept that I have tried to disambiguate in an article called "Sex, Status, and Seidh: Homosexuality in Germanic Religion" (1997). The term *ergi* was used as an insult, implying that one takes the receptive role in sex. Snorri's statement that formerly both men and women learned seidh but that by his time it was considered so *ergi* that it was only taught to priestesses (*Ynglingasaga* 7), indicates a decrease in status for women and any quality associated with them, possibly stimulated by the growing influence of Continental European Christian culture.

One of Odin's bynames that has puzzled students is "Jalk," translated as "gelding," which is surely one of the last terms one would expect to apply to the god. I am not alone in suspecting that this is the name he might have used on Samsey Isle.

Seeking the Seeress

If the völur of Samsey Isle sound like hedge witches, the Völva who speaks the prophecies of *Völuspá* seems to be considerably higher in status and nobler in kind. From the authority with which she demands whether Valfather wants her to recount the tales of ancient times to the final prophecy of Ragnarök, she lays it out in soaring poetry. She knows where Odin's eye is hid. She knows that Baldr will die and who will avenge him and the dreadful list of disasters that will herald the doom of the gods. And she is rewarded (*Völuspá* 29).

> The father of armies gave rings and necklace,
>
> (from her he) got spae spells and spae magic.
>
> She sees widely over the worlds.

We do not know when and why Odin sought her counsel, but we do have some background for the other poem in which he seeks out a seeress. In *Baldrs Draumar* (the Dreams of Baldr), the gods meet to discuss why Odin's son is having bad dreams. When no one can explain them, Odin (traveling under the name of Vegtam) saddles Sleipnir and rides to the grave-mound of the Völva who is buried outside the eastern gate of Hel. As we know from *Hávamál*, he has spells that can compel the dead. He uses them to summon the seeress, who rises from her grave, complaining loudly at being disturbed. He asks about Baldr, and she foretells the whole story, until at last she realizes to whom she is talking and with an exchange of insults sends him on his way.

The fact that Odin is told exactly what will happen by the Völva and yet does nothing to prevent it is one of the mysteries of Norse mythology. One senses not only ambivalence in not only the motivations of Baldr's parents but also the workings of a wyrd so powerful that it binds even the highest gods.

In Wagner's *Ring* operas, the role of the Völva, who for some reason known only to Wagner is referred to as the Vala, is filled by the earth goddess Erda, summoned by Wotan at the beginning of act 3 of *Siegfried*. Their conversation is unproductive, since she first asks why Wotan has not gone to Brünnhilde for counsel. When he explains that the Valkyrie has been punished for disobedience, Erda grows confused, and when he asks how Wotan can avoid the coming destruction, she goes silent. Disappointed, he sends her back to sleep, proclaiming that he will cease to fight fate and allow Siegfried, free of the gods, to deal with the Ring.

As for Brünnhilde, we will see her and the valkyries again in chapter 7, when Odin goes to war.

Mortal Meetings

It is interesting that so many women are attracted to Odin, given that he is so masculine a god. Based on many conversations, my impression is that women, on the whole, may actually find it easier to connect with him than men do. In *That Hideous Strength*, C. S. Lewis has a character observe that we are all feminine in relation to God. I think that (except when he himself is being *ergi*) that may also be true of mortals who encounter Odin.

As we shall see in chapter 7, the *wod* ecstasy of the berserker was usually a masculine path, but these days, men as well as women are socialized to value calm and control. Whereas a woman who knows how to consent can open herself to Odin's ecstatic energy, when that divine wind begins to blow, many men react by trying to resist its power. Usually, the best advice is to either (try to) cut off contact with the god entirely or, as Heinlein used to put it, to "relax and cooperate with the inevitable." Sara MacLachlan's song "Possession" was not written about Odin, but it expresses quite vividly the way some people feel toward him.

A woman may relate to Odin as an employer or a guardian, as a daughter to a father, or as a lover. This account describes the experience of one young woman who is just beginning to work with him.

> My first experience with Odin was this: one summer day I was taking a shower and all of a sudden this really beautiful, strong tune came into my head (mind you, I don't write songs), and I was just like "Okay, cool" and kind of brushed it off. That night this really intense energy filled my room and Odin showed up and my first reaction was "Fuck," just because the energy was so intense; I was a little bit scared. I asked if he wanted me to write him a song, he replied "Yes," and I got on writing that song.

> My first few times interacting with Odin were generally characterized by that intense energy and me being intimidated by it. About a year after Odin first showed up in my life, I went to an Odin devotional and that totally changed how I view him and how I interact with him now. During the devotional, Odin gave me some tools to help deal with some issues that were/are really

hard for me. That night, I saw that Odin was much easier to connect with than I thought, he was very willing to help me with the things I needed help with, and to top it off loves math like I do.

I am beyond happy I went to the Odin devotional, as I now feel much more connected to him and feel much more comfortable actually working with him. Also, truthfully, at the devotional he still said/did things that could have been scary, but really they just pushed me to move through fear, so I guess it's much more my perspective of him that has changed, and since the devotional, I have started wearing a valknut and got a statue of two wolves for my altar, so I have been converted to an Odin fan.

For some, the experience of connecting with the god while in a trance state can have a sexual component, as energy flowing through the body may activate those centers as well. One priestess of Odin, asking for insight, received the following comments as dictation.

I take it what you want is how to pursue that ecstatic moment when all else drops away . . . and in nine easy lessons. Well, I'll give it to you in one: *ergi*. Reflect on this, this receptivity meant by the word. Think of it, not as unmanly, but as unmanning—the difference is profound.

Make of yourself a vessel. A vessel for what? Well, if you would experience the ecstasy of being one with a god, then you must be open to them, and that to which they connect. . . . Yes. You must make the way for the sea to be poured into a thimble, for the stars to all be held in a bucket of milk. You must make of yourself a vessel for *the universe entire*, and that is no small thing.

But that is what you seek, that is the way of it. Reflect on the concept of receptivity, and hollow yourself out so that your essence is . . . passive. Not unresponsive, but able to move out of the way. You can use Us to fill in what has been made empty by your own passing. Like any other act, it will be difficult on the first attempt. Like the nervous virgin, you will be tight and cannot hold much (and I have known very many spiritual virgins . . .). But, as you grow, the more you hold, the more you *can* hold, and the sooner you will attain that which you seek.

Still, it's very much like sex, so if you have hang-ups about that, they may come to haunt you here. They will come and live with you, filling up that space where you would have us live, where you would put all the universe you can stand. And that . . . will not do. But to open the way to ecstasy, make of yourself a vessel. Even I have done it, from time to time . . . although you can well imagine I can hold a *little* more than the average one of you, yes?

When you allow the universe, All that Is, to penetrate you for even one shining moment . . . or, by proxy for it, any of Us . . . you learn a little better how to respond to it the rest of the time. That's how you respect us in the morning: by remembering how to talk to us waking as well as you do when sleeping or meditating. Sex is good. Moments of mind-shattering ecstasy are wonderful (and I'm an expert). But it's the respect in the morning that really gets the job done as far as we're concerned.

Do you understand? It's important, it's what keeps the task going once the fun is just a memory.

Some women have made a formal commitment as a Godspouse. In *Flateyjarbók,* there is a story in which a temple of Frey is managed by a priestess who is known as the god's wife. There are also peasant traditions from Denmark, in which a maiden was "married" to a figure made from the last sheaf, representing Wodan and called "the Old Man" (de Vries 1931). So far as I know, the first to actually go through a marriage ritual with Odin in modern times was Freya Aswynn, author of *Leaves of Yggdrasil* and *Powers and Principles of the Runes.* She began to sense Odin's presence in the early 1980s, when she was still practicing Wicca and the Western Mystery tradition, and dedicated herself to him. In 1993, she suffered a psychic assault that "astrally" disconnected her. This is how she describes it.

> One day I woke up and Odin was gone! So far as I was concerned, I was finished and ready to "go and see him in person" and find out what the f*** was going on. As I was contemplating my one-way ticket to Asgard, my wolf brother rang up with some question or comment about Valkyries, and he intuited that something was very wrong.

> He went out on a vision quest and contacted Odin about this matter. Odin showed him a little crusted cap of some rust colored material on my crown chakra. Kveldulfr was instructed by Odin to strike it with Gungnir, the cap burst apart and I was back to normal. I was however very anxious about the fact that any asshole with a grudge could disconnect me from Odin, my Inner Plane contact. I was thinking about finding a way to eliminate this possibility forever, well at least for this incarnation. I had the idea, but not quite the audacity, to suggest it.

> I had read in Voodoo literature that devotees sometimes "married" the Loa. At the same time, I knew that in Sweden in the Middle Ages a female priestess

was considered by all to be the bride of Frey and drove around with a cart and Frey's statue. When I very subtly questioned Kveldulfr, by coincidence he had come across "Contributions to the Study of Othin" by Jan de Vries. In this was mention of a ritual involving the "last sheaf" and Wodan. After due consideration and various consultations, we decided that this was the only way for me to progress, both esoterically as well as for personal spiritual growth. On the 28th of November 1993, with a small circle of kinsfolk in attendance, I was married to Wodan. The ceremony was based on a traditional agricultural harvest rite, written and researched by Kveldulfr Gundarsson. The vows I took are personal.

From the beginning in '83, I somehow always was aware of his presence. This became even stronger after the wedding until 2002 or thereabouts, then life went to shit and I had to fight for my survival in the mundane. He was still there though. I always had and have access to His guidance and I even surprise myself as to the accuracy of my Rune Readings. In addition to this, I have ever since my wedding been in excellent health considering my age, which is sixty-seven.

The role of god-spouse is not an easy path. In recent years, the idea has been adopted by people from a number of Pagan traditions, working with various deities. It involves the same level of commitment as a monogamous human marriage, or perhaps more, since so much of the relationship is interior. In Voudoun, marriage with one of the loa (the Powers of that tradition) is modeled on a human wedding, with a marriage contract that lists the responsibilities of each partner. This is actually a good idea when making any kind of oath to a god, especially to Odin, who will hold you to your word even if you didn't necessarily understand what you were letting yourself in for. On the other hand, just as a mortal marriage may come to an end when one partner moves on, even those who have made a public and formal commitment to Odin sometimes find that he has released them or even passed them on to another god. Except in his relationship with Frigg, he is not noted for fidelity.

For a deeper discussion of oaths and initiations, see appendix 1.

I myself have never been called to make this particular commitment. By the time I realized how deeply connected to Odin I had become, a formal recognition seemed redundant. My status is more like that of one of his old girlfriends, and I think that leaving me with apparent freedom makes it easier for him to work through me in connecting to other Powers.

Odin may not be visible, but a relationship with him is very real and may cause difficulties in the human partner's other relationships. Taking this step requires careful negotiation. For a discussion of the issues, see the collection of articles under the link for godspousery at *https://darkam-berdragon.wordpress.com,* especially those from Beth Lynch.

Oski is the Desired One, but what do we desire? We have spoken here of Odin and women, but gender is not relevant when an empty heart desires to be filled.

The gifts we ask of him as the Jul being are not the ones we want when the crops have failed or the foe is at the gates. When Odin follows his desires, almost invariably it is because a greater purpose must be served.

Practice

1. Hold a dinner party for Oski.

The dinner can be for two or a feast to which you invite others who honor him. Set a place for each guest, including one for the god. At one ritual that happened to be on Sadie Hawkins Day (February 29), we also set places for each of the goddesses with whom Odin has a relationship.

As you eat and drink, tell stories that honor him. A color scheme of blue and silver will set the scene. Serve whatever delicacies you feel he would like. Drinks may include red wine, akvavit, or mead. When dinner is over, set the contents of Odin's plate outside where they may be consumed by local ravens and wolves or their equivalents.

2. Bless a cup of mead, then sit down and write a poem.

It does not have to be complicated—free verse or simple four-beat alliterative lines like the ones in the poem below will give you the right to taste the mead. The topic can be Odin, or love, or simply something that moves you.

3. Fifth Night Meditation: The Desired One

Set up your altar as usual and light an orange candle. You may combine this practice with the feast for Odin described above. Then say:

Odin, by these names I call you:

Oski (God of Wishes, Fulfiller of Desire)

Sadh or *Sann* (True One)

Thekk (Pleasant, Much Liked, Clever)

Unn or *Udh* (Lover, Beloved)

Njótr (User, Enjoyer)

Glapsvidhr (Seducer)

Oski, our/my desires fulfilling,

Welcome, Wish-father, to our/my hall!

To Thy delight let us/me drink deeply—

Thekk, our/my thanks we/I offer thee!

Or

Wild as the wind Your ecstasy,

Deep as the sea my desire.

Solid as stone Your love for me,

my need more fierce than fire.

This moment is set apart for you,

I open my heart and my hall.

Joy is a gift I give back to you,

Odin, I offer You all.

Close your eyes and think about what you have just said. What things do you desire—the desires that are created by *need* not frivolities. What do you want and why do you want it? Who would it benefit, and what would you be willing to give to the god to achieve your desire? When your thoughts are clear, sit quietly, counting your breaths and opening your heart for his reply.

The head-Ransom

Lord, hearken to't

(Well beseems that),

What song I've wrought,

If there's silence got.

Most men heard say

How the King made fray;

But Odin saw

Where the slain men lay.

Wax'd rattle of swords

With clank of wards;

Sour wax'd round Lord:

Lord ranged for'rd.

Heard was the croon

Of the iron-storm's tune:

Sword-river's moan,

Where the spate swirl'd down.

No jot waver'd

The web dart-broider'd,

Where the King's merry

Spear-fields serry,

In bloody shallows

'Neath banners wallows

Seal's plain, and thunder

Gives tongue from under.

On the shore the folk sink

'Neath javelins' clink,

Loud fame gat

Eric from that.

—verses from "The Head-Ransom"
by Egil Skallagrimsson, translated by E. R. Eddison
(1930, 1968)

Fig. 14. Sigfather

chapter seven

Battle God

Egil Skallagrimsson is one of the most striking figures from the Icelandic saga era, a truly Odinic hero. We saw something of his rune lore in chapter 4, but he is best known as a skjald and warrior. The verses above are from a poem called "The Head-Ransom," written while he was a prisoner of his enemy King Eric Blood-Axe to persuade the king to let him go free. Translated by novelist E. R. Eddison, it captures the gusto with which the Viking Age skjalds celebrated war and the kings who waged it.

As Victory father, Odin provided battle magic, protection, and advice. He is the patron of the bear-sarks and the wolf-coats who were used as shock troops in battle, and lord of the einherior, the heroes who wait for Ragnarök in Valhalla. Today, this aspect resonates with people in the military or other professions involving stress or danger and can be an inspiration to men in prison as well.

The Father of Armies

In Price's list of Odin's names, those relating to warfare comprise 25 percent of the whole. This total is hardly surprising, considering that the people who most often made war were also the people who paid the poets, who, in turn, must have spent a lot of time thinking up new and different ways to refer to the god to whom their patrons sacrificed for victory. The selection of names discussed below covers the variety of martial roles that Odin mastered.

As a leader of armies Odin is *Herjafadhr* (Army Father) along with six other names with the element *her*, a term originally referring to a troop of raiders rather than a formally organized army. Kershaw (2000, 17) defines him as having originally been the mythical leader and personification of the *herr*. He is also *Ófnir* (Inciter), *Hvatmódh* (Whet Courage), *Sigfadhr* (Victory Father), and eight other names that include *Sig*. Among combat names, we find *Atrith* (Attacking Rider), *Geirdrottin* (Lord of the Spear), and eight other names with "spear" as an element. The spear Gungnir is Odin's emblematic weapon. He is also *Göllnir* (Battle Screamer), *Herteit* (Glad in Battle), *Hildolf* (Battle Wolf), *Hjalmberi* (Helmet Bearer), *Járngrím* (Iron Mask), *Svölnir* (Shield Bearer), and *Vidhurr* (Killer). Names that indicate his role in battle magic include *Haptagudh* (Fetter God) and *Hramm* (Fetterer, Ripper), and possibly *Gunnblindi* (Battle Blind) and *Herblindi* (Army Blind).

Interestingly enough, despite all these titles, in the mythology the only fight in which we see Odin personally taking the field is the one in which he faces the Fenris Wolf at Ragnarök, the fight that he will lose. Thor fights giants in single combat, Snorri says warriors should call on Tyr, and in *Skirnismál,* Frey is called "general of the gods." Yet it is Odin to whom kings sacrificed for victory.

For an image of the god in this role, look online for the Arthur Rackham picture of Wotan galloping off to punish Brünnhilde for disobeying him (from the illustrated libretto for Wagner's *Die Walküre)*.

Battle Magic

The spells at the end of *Hávamál* describe the kinds of aid Odin can give. Some of them are protective. Spell number three blunts the blades of enemies so they will not cut. Number five stops arrows in flight. With the eleventh and thirteenth spells (*Hávamál* 156, 158), Odin protects his followers—

> I know an eleventh, if I shall to battle
>
> Lead old friends,
>
> Under shields I sing, and they fare with might,
>
> Whole (healthy) into battle,
>
> Whole from the battle,
>
> Whole wherever they walk.

But as we see from the names listed above, despite all the spear shaking, it is mind power that Odin uses to bestow victory. Odin whips up the spirits and courage of the side he favors, while he blinds the minds and binds the limbs of the foe. When Sun Tzu says in *The Art of War* that subduing the enemy without fighting is the supreme art of war, he is talking about the psychological element in warfare that can overcome physical advantage.

There are two parts to that equation. Standing fast while you face a line of other people who seek to kill you takes the conviction that your leader is worth following, that the people standing with you in the line are worth dying for and feel the same about you, and that you yourself are the "scariest M—F— in the valley." It helps if you believe that the gods are on your side. In *Ynglingasaga* 2, Snorri describes Odin's ability as a morale builder:

> Odin was a mighty warrior who had wandered far and
> won for himself many kingdoms; he was so victorious
> that he won every battle, and through that it came about
> that his men believed he must needs be winner in every
> fight. It was his wont when he sent his men to battle or
> on any other journey to lay his hands on their heads and
> give them his blessing; they then believed that all would

go well with them. And so it was with his men: when they were hard beset on sea or land, they called on his name and always thought they got help from it; in him had they all their trust.

In the film version of Tolkien's *Return of the King,* at the beginning of the battle of the Pelenor Fields, King Theoden rides along the line of Rohirrim riders, tapping their spears with his sword and thereby transferring his luck to them in just this way.

As we can see from this account by John T. Mainer, Odin continues to help warriors today.

My first encounter with Odin was deeply moving, and embarrassing; the former because of the changes it made in me, the latter because I was ignorant for a long time about who had taken a hand. In 1988, I was two-thirds of the way through basic training in the Canadian Armed Forces. Those who were going to drop, had dropped, and we were culled from a company down to an over-strength platoon. Those who were left were going to go all the way, they were stripped down to the core of who they were, had been tested to their limits and there was no give in any of them. I knew them all as worthy, and I wanted to open to them, but I could not. The failing was my own, which actually made it harder to accept. I had training in Go-Ju Ryu karate and Tai-Chi so I was attempting to use eastern meditation techniques to deal with my growing anger issues and problems opening up, but without much success.

I was sitting on a large boulder out back of C Barracks, on the hill above the Regimental HQ, when I slipped from meditation into vision. You have to understand, I had no knowledge of the centre boss shields used by our ancestors, and when I thought of shields, my thought was either Roman tower shields, Greek or Celtic arm strapped heavy round shields, so what awaited in my vision didn't make much sense at the time. I saw a shield wall, the men and women in it were my platoon, and they were fighting hard against a foe that outnumbered them greatly. Their wall was strong, and they were splendid warriors, but they were getting cut down because at the centre of the line was an empty file; my place. I knew the place was mine, and without my shield and spear they were falling. I could not advance and take my place, nor could I bear to watch them get cut down because of me. In my shame I turned to find a man, white haired and wild bearded. He had a dark blue hat pulled low over his face, and a dark blue (not Navy blue, just darker than royal blue) battered cloak. One blue eye blazed with utter contempt and fury at me and I literally stepped back from the force of it.

He asked me why I tarried here when my comrades were dying, did I not want to go to them and take my place? I lost it, and screamed at him that I CAN'T. He asked again if I wanted to, and this time I just nodded. Then he said simply, "Then join them" and without a word of warning, or me ever being aware that he held one at all, suddenly he plunged a spear gripped in his right hand through my chest. The head was broad, flaring near the base and you could see the hammer marks on it. It drove through my chest, splitting my breastbone from just below the nipple line, and blasting out my back.

I came out of the vision like a shot, fists raised, heart hammering painfully in my chest, every single muscle in my body hard and tensed and my adrenaline in full fight/flight mode. From that day forth, the barrier that had always prevented me from connecting was gone, and I bonded to my basic training group and the others of the Regiment as I had bonded to no one before in my life save blood kin.

The changes in how I interacted with everyone after that point made it essentially a new life, and I still had no clue who had done this. I chanced to be without a book on my way to campus for school, when I stopped at a used bookstore to buy something to read. I saw a picture of the one eyed bastard who stabbed me, and the title of the book was *Brisingamen*. Written by Diana L. Paxson, ironically before she was heathen, the book told of Odin and the gods in modern context and all it took was the name before the penny dropped. It had been Odin who had found and fixed me.

Being a university student and soldier, I went to the library, found the *Hávamál*, and read for the first time a moral code that spoke to my soul. In the words of the wanderer, in the teachings of the Feeder of Ravens, I found the teachings I had been searching for that could bring all the warring parts of me, soldier, scholar, poet, into one cohesive whole.

Note that John had this experience a year after my own encounter with the god and more than twenty years before we actually met. Odin seems to have started recruiting in earnest about then.

Thanking "Battle Glad" is easy when you win, but there is a deeper level of commitment in which you continue to stand fast even when it becomes clear that Victory father is not going to give you the victory.

A case in point is the Battle of Maldon, in which an Anglo-Saxon earl makes the mistake of letting the Viking raiders cross to solid ground so they can have a fair fight. He gets killed, leaving his followers to decide whether to abandon his body or keep faith with their lord and each other by defending it. The words of the old retainer Byrthwold ring out with the clash of steel (Griffiths 1993, 312–13).

> *Hige sceal þe heardra, heorte þe cenre*
>
> *mod sceal the mare þe ure mægen lytlað*
>
> Mind shall be harder, heart be keener,
>
> Courage shall be more as our might lessens.

This is a colder kind of courage, based not on the assurance of victory but on honor, on keeping troth with your fellows, your god, and your highest self, the kind of bravery that will be needed at Ragnarök.

The other part of Odin's magic turns this around. In *Ynglingasaga* 6, Snorri tells us, "He could make his foes blind or deaf or terrified and their weapons were as nothing more than sticks." We know from the fourth spell in *Hávamál* that Odin can free himself (and his followers) from physical fetters. The names *Haptagudh* and *Herblindi* tell us that psychically, as well as physically, he can apply them to others. The variety of weird-looking gear warriors have added to their armor over the centuries suggests that psychological warfare is ancient. If hearts beat faster when Victory Father incites a battle, the blood grows cold when he takes that power away. It may be more glorious to fight a worthy foe, but it is easier to defeat an enemy who cannot fight back. There is no more dangerous enemy than the one that strikes from within.

Odin's other main role in warfare is to advise. This is seen most clearly in Saxo's story of the death of King Harold War-Tooth (Grammaticus 1905, *Gesta Danorum* 1, 8). Odin has previously taught Harold the secret of the *Svinfylking* (Swine array) battle formation, which is a wedge in which each successive row of men is doubled. It is known from many cultures and was a favorite formation of the German tribes who fought the Romans. When Odin, taking the role of Harold's charioteer at the Battle of Brávellir, tells him that his opponent, Hring, has drawn up his men in the wedge formation, Harold realizes that his enemy could only have learned it from Odin and that the god has therefore abandoned him.

Battling with the Bears, Wandering with Wolves

But Odin has yet another weapon. Snorri also tells us that "his own men went about without armor and were mad like hounds or wolves, and bit their shields and were strong as bears or bulls; they slew men, but neither fire nor steel would deal with them. This was called a berserk's-gang" (*Ynglingasaga* 6).

The figure of the berserker has fascinated fighters and scholars alike, inspiring a variety of speculations as to the condition's cause ranging from consumption of *Amanita muscaria* (fly agaric) or alcohol to various mental or physical conditions. Jesse Byock (1993) proposed that it might have in some cases been a symptom of Paget's disease, a condition involving uncontrolled skull growth. At the end of *Egilssaga*, we're told that a hundred and fifty years after his death, Egil's body was exhumed and his skull found to be abnormally thick and hard.

The berserk fit is a state of altered consciousness in which the fighter is consumed by a fighting madness in which not only can he accomplish feats that are beyond his usual strength but he is also impervious to pain. The Roman poet Lucan, writing about the wars in the Alps during the early second century BCE, refers to what he called the *furor Teutonicus* to describe the fighting style of the German Teutones. In Viking tradition, berserkers identified with bears—wearing an actual or magical bear sark (skin)—or were *ulfhedinn*, wearers of the wolf jacket.

Old Norse literature is rich in stories of shapeshifting and words derived from the *hamR* root, including *hamfarir* (shape journey), *hamrammr* (shape strong), *hamask* (to fall into a state of animal fury), *hambleyna* (leaper out of his skin), and *hamslauss* (out of his shape). In the sagas, shape changing generally is used for fighting, although it may also be used for information gathering. As we saw in chapter 3, Odin was said to have the power to take the form of a bird or beast while in trance and in that shape to journey in the inner and outer worlds (*Ynglingasaga* 7).

We find another such example in *Hrolfkrakisaga*, in which Bodhvar Biarki fights for his king in the form of a great red bear, while his body remains in his house, apparently asleep. When his friend comes to find out why he is not at the battle, he "wakes up," and the bear disappears. This is also presumably what is going on when Dufthak and Storolf fight in the shapes of a bull and a bear (clearly their antipathy predates the struggles of the stock exchange) in the *Landnamabók*.

A description of a berserker can be found in chapter 7 of Saxo Grammaticus's (1905) history of the Danes.

> When Hardbeen heard this, a demoniacal frenzy suddenly took him; he furiously bit and devoured the edges of his shield; he kept gulping down fiery coals; he snatched live embers in his mouth and let them pass down into his entrails; he rushed through the perils of crackling fires; and at last, when he had raved through every sort of madness, he turned his sword with raging hand against the hearts of six of his champions. It is doubtful whether this madness came from thirst for battle or natural ferocity. Then with the remaining band of his champions he attacked Halfdan, who crushed him with a hammer of wondrous size, so that he lost both victory and life; paying the penalty both to Halfdan, whom he had challenged, and to the kings whose offspring he had violently ravished.

Even when they went to battle in groups, the bear-sarks fought as single champions. The wolf-jackets, following the habits of their totem, may have worked together in a more organized fashion. A 7th century bronze helmet plaque shows a one-eyed warrior dancing with a man in a wolf skin and may represent a ritual. King Harold Fairhair had a group of ulfhedinn, and in a praise poem for the king by Thórbiörn Hornklofi, they are described as fighting with shield and spear in a closed group. In *Hrolf Kraki's saga*, the kings of Sweden and Denmark both have bands of a dozen berserkers in their retinues. Kris Kershaw (2000, 58) suggests that fighting a berserk was part of a ritual in which a youth proved his manhood. He believes that the Indo-European forerunner of Odin may have been primarily associated with wolves and discusses a variety of wolf cults from Anatolia, Greece, Ireland, the Slavic lands, and India. In Norse tradition, the best known "wolf warriors" are Sigmund and his son Sinfjotli.

> Now one day they went again to the forest in order to find themselves riches, and came to a cabin, and in the cabin there were two men asleep, wearing heavy gold rings. An evil fate had overtaken them, for there were wolf skins (*ulfahamr*) hanging above them in the cabin. They could shed the skins once every ten days. They were princes. Sigmund and Sinfjotli got into the skins, and could not get out of them again—the strange power was there, just as before, and they even howled like wolves, both understanding what was being said. (*Volsungasaga* 8)

In *The One-Eyed God*, Chris Kershaw explores an early Germanic tradition of warrior training called the *mannerbunde*, based on accounts of warrior training in various German tribes in Tacitus's *Germania*. The mannerbunde was

> a cultic warrior brotherhood of young males, bound by oath to a god and to each other and in ritual union with their ancestors, in training to be the men, or the leading men, of their society. The word is used of age-set systems in which the military aspect of the youths' formation is particularly important. It is not an ideal term: the youths are not men yet; they are in process of becoming men. (Kershaw, 2000, xi)

He goes on to compare the customs described by Tacitus with ethnographic studies of warrior societies from the Vedas and ancient Greece to the Masai, involving masks; animal identities such as the dog, wolf, horse, and bear; and a cult in which, through the young men, the ancestors live again. Typically, for a good part of the period, the boy lived in the forest like the beasts of the forest; he became a hardy and crafty hunter and fighter. When a tribe went to war, these youths were used as shock troops and guerrillas, painted black, often masked, and revved up by ritual to become an army of the dead and thus immortal.

Anyone who has raised boys can appreciate the benefits of a system that gets them out of town during the years in which their growing strength and raging hormones are most likely to get them into trouble. Going into the army can serve the same purpose today. In the system described by Tacitus, once the young warriors had settled down, they were able to go home and become responsible members of society. In the Chatti tribe, certain warriors continued in this status instead of returning to the tribe and served as trainers of boys lifelong.

The altered state of consciousness that is Odin's gift to his warriors does not always involve chewing on one's shield, as we see in John T. Mainer's account of his first battle.

> My first firefight was my worst. We were deployed as communications support for a multi-national peace-keeping force. Our security element was not drawn from NATO countries, and our confidence in them was low. As a result, we did one shift on communications, one on guard, and one off. I was off shift, sleeping, deeply fatigued from running two on/one off except when our moves happened in the off shift. Then, instead of sleep, you did transport and digging new generator pits and fighting positions.

> The call to stand-to took me out of a deep sleep. I was dragged from my position, run to a slit trench and dropped there alone by an NCO who went to drag

another warm body to the next position. I had no idea what the situation was. I was facing our supposed rear, with no idea what my safe arc of fire was, no communication, and only the sound of gunfire getting closer as a guide. It was night. Each of us might as well have been on the moon, we were so isolated. The traditional strengths of a soldier were stripped from me as I had no idea what was going on, no idea what, besides defending our location, my tasking was, where friendlies or enemies were, or what changes had been made to our ROE now that we were under direct attack. We had no night vision gear in those days. I was alone in a slit trench, a firefight happening in the tree line. No idea what to do at all. Fear paralyzed me and I had bile in my throat. I did not pray for safety, or even victory. I asked Odin, Sigfather, Victory Father, to understand what was happening.

You do not seek out the combat arms of the Service if you do not wish to test yourself in combat. I had sought this test, had thrown myself into the training and preparation for this moment. I had all the tools, but no idea how to use them, or which to bring to bear. All of this was within me when Odin came upon me to fill in the blanks, to fill me with the ice-rage, the battle coldness. I felt it come upon me and the night, although still broken by flashes of fire and sound, seemed to grow almost still. I felt a joy rise up in me and I felt my thoughts guided to consider a number of points one by one.

I focused on sound first. I noted the familiar timbre of our own weapons, noted the two groups fighting to our rear, the right-most group sounded like the familiar sounds of our own munitions. The left group did not. I then felt my eyes drawn to consider the muzzle flashes.

Flash suppressors do not hide the flash of burning propel-
lant. You can't do that. What they do is side-scatter the
blast to reduce the long tongue of flame that allows you
to accurately back-plot the shooter. There is a pattern
familiar from a hundred exercises of our own weapons
firing in the dark. The right-most group had that. The
left-most group did not.

At that point the pattern of the battle unfolded for me.
I felt the joy fill me. The fear was not gone, but what it
was now wove with the joy into something new. I fired
every two or three seconds in steady aimed fire. Many
of those points of fire that I back-plotted and engaged
stopped firing, either taking cover or downed by my
rounds.

To be filled by the Battle-Glad, to embrace the ice rage,
is not to be faster, or smarter, or stronger. It is to let
everything non-essential drop away. Your training, your
instincts, they remain. What the berserker feels is what
the Japanese might understand as Mushin; no thought.
What Miyamoto Musashi called attitude-no attitude,
neither focused on attack nor on defense, simply riding
the tides of battle like a raven rides the wind, instinct
and training merging to allow you to act without
thought as smoothly as if you had drilled this specific
maneuver a thousand times before.

There is a saying in the community—slow is smooth,
smooth is fast. It is not that berserkers move faster. It is
that in the Ice Rage, or Mushin, as the Japanese Kendo
community would know it, you do not waste thought
or motion. You move at appropriate speed. You have let
go of all extraneous awareness and only those things of
tactical importance are left in your sight. You are only
seeing and focusing on those things your long training

and instinct have taught you are important, and only judging them on the criteria that you have trained yourself to consider.

Your decisions are not robotic. They are more instinctive, like a hunting wolf. There is no hesitation. This gives the impression of thinking swiftly when what is really happening is that you have shut down all non-essential thoughts so that from your perspective you have a lot of time to consider the information you are taking in. You do not have to rush your decisions, they simply flow. Fear is fuel. Pain is simply noted, frequently also as fuel. Otherwise they are part of the data that you have quit paying attention to while you are busy. When you are finished, there is a euphoria.

When that is done, there comes the energy crash and tendency to brood as the things you ignored now take their turn to play across your thoughts. Nothing is free. The gifts of the Battle-Glad are like any other coping mechanism. They give you a gift with one hand and submit a bill with the other.

On balance, they are worth it.

Men of Odin

Soldiers are not the only ones who encounter Odin as a warrior. Many men identify with and admire Odin, but working with him can actually be harder for males. Looking at the lore for stories about heroes associated with Odin, including Sigmund and Sinfjotli, Starkad, Hadding, Harald Fairhair, Helgi Hundingsbane, and Egil Skallagrimsson, will give you a sense of the benefits and hazards of the relationship.

Some people are immediately drawn to Odin, while others, like Deryk, find that he has chosen them.

Now when I joined ADF (Ar n'Draoicht Fein, a Pagan church based on ancient Indo-European traditions), I originally planned on going Celtic, since it was part of my ancestry and I figured it would be appropriate. . . . Well then the All-Father decided to come and pay me a visit and explain a few things to me. Sometimes he will shove me in a direction to work on something and when I screw it up, I hear laughter and occasionally as I muddle through it I hear "Are we learning yet?" I have zero complaints about the relationship, and I know he has been around me my entire life, just a figure mostly unnoticed in the background. I don't believe it is necessary to have a personal relationship with the kindreds, just take your time making offerings and praise and if something starts to develop, and you're interested in that happening, then continue it. In my daily devotional, I pray to sixteen gods and the three Norns . . . as well as the ancestors and wights.

It is important to note that Odin does not necessarily require an exclusive commitment. For some people, *henotheism,* in which one recognizes all the gods but worships only one, is the best path, but for others, Odin may be the most important but is not the only god. In fact, in my experience, Odin promotes communication not only with other deities in the Norse pantheon but even with other pantheons. Connecting with them through us is one way he learns. Heathenry is, after all, a polytheistic religion.

I find some support for this view in *Völuspá* 23, which tells us that the war between the Æsir and the Vanir was about whether the two groups should share "wassail"; it ended with an alliance in which Njordh, Frey, and Freyja became part of the Asgard community, receiving equal honors as they do today. In book one of Saxo's history of the Danes, when Odin leaves Asgard, a person called "Mid-Odin" takes over and decrees that all the gods should receive separate offerings instead of sharing. Odin reverses this ruling when he returns.

Some of my best opportunities to observe the ways in which men react to Odin have been at Trothmoot, the annual meeting of an international Heathen organization, the Troth, that is held somewhere in the United States each June.

The high point of the moot—a conference that includes meetings, workshops, and rituals—is the Saturday night Grand Sumble, a practice that descends from the same traditions as toasting at a banquet, and the Greek symposium. In its most typical form, a drinking horn full of mead is blessed and carried around the circle three times. In the first round, each participant drinks to a goddess or god. In the second, we toast our actual ancestors or people from the past whom we admire. In the third, people can toast other living humans, but this is also the place to boast of one's accomplishments or to take an oath. In Heathenry, oaths are very serious business, since the "luck" of those who bear witness is linked to the outcome. For this reason, one of the group is designated as *Thul*, or Speaker, one of whose jobs is to challenge any oath that seems foolish, dangerous, or impossible.

From time to time, someone, usually a young man, will stand up and try to dedicate himself to Odin. The declaration is often greeted by a groan, followed by a challenge from the Thul. The trouble with an oath to die in the trenches for Odin is that he may just take you up on it. I know quite a few people who have sworn themselves to Odin (and some who have found themselves in his service without ever actually having formally agreed), but when the community consents to bear witness, it is because they know that the individual has studied the lore, developed a relationship with the god, and has a clue as to what he, she, or they are getting into.

I remember how everyone laughed when a young man who attended one of our oracular sessions stated that he was thinking of going into police work and wanted to know whether Odin would protect him. The problem with serving the Giver of Victory is that he grants victory for his reasons, not ours. As you shall see in the discussion of Odin as the Stirrer of Strife, he is a god who often seems to feel that the end justifies the means. We had to explain to the young man that Odin might well protect him, but the god would also sacrifice him if some greater purpose required it. The path taken by those who enter law enforcement or the military implies that they are willing to lay down their lives for those whom they are sworn to protect. Swearing that oath in the name of Odin does not mean you will be safe, but it does improve the odds that if you die, it will be for a good reason.

If you are thinking of getting involved with Odin, this advice from Hrafnskjald, given in an e-mail on the Troth members' list, is worth remembering:

1. Just because he asks doesn't mean you have to agree. You have, and should respect, your own boundaries and limits on what you are willing to do. We are not slaves to the gods, nor their masters, but rather the relationship is one of mutual consent. Don't feel afraid to push back or say no if something feels wrong.

2. Don't feel pressured to agree to any deals, make any oaths, etc., until you know what is right for you. You'll know when it's right because at that point you won't have any hesitations.

3. Our gods are not picky when it comes to the details of rites, especially for people just starting out; rather, the *intention* is what is key. Respect yourself, and them, and you won't go wrong. They want us to do worthy deeds and live lives that improve our communities and the world, and they can be great allies in life's struggle. The image here is more of a parent teaching a child to read and less of that same child taking a standardized test on reading: you might make mistakes as you learn, but that's okay.

4. Breathe. You are still the person you were, only you have new insights and some new friends.

There are other situations in which one might need the kind of courage that Odin can give. The first type of Heathenry to gain a foothold in prison culture was "Odinism" as taught by the Odinic Rite, an organization founded in the United Kingdom in 1973. Many incarcerated men have found the Viking virtues of courage, strength, dedication, and self-discipline an inspiration in their struggle to survive. Unfortunately, the Odinic Rite's founders had links to neo-Nazis, and this interpretation of Heathenry gives white prisoners an ethnic identity in a prison population that often (apparently with the tacit support of the authorities) seems to be divided along racial lines.

For this reason, many Heathen groups avoid prison work and ex-prisoners. However, eventually some of those who learn about Heathenry in prison are going to come out. In recent years, inclusive organizations such as the Troth have begun "in-reach" programs, providing materials and counsel so that ex-prisoners understand that racial separatism is *not* a Heathen virtue, no matter what they had to do to survive inside.

Working with Odin can be challenging. I am grateful to one correspondent, Connor McOdinmahon for sharing this prayer:

> Hail Odin . . . Odin, why?
>
> The struggle is at times incomprehensible,
>
> I question whether I am being made stronger or being slowly killed,
>
> I question the plan, but my faith does not waver,
>
> Great Odin, bringer of glory, I ask you do not give up on me,
>
> Through the pain, the blood, the agony, and the inner turmoil,
>
> I'm battered, I'm bruised, but I'm still here, still standing,
>
>
> And it's to you I look above all,
>
> You have me on my spear, and I am bleeding like never before.
>
> The darkness of Ginnungagap can be heard, it's so intense,
>
> Inspire me to reject the turmoil and pull myself off my spear,

Inspire me to get off the tree and hit the soil,

Throughout the struggle and the questions, and though the night remains,

My trust, faith, and fealty do as well.

Here they are, here they stay.

Great All-father, I ask and plead for your strength and inspiration.

When I wrote to him, asking if I could quote this in the book, he replied with the following:

> Something WEIRD happened after I sent out that Odinic dedication/call/prayer. I'm still digesting it, physically, mentally, spiritually . . .
>
> Long story short . . . hit a VERY low point, practically cracked, poured out the Odin prayer (which I barely even remember doing, it was so spontaneous and I was in such a distressed mental state), and a few interesting things, in a good way, happened. After a desperate job search (thousands of applications all over the world, and I have multiple degrees in business strategy), it was like calls and emails started rolling in like never before out of nowhere.
>
> And the craziest thing . . . after I sent that out, I put my Odin mini-statue right by my monitor, looking directly at me, and wrote like I've never written before. Business articles, history, Asatru-related, etc., . . . they flowed out like CRAZY. I've been working on a novel for about four years now, and finally feel I'm able to complete it. It's just a weird feeling, Diana.
>
> I've also met more friends in the last several days than the last several years.

I cannot promise that Odin will always provide such a spectacular answer to your prayers, but sometimes, the stroke of his spear will set you free.

Practice

1. Read any or all of the following:

Egil's Saga, either the Penguin edition translated by Bernard Scudder, or my favorite, the one translated by novelist E. R. Eddison.

The Saga of the Volsungs, translated by Jesse Byock, Penguin Classics—lots of Odinic heroes.

The chapters featuring the Rohirrim in *The Two Towers* and *The Return of the King,* by J. R. R. Tolkien.

The Broken Sword, by Poul Anderson, Del Rey Books, 1954 (reissued in 1981). This is the book that turned me on to Germanic culture.

The Dragons of the Rhine, Diana Paxson, William Morrow, 1995. This is the middle book in my *Wodan's Children* trilogy and the one with the most battles. The other two books are *The Wolf and the Raven* and *The Lord of Horses.*

The High King of Montival, by S. M. Stirling, RoC, 2010, or anything else in the Emberverse saga. Stirling does great battle scenes.

2. Get (back) into shape.

Exercise. If you have trained in a martial art, continue, or consider resuming it or take up a new one. If you are already fit or just getting into shape, add a spiritual dimension to your practice. Before you begin, do some conscious breathing. As you move, open your awareness to your surroundings and to the spirit of Odin within you.

3. Find a battle that needs fighting.

Not all wars are won with weapons. It takes a different kind of courage to fight for the rights of minority groups and environmental protection. My belief is that Odin is particularly concerned about threats to the ecosystem in which we and our civilization and religion evolved. For more on this, see chapter 9. You will also find a battle song, the "Gjallarhorn Alliance Anthem," in appendix 2.

4. Sixth Night Meditation—The Warrior

Set up your altar as usual and light a red candle. If you have a favorite or ritual weapon, have it there as well. Whisky would be an appropriate drink to pour. Then say:

Odin, by these names I call you:

Herjafadhr (Army Father)

Ófnir (Inciter)

Hvatmódh (Whet-Courage)

Sigfadhr (Victory Father)

Atrith (Attacking Rider)

Geirdrottin (Lord of the Spear)

Göllnir (Battle Screamer)

Herteit (Glad in Battle)

Hildolf (Battle Wolf)

Hjalmberi (Helmet Bearer)

Járngrím (Iron Mask)

Svölnir (Shield Bearer)

Vidhurr (Killer)

Haptagudh (Fetter God)

Hramm (Fetterer, Ripper)

Herblindi (Army Blind)

What battles do you face? What threatens you or those you care for? Who are your enemies and why do you consider them foes? Remember that some battles are fought within. Think about this carefully and consider how much and what kind of force is appropriate to use in opposing them. Make a plan of attack.

If, on reflection, you conclude that you are justified in calling on the Father of Armies, chant this prayer to the rhythm of marching feet until you feel your heartbeat speed. As you do so, bring to mind your enemies and the reasons you must oppose them.

Exalted by hate

Our enemies wait.

Baleful, they boast

And gather their host.

Whet-Courage call

Fight-frenzy for all.

Incite the attack

And help us fight back!

As they abide

Blind in their pride.

Fetter the foe,

Lord, lay them low.

Sigfather, shield

And we shall not yield.

Strong may we stand,

Warding our land.

Battle-Glad bless

us with success.

War-father, hear,

Odin, be near!

Focus your passion. Visualize the result you desire. Let the chant build until you sense it is time to send it like a spear against your foe. When you are done, pay attention to your breathing, slowing it until you are aware of your surroundings again.

Then take action! Make a list of the things you are going to do in the real world (while staying within the law) to put your money where your mouth is. For instance, if your attack is directed against those who harm the environment, use your voice, your resources, and, if necessary, your body to support the efforts of environmental organizations and communities.

Bolverk and the Thralls

Odin departed from home and came to a certain place where nine thralls were mowing hay. He asked if they desired him to whet their scythes, and they assented. Then he took a hone from his belt and whetted the scythes; it seemed to them that the scythes cut better by far, and they asked that the hone be sold them. But he put such a value on it that whoso desired to buy must give a considerable price: nonetheless all said that they would agree and prayed him to sell it to them. He cast the hone up into the air; but since all wished to lay their hands on it, they became so intermingled with one another that each struck with his scythe against the other's neck.

Odin sought a night's lodging with the giant who is called Baugi, Suttung's brother. Baugi bewailed his husbandry, saying that his nine thralls had killed one another, and declared that he had no hope of work-men. Odin called himself Bölverkr in Baugi's presence; he offered to undertake nine men's work for Baugi, and demanded for his wages one drink of Suttungr's Mead. Baugi declared that he had no control whatever over the mead, and said that Suttungr was determined to have it to himself, but promised to go with Bölverkr and try if they might get the mead. During the summer Bölverkr accomplished nine men's work for Baugi, but when winter came he asked Baugi for his hire.

Then they both set out for Suttungr's. Baugi told Suttungr his brother of his bargain with Bölverkr; but Suttungr flatly refused them a single drop of the mead. Then Bölverkr made suggestion to Baugi that they try certain wiles, if perchance they might find means to get at the mead; and Baugi agreed readily. Thereupon Bölverkr drew out the auger called Rati, saying that Baugi must bore the rock, if the auger cut. He did so. At last Baugi said that the rock was bored through, but Bölverkr blew into the auger-hole, and the chips flew up at him. Then he discovered that Baugi would have deceived him, and he bade him bore through the rock. Baugi bored anew; and when Bölverkr blew a second time, then the chips were blown in by the blast.

Then Bölyęrkr turned himself into a serpent and crawled into the auger-hole, but Baugi thrust at him from behind with the auger and missed him. Bölverkr proceeded to the place where Gunnlöd was, and lay with her three nights; and then she gave him leave to drink three draughts of the mead.

—Snorri Sturlusson, *Skaldskaparmál* 1,
translated by Arthur Gilchrist Brodeur (1916)

Fig. 15. Bolverk

chapter eight

Bale-Worker

Much as we would prefer to view Odin as the ruler, the lover, the master of magic and wisdom, or patron of heroes, he can also be a god for whom the ends justify the means.

Under "Trickery-names," Price includes *Bölverk* (Bale-work), *Ginnarr* (Deceiver), *Skollvald* (Treachery Ruler), and *Svipall* (Changeable One or Changer), to which we might add the modern "Mind-fucker" and "Odin, you bastard." In this context, I also include some of the Frenzy and Anger names, such as *Ygg* (the Terrible One), *Gapthrosnir* (One in Gaping Frenzy), *Vidhur* (Killer), and *Báleyg* (Blaze Eye). Mr. Wednesday, with all his intricate plotting, might fit in this category as well. I am still trying to decide. In a discussion on the online blog *Quora*, Edward Conway (2015) defines Odin as a god of "Death, transformation, and black ops."

As we have seen, before Odin comes to Gunnlödh as a lover, he is Bölverk, who tricks the thralls into killing one another. In the sagas, he is often accused of treachery and deception. Admittedly, some of those who complain are kings who have vowed themselves to the god and are now trying to get out of the deal, but Odin's other identity as Ygg, the Terrible One, cannot be denied. We recognize and respect these aspects of the god. If we are wise, we do not use these names to invoke him, but it would be hypocritical as well as dangerous to ignore them.

Glapsvidh, the Seducer

I say this openly, for I know both sexes.

A man's mind is fickle with women.

When we speak most fair, our thoughts are most false

Which deceive the hearts of the wise.

—*Hávamál* 91

Odin says it himself—he has a bad reputation with women. He called himself Bölverk when he destroyed the thralls and got the help of Gunnlödh's uncle in his quest for the mead of poetry, but it is as Glapsvidh the seducer that he takes the form of a serpent to penetrate the mountain. One does not have to be a Freudian to interpret the imagery. I have shared my own interpretation of what happened next in the poem that precedes chapter 6, but even the lore agrees that it was a seduction rather than rape.

In *Hávamál* 104–110, Odin discusses how he reached the cavern in which Gunlödh guarded the cauldrons and carried the holy mead away. He boasts of his achievement, but he accuses himself of rewarding her goodwill with evil and leaving her with a heavy heart and, worse still, of breaking an oath to do it.

On an oath ring I know that Odin swore,

how shall his troth be trusted?

Suttung he robbed and took his sumble [the mead].

And sorrow to Gunnlödh.

—*Hávamál* 110

Odin's dealings with giantesses seem to have been more or less on equal terms, but his relationship with Rind, who was either a goddess or a human princess depending on whether you are reading Snorri or Saxo, is among the worst examples of the means being excused by the end. His purpose was to beget his son Váli, the destined avenger of Baldr. According to the skjald Kormák Ögmundarson, "*seidh Yggr til Rind*"— "Ygg worked seidh on Rind" (*Skaldskaparmál* 2).

In book three of Saxo Grammaticus's *Gesta Danorum,* we get the full story. After the death of Balderus, Othinus (Odin) goes to Ruthenia, where he adopts several disguises to court the princess Rinda. She rejects him in all of them, but when Odin inscribes runes on a piece of bark and touches her with it, she goes mad. This would be a rune spell, but taking the shape of a woman healer called Wechsa would definitely be classed as seidh. In that form, he tells the king that his daughter can only be cured by a medicine whose effect is so violent, she has to be tied down. Once Rind is immobilized, he rapes her.

According to the *Baldrsdraumar,* this is the only way Baldr can be avenged. When the resulting child, Váli, is only one day old, he fulfills the prophecy made by the Völva and slays Höd, by whose shot Baldr was actually killed.

The Stirrer of Strife

Odin can also be accused of ill treating men. In *Lokasenna* 22, Loki charges Odin with giving victory to the weak rather than rewarding the better warriors. Actually, if we examine the stories told about both Odin and Loki in the lore, we find that Loki's mischief generally results in benefits to the gods. It is Odin whose history includes deceptions and betrayals.

The hero Starkad is another whose story is known both from the sagas and the *Gesta Danorum.* In *King Gautrek's Saga* 7, he is the sworn champion of Vikar, king of Agder in Norway, whom he has served since he was a boy. When they are on the way to attack another kingdom, the winds turn against them, and they have to anchor near some islands. Divination indicates that to get a wind, they must sacrifice a man to

Odin. Unfortunately, when they draw lots, the choice falls on the king. Nobody likes that idea, so they decide to wait till the next day to decide what to do.

That night, Starkad is wakened by his foster father, Hrosshársgrani ("Horsehair moustache," elsewhere given as a name of Odin), and follows him to a clearing where eleven men are sitting. They hail Hrosshársgrani as Odin and declare that they are met to decide the fate of Starkad. Because Starkad's grandmother preferred a giant (also named Starkad) to Thor, the god (or the man possessed by Thor) declares that Starkad will have no descendants. Hrosshársgrani/Odin replies that he will have the lifespan of three men, to which Thor counters that Starkad will commit a foul deed in each one. The two gods continue trading gifts and curses, and when all is done, Starkad finds out that his first foul deed is to send the king to Odin as the lot required. Hrosshársgrani/Odin gives him a spear that appears to be a reed and sends him back to bed.

In the morning, the king's men decide to hold a mock sacrifice, and Starkad tells them to find a tree with a slender branch and get him a piece of stretchy calf gut.

> "Your gallows is ready for you now, my lord," he said to King Vikar, "and it doesn't seem too dangerous. Come over here and I'll put a noose around your neck."
>
> "If this contraption isn't any more dangerous than it looks," said the king, "then it can't do me much harm. But if things turn out otherwise, it's in the hands of fate."
>
> After that he climbed up the stump. Starkad put the noose round his neck and climbed down. Then he stabbed the king with the reed-stalk. "Now I give you to Odin," he said.
>
> At that Starkad let loose the branch. The reed-stalk turned into a spear which pierced the king, the tree

stump slipped from under his feet, the calf guts turned into a strong withy, the branch shot up with the king into the foliage, and there he died. Ever since, that place has been known as Vikarsholmar. (Pálsson and Edwards 1985)

Not too surprisingly, this makes Starkad a "much-hated man" in Norway. The poem he wrote while in exile expresses his pain

> Against my will   I gave to the gods
>
> My true lord Vikar   high on the tree:
>
> Never such pangs   of pain for me
>
> As when my spear   slipped into his side.

With the best will in the world, I find it hard to interpret Vikar's death and Starkad's pain as anything but collateral damage from a competition between two gods, unless it is intended as a caution against trying to outwit fate. King Vikar is portrayed as a model ruler, so perhaps this is Odin's way of inviting him to Valhalla.

If Ragnar Lothbrok of the *Vikings!* TV series is an Odinic hero, it is probably the god in his aspect of Bolverk who is writing his script. The series concatenates Viking history from the late 8th through the 10th centuries, linking figures separated in time and space into a single storyline. Ragnar, unable to get men to help him punish King Ecbert for killing the colonists the Vikings had left in England, seeks his own death there, knowing that his sons will be bound to avenge him. The "Great Army," that according to the *Anglo-Saxon Chronicle* was led by Ragnar's sons, conquered much of Northeast England. It was eventually defeated by Afred the Great (who in the TV series is still a child). The peace terms established the Danelaw under Viking control.

In chapter 7, Odin was praised as the giver of victory, but what happens when he turns against you? In the *Saga of Hrolf Kraki and His Champions* 46, King Hrolf and his picked warriors are riding through the countryside. They stop at the steading of a man who calls himself Farmer Hrani ("Blusterer"), who offers the king a sword, a mail coat, and a shield. When the king calls them "monstrous" and refuses to take them, the farmer, offended, responds, "You are not being so clever in this matter, King Hrolf, as you probably think you are, and you are never as wise as you imagine."

After this, the king decides it is best to leave. As they go riding down the road, Bodhvar Bjarki, the greatest of his heroes, gets to thinking:

> "Sense comes late to fools, and so it comes to me now. I fear we've not been terribly wise, for we turned down what we should have taken, and chances are we've turned down victory."
>
> King Hrolf says, "I suspect the same, because this must have been old Odin, and he certainly was a one-eyed man."
>
> "Let's turn back as fast as we can," says Svipdag, "and see." They go back now, and by then both farm and farmer had disappeared.

Bodhvar observes that perhaps they should avoid fighting in the future because it's unlikely to go well for them, in which he is quite correct. The plot thickens, and soon King Hrolf and his champions are embroiled in what will be their final battle.

Once more Bodhvar comments:

> "Here have many men assembled against us, nobles and commoners, who press from all sides, so that shields can hardly hold them back, but I can't spot Odin here yet. I have a strong suspicion he'll be lurking round here somewhere, dirty treacherous devil that he is, and if anyone could point him out to me, I'd squeeze him like any other miserable measly little mouse, and I'll have

some none too reverent sport with that nasty venomous creature, if I get a hold of him, and who wouldn't have hate in his heart, if he saw his liege lord treated as we see ours now?"

Hjalti said, "It is not easy to bend fate, nor to stand against nature." And with that their talk was done. (*Saga of Hrolf Kraki and His Champions* 51)

As poems like the *Eiriksmál* and the *Hákonarmál* make clear, Odin harvests heroes for Valhalla, for "the wolf gapes ever at the gates of the gods," and if the Viking delight in warfare does not provide sufficient carnage, as Ofnir, Odin is quite capable of inciting more.

The *Sörla Thattr*, a tale from the medieval *Flateyjarbók,* presents a slightly euhemerized story in which the goddess Freyja is a concubine of Odin. She has acquired the splendid necklace (Brisingamen) by sleeping with the four dwarves who created it. Odin orders Loki to steal it from her and bring it to him. In a version of the story mentioned in *Skaldskaparmál,* the gods Heimdall and Loki fight in the form of seals. Heimdall wins and returns the necklace to Freyja.

In the version of the story told in the *Sörla Thattr,* to regain the necklace Freyja must use her magic to cause two kings and their armies to engage in an endless battle. This is accomplished when King Hedin abducts King Högni's daughter Hild. For 143 years, they fight to the death each day and rise with the dawn to repeat the battle, until a Christian retainer of King Olaf Trygvasson arrives. His blessing is apparently enough to put the combatants to rest.

This eternal battle reflects the daily combats of the einherior at Valhalla. It may represent a clouded memory of Odin's division of the slain with Freyja, or it may be just another device to gather warriors to fight at Ragnarök.

Baldr

There is one more deed that might be counted as a betrayal, and that is the death of Baldr. When Baldr starts having bad dreams, Odin rides to Hel to consult the Völva who is buried by the eastern gate. She not only says who will kill Baldr, but as we have seen above, she tells Odin who will avenge him. In his description of Baldr's funeral, Snorri says that Odin took his death hardest of all, because he knew how much Baldr would be missed (*Gylfaginning* 49), but despite the Völva's prediction, his father does nothing at all to prevent the tragedy.

Perhaps the most interesting thing about Baldr's ending is the question with which a disguised Odin wins the riddle contests with the wise giant Vafthruthnir: "What did Odin himself say into the ear of his son before he mounted the pyre?" (*Vafthruthnismál* 54)

This is the great unanswered question in the Old Norse lore, which has not prevented modern Heathens from wondering. One of the more popular speculations starts with the fact that although Baldr is dead to the world we know, in the global reset that takes place after Ragnarök, both he and his slayer will return to reign. Only in Hel can he be preserved until that time comes. This is the knowledge that keeps Odin silent, the grief that he forever bears.

I considered putting the discussion of "wod" in this chapter, but it seems to me that it is not in his moods of frenzy that Odin is most terrible, but in the moments when he is most dispassionate, subordinating all his other aspects to the claims of overriding Need.

Ygg in the Modern World

I like to think that when the old gods were forbidden and the temples pulled down, Odin went underground, surfacing from time to time to inspire the ferment of invention that led to the scientific method and the modern world. In the 19th century, Victory father and the Wanderer appeared in the operas of Wagner. In 1936, Jung described the return of Ygg in his disturbing essay, "Wotan."

Jung characterizes Wotan as "a restless wanderer who creates unrest and stirs up strife, now here, now there, and works magic. . . . He is the god of storm and frenzy, the unleasher of passions and the lust of battle; moreover he is a superlative magician and artist in illusion who is versed in all secrets of an occult nature."

And he is, in Jung's view, the expression of the *furor teutonicus*. "Apparently he really was only asleep in the Kyffhauser mountain until the ravens called him and announced the break of day. He is a fundamental attribute of the German psyche, an irrational psychic factor which acts on the high pressure of Civilization like a cyclone and blows it away"(-Jung 1936).

To continue Jung's analysis, "All human control comes to an end when the individual is caught in a mass movement. Then, the archetypes begin to function, as happens, also, in the lives of individuals when they are confronted with situations that cannot be dealt with in any of the familiar ways. But what a so-called Fuhrer does with a mass movement can plainly be seen if we turn our eyes to the north or south of our country [Switzerland]." To Jung, writing in 1936, this was a specifically German phenomenon. In 2016, we saw that a state of fury focused on a charismatic leader can possess large numbers of people in the United States as well.

To call the Terrible One an archetype does not mean he is not real or perhaps even sometimes necessary. But Odin's other aspects must be summoned to balance his power.

Prisons are another environment in which the Bale-worker may appear. Odin is one of the most popular gods among incarcerated Heathens. Prison art shows him heavily muscled and impressively armed. Given the extent to which our perceptions can be shaped by our environment, I find this comment from Rory Bowman illuminating.

> My strongest and most direct experiences with such a spirit have been decidedly unpleasant. The strongest of these came the only time I was in jail. I was in for just over 100 hours, and had dreams about 72 hours in of a strong sense of a spirit that seemed to present as Odin.

It was fairly foul-tempered and hostile to Jahweh and both Christians and Jews. I didn't want anything to do with it, but was quite surprised to have such a strong experience, especially in that setting.

I have since done some "in-reach" work in state prisons, and have felt a similar force "inside," but not as strongly or distinctly. Based on those experiences, I have a sense that there is something inside prisons which identifies as Odin, and which is not kind but mostly self-serving and very interested in recruiting. I suspect that force may be what many racist "Odinists" are connecting to, and I want nothing to do with it. I want whatever it was which presented to me as Odin in those contexts to stay far away from me, and I plan to keep a conscious and respectful distance away from it. What my direct experience leads me to think of as a visceral experience of "the Odin force" is nothing I want anything to do with, because I think it is looking for pawns and weapons rather than kinsmen and allies.

For many years, the Heathens who were doing prison work tended to be those who viewed Heathenry as a Northern European religion that could serve as the focus for a "White" identity, sometimes a necessity in institutions where prisoners are controlled by encouraging them to divide up along ethnic lines. For the same reason, most inclusive Heathens avoided prison ministry. More recently, the realization that some of these people may want to interact with other Heathens when they get out has inspired an increasing number of Heathens who are not racists to work with them.

When I turned my correspondence with a prisoner into a book (*Working Within*), I discussed how to practice as an individual. Improved laws protecting prisoners' religious rights have allowed the development of prison kindreds, and for several years I have been conducting services in a federal institution twice a year. It is an environment that puts a high value on Odin's strength and power. His fury, though attractive, is a danger.

Compelling as Odin may be, he is not for everyone. In describing his search for a patron deity, Olin Hemingway wrote,

> Of course, I wanted it to be Odin. He's got all the best lines and all the best toys and the best seat at the best hall in the best world. . . . There is an undeniable coolness factor involved, from the eight-legged horse to the magical spear to the ineffable wisdom that must accompany the empty socket beneath that wide-brimmed hat.
>
> Long story short, it was Freyja who reached out and inexplicably proved herself to me, and I've been with her ever since, so it is from that vantage point that my opinion of Odin has moved from stories to scripture, so to speak. In him, I see tale after tale of bad behavior, with the same consequence that those of Yahweh had upon his people. I see him starting wars, disregarding his word, being kind of a d*** to his sons, competing against his wife and taking my lady from her home as hostage (something no other being in the nine worlds could do). I see him being taught the art of seidh, and compelling her to (yet again) cause interminable war. Indeed, for the most part, I identify the Æsir as a group with death and dismemberment and other undesirable things, just as I look upon the Vanir as members of a house with beauty, plenty and life.
>
> I believe he gives good advice, but I wouldn't trust him with my sister. . . . It wouldn't shock me either to find that Odin was indeed an ancient warlord, perhaps even a devotee of the Lady, whose legend supplanted its rivals until they seemed or became equal; but in the end, it feels like I have a universal pass from her, so it doesn't matter so

much to me either way. Whether a shaman hung himself on a tree, or a god upon the universe, he seems as though made of whispers on the tongues of travelers, and there is an open invitation still standing for a visit.

Even those who are drawn to Odin may find themselves in danger. Those who have worked with him for a while may be called to counsel others who are struggling with the impact of having their minds blown by that mighty wind. Here are some more comments from Lorrie Wood.

> If you're looking for the answer to, "Which Odin is the mindfucker?" The answer is yes. They ALL are. Is Mindfucker appropriate, if not directly attested? By me, yes.

> Sometimes you crack an egg, it's a mess. Sometimes it's an omelet. Head-cracking—whatever little damage was needed to open awareness to a worldview outside the one you were handed—is this way: when you knock on a door to open it, sometimes you think you're gently rapping but whoops it's a battering ram. Idiots like me try to mop up the messes and make soufflé, which after a few times comes with the hard-won understanding that THIS one ain't coming together—or it's not my mess to tidy, or whoops I don't actually know wtf to do with duck eggs as my specialty is raven eggs, etc.

> . . . it's a hobby. >.<

> That all being said, there are a few I know who took his touch extremely poorly, and who, despite needing professional help, have run through whole Rolodexes of priests of all faiths and found either no good counsel, or no counsel they were able to put into action. I *also* learned when to say "Nope, sorry, this is beyond my capabilities as an ad hoc pastoral counselor, here are

pagan-and-heathen-friendly professionals, best of luck." Boundaries are awesome and completely within my praxis. :P

(Contrariwise, I also sometimes ignore my own damn advice.)

And, yet, sometimes the wrestling match with the god ends happily. In an article titled, "How I found Odin and what he did to me when he caught me," Bari, a very talented healer and teacher, describes her mostly painful contacts with Odin during a lengthy spiritual journey that culminated at an oracular ritual at the 2006 PantheaCon, a Pagan festival held annually in San Jose, California. It should be noted that although Odin claimed her, it was not an exclusive contract, and she has continued to work with other Powers.

> I knew it was time to ask my question. The woman before me had asked to speak with Odin, who promptly began riding the seer. The querent stepped down, and I stepped forward. Before I said anything, the seer said in a booming voice, "Well, hello!" with a leer (obviously still channeling, obviously having recognized me). I started to shake and realized I was very frightened. I approached and said, "I am scared to be here but I am fairly certain Odin contacted me during the Blót on Friday and told me he had a message for me. I am here to receive that message."
>
> He laughed and pointed at me and said, "By the way, you're mine."
>
> My whole body started shaking hard and I felt like something cracked open, and I started crying.
>
> "Oops."

"I've been running from you for so long."

Aloud, I heard, "It would go easier for you if you were to stop running, I think." And in my heart, I also heard, "Stop crying, you knew this was coming."

I told him he'd hurt me and that I need him to be more gentle with me. He told me I had to tell him when he was being too rough. I thanked him and stepped down.

When I stepped back I had several folks rally around me to talk me down. I definitely appreciated being told that I didn't have to do anything I didn't want to do, not to be a scared rabbit, that even us small furry folks have teeth and claws. Several women came to me to say they were his as well, and welcome to the family. I was so overwhelmed I didn't really know what to do: I was furious and felt manipulated, but I also felt incredibly honored and loved, I felt grateful for the community magically showing up—and I felt trapped and uncomfortable and very exposed. I knew he'd done an end-run with me—I had refused to talk to him for so long that the only way he was going to get me to sit still long enough to have this conversation was to do it in a very public place, in front of a room full of people where I couldn't deny what had happened.

Is Odin a savior or a deceiver?

Yes.

Are his deeds always justified?

Refusing to act has consequences, too.

Does the end justify the means?

Prime Minister Churchill thought so when he decided not to warn the people of Coventry about the coming German air raid because doing so would have revealed that the British had cracked the German code. President Truman thought so when he authorized use of the atomic bomb. They did not make these decisions lightly. When Odin is Bölverk or Ygg, the suffering he causes torments him as well.

Practice

I have no exercises for connecting with this aspect of Odin except, perhaps, a recommendation to find a good book on history and contemplate the long-term effects of drastic interventions. For those caught up in it, the destruction is terrible, but eventually something new emerges that, if not better, at least allows the evolution of new and different ways.

The problem with trying to work with Bölverk is that he *is* treacherous. The trick that brings down your enemy is just as likely to take you with him. The politicians who call for Change! without calculating the cost terrify me. Odin gives victory to suit *his* purposes, not ours. Sometimes today's defeat paves the way for a greater good tomorrow, but that doesn't change the suffering of those in the way. We cannot see all ends. I am not sure that Odin himself can see all ends. He is an opportunist, who will do his utmost to turn both good and evil to the service of evolution.

I have been in situations in which I was sorely tempted to invoke Bölverk. In the end, I didn't do it, because I did not have the courage to trust the outcome, knowing his solution might destroy me and mine as well. I actually think that if you want to play a trick on an enemy, calling on Loki might be safer.

Seventh Night Meditation: Bolverk

Set up your altar as usual and light a brown candle. I do not invoke Odin by his baleful names. Instead, I offer the following prayer.

> Hail to Odin, god of many names.
>
> This is what I ask:
>
> Turn away your face of Terror.
>
> From my own bale-works bring blessings.
>
> Change my choices when they go awry.
>
> Truth reveal when words betray me
>
> And deeper good beneath deception.
>
> May stirred strife spur me to ambition
>
> To strive, to struggle, and not to yield.

Wodan's Hunt

(to the tune of "St. Stephen"; for music, see appendix 2)

Wodan is a holy god,

and stark with Áses might.

'Tis sung how Baldr's horse he did heal

before the great gods' sight.

Yet swiftest of all, his own steed,

Old Sleipnir, dapple grey,

When winter winds begin to howl,

He rides 'til break of day.

O mortal man, you may well fear

When the host rides through the sky,

And crouch beside your fire warm,

When Wodan's Hunt rides by.

Now ale is poured and coals aglow,

And clan sits by the hearth,

The Yule log is burning bright,

Of food we have no dearth.

We set out offerings for the Host,

Hung from the old dark yew,

The apples red and braided bread,

And horns of frothing brew.

O mortal man, you may well fear

When the host rides through the sky,

And crouch beside your fire warm,

When Wodan's Hunt rides by.

The winter night is wild with snow

That shrieks about the roofs.

We hear the riders' wailing horns,

we hear their dreadful hooves.

The trolls all rage and furious run,

From howe to howe they howl,

And alfs ride forth from mounds' high tops,

Beneath their pale cauls.

O mortal man, you may well fear

When the host rides through the sky,

And crouch beside your fire warm,

When Wodan's Hunt rides by.

The ghosts awake to mount their steeds,

The slain from restless sleep.

They gather all in Wodan's train

To fare from keep to keep.

And some we know will ride this night,

As empty lie their beds,

The stable doors will hang ajar,

The horses bear the dead.

O mortal man, you may well fear

When the host rides through the sky,

And crouch beside your fire warm,

When Wodan's Hunt rides by.

— Kveldúlfr Hagen Gundarsson

Fig.16. Odin rides with the Hunt

CHAPTER NINE

God of the Dead

Cattle die, kinsmen die,

You yourself will die.

But fair fame dies never,

For the one who wins it.

—*Hávamál* 76

I f there is one quotation most Heathens know, it would be the one above. These words of the High One are taken as a call for courage, but they also have implications for the way we think about death and about Odin as a god who is as concerned with the dead as he is with those who are living. Stephan Grundy interprets Odin's blue-black cloak as the *livor mortis* from pooling blood that colors the back and shoulders of a corpse that has been lying on the ground.

As it happens, I began working on this chapter on Hallowe'en, an appropriate time to consider Odin in his aspect as a scary, one-eyed death god. Several of his names confirm his claim to this role. Price lists ten "Gallows-names" for Odin. As *Hangatyr* or *Váfudhr* (Dangler), he is the god of the hanged who knows how to make them speak, whether they were strung up for a crime or as an offering. Twelve names show him as Lord of the Dead. As *Draugadrótin*, he is the ruler of the Draugar, a particularly nasty type of Norse zombie. As *Hléfödhr* (Mound Father), he wards those whose bodies or ashes are buried in the earth; and as *Valfadhr*, he is the Father of the Slain who presides over his chosen warriors in Valhalla. As we see in the song that introduces this chapter, on stormy winter nights, Odin leads the Wild Hunt that brings both death and blessings.

How central are these aspects to Odin's nature? The worlds between which Odin walks include those of the living and the dead. In *The Cult of Ódhinn, God of Death*, Grundy (2014) argues that Odin's original and primary function was as a death god and shows how Odin's other aspects could have developed from this role. I highly recommend this book, which explores aspects of Odin's nature often skipped elsewhere. It is academic in style, but now that so much of the Old Norse literature is available online, you can look up the quotes in translation.

Wolves and Ravens

For a first clue to Odin's role as a god of death, let us consider his animal companions. Odin's wolves are called *Geri* and *Freki*, "Hunger" and "Greed." Today, most of us see wolves and ravens in a positive light. Wolves are canny beasts with an admirable social organization whose example may well have shown early humans how to work together to hunt.

Ravens are known for their brilliance at solving problems, but what Huginn and Muninn are usually thinking about and remembering is where to find things to eat. In the wild, ravens will often raise a clamor of cawing over the body of a fallen animal in order to attract the wolves, who can tear open the body, so that the ravens can get at the soft bits. Both creatures are highly effective and opportunistic scavengers, and in the old days, human bodies were among their favorite foods.

When Odin stands below the scaffold to talk to the hanged man, a raven is probably sitting atop it, waiting, as they do in the song "The Twa

Corbies," to pluck out a "bonny blue eye." When men were sacrificed to Odin, they were hanged as well as stabbed, and the ravens always came.

Odin is *Hrafnagudh* (Raven God), *Hildolf* (Battle Wolf), and *Kjallar,* the one who nourishes the carrion eaters. The real banquet hall for both wolves and ravens is the battlefield, as in this poem by the late Paul Edwin Zimmer (1979):

> The Dead lie in silence upon the cold ground,
>
> And the calling of Ravens is all of the sound.
>
> When the Heroes have fallen, the birds *always* know—
>
> And the hunger of Ravens their Honor shall show.
>
> The Black Bird of Odin, who blesses the slain,
>
> Shall rise filled from the field where the Heroes have lain;
>
> Where the Valkyrie bears men's souls on her swift steed,
>
> The Ravens shall thank them, as they wing down—to feed.

Hangatyr: Gallows God

> I know a twelfth, if I see in a tree
>
> A hanged corpse dangle,
>
> I cut and color certain runes
>
> So that man walks
>
> And talks with me.
>
> —*Hávamál* 157

The ability to reanimate and speak to the dead is a mighty magic, and of all the dead, those who died on the gallows are the closest to the God of the Hanged. There are two reasons for this. First, as we have seen, Odin himself was hanged on the Worldtree, and speared as well. We know from the history of Starkad and other references in the sagas that this was the traditional mode of sacrifice to Odin, so when the god proclaims that he was sacrificed to himself, he is speaking literally.

A second reason might be that tightening a noose stops the breath. It was Odin who gave humans that gift in the first place. What does it mean that he can still make a man speak when the breath has been taken away?

And why, if the sacrifice has been hanged, is he also pierced by a spear? Odin's own dedicated weapon is the spear Gungnir. In sources from the 1st century through the Viking Age, there is abundant evidence that casting a spear over the opposing army dedicated them to Odin. Not only did the god claim the battle dead, but any surviving foes might be hanged afterward as an offering.

As a god of death, Odin is most present at the moment of dying, the stabbing anguish of the convulsing heart, the last struggle for breath. He is the giver of önd, and wherever the breath goes, he goes as well. The dead are without breath, but as they experience further transformations, they know the god after another manner.

In chapter 5, I quoted the first part of a poem by Fjolnirsvin in the form of a conversation with Odin. This is the remainder, in which Odin replies, and the imagery of the Odinic sacrifice leads to a confrontation with death.

II. Oðinn

When I manifest fully, I will bring your death,

which you await

like bride awaits bridegroom,

kindling wants fire,

drink cries out for fermentation.

not what comes after

(though much comes after)

but the moment of transition itself,

in which I am sovereign.

Maker of bounds, transgressor of limits,

trickster, I

lead all your chances

to that quick terror

to that ecstasy

when noose tightens on the beam

when reed becomes spear,

iron parts rib,

and point crosses perpendicular flesh.

III. Me

Let me not (Oh, let me!) pray too much.

"Gift calls out for gift."

Is it better to remain ignored

or chance destruction from what is given in return?

Valhalla

In previous chapters, we encountered Odin as a god of war and battle frenzy and a Stirrer of Strife. But *why* is he so bloodthirsty? The role in which he is most often connected with the dead is as *Valfadhr*, Lord of *Valhalla*, the hall of the slain, where the *einherior*, the "only," or perhaps, "number one" warriors, feast all night and fight all day. A euphemism for death in battle is "to visit Odin," or "to be Odin's guest."

Popular belief has it that the ambition of all Norsemen was to join him there, however Viking Age concepts of the afterlife included a number of options, including joining one's ancestors in Hel, reincarnating in the family line, or becoming one of the spirits of the land. As an afterlife destination, Valhalla is "invitation only," a very exclusive club to which Odin admits only the most heroic of the slain.

Sometimes Odin delivers the invitation in person, as in *Volsungasaga* 11–12.

> The battle had been going on for some time, when a man came into the fight. He had a wide-brimmed hat that sloped over his face, and he wore a black hooded cloak. He had one eye, and he held a spear in his hand. This man came up against King Sigmund, raising the spear before him. When Sigmund struck hard with his sword, it broke against the spear. Then the tide of the battle turned, for King Sigmund's luck was now gone, and many of his men fell. The king did not seek to protect himself, and fiercely urged his men on.

When night falls, Sigmund's wife searches the battlefield and finds him dying from many wounds, however he refuses to let her treat him, because Odin has broken the sword that the god himself once gave him. "Odin does not want me to wield the sword since it is now broken. I have fought battles while it pleased him. . . . But my wounds tire me, and I will now visit our kinsmen who have gone before." While the saga does not specifically mention Valhalla, Sigmund is of Odin's line, and we can assume they all ended up there.

More often, it is the valkyries who deliver the invitations. If there is one image familiar from opera, it is that of the Valkyrie, usually portrayed as a busty soprano in a breastplate and winged helmet, shrieking syllables that, as Anna Russell points out in her discussion of the *Ring* cycle, are untranslatable because they don't mean anything. When you look at the lore, the valkyries become both scarier and more interesting.

Odin names thirteen valkyries in *Grímnismál*. Snorri adds a few more. As translated by Orchard (2011), they have meanings like "Wielder," "Brandisher," "War," "Strength," "War Bindings," "Spear Waver," and "Shield Truce." Fulfilling Odin's will, they are the Choosers of the Slain. They may also have a role in battle. In the *Germania* of Tacitus, we hear of a tribal woman who watched the battles, shrieking to terrify the foe. In the Helgi poems, human women with the title of valkyrie send their fetches soaring above the battle, working spells. Given that at least one valkyrie name refers to binding, as workers of war magic they may be extensions of Odin's powers.

In Anglo-Saxon spells, we find the *waelcyrge,* sometimes used as a gloss for the Classical Furies. In the spell against rheumatism, some see them in the screaming "mighty women," who send invisible spears to cause pain (Storms 1949, "With Faerstice"). The other job of the valkyries is to serve mead and ale to the heroes. The figures of women carrying drinking horns that appear on memorial runestones may represent valkyries, although this task was part of the role of a woman of high status, who performed it to honor heroes and promote peace within the hall. These stones are also the source of the valknut, the symbol of three interlaced triangles that has been adopted as a tattoo by some who dedicate themselves to Odin.

So who gets on Odin's A-list, and why? In the euhemerized history of the gods in *Ynglingasaga* 9, we learn that

> Odin died in his bed in Sweden, and when he was near
> death he had himself marked with a spear point and
> dedicated to himself all men who died through weap-

ons; he said that he should now fare to the Godheims and there welcome his friends. . . . The Swedes often seemed to see him clearly before great battles began; to some he gave victory, but others he bid come to him; both fates seemed good to them.

One mortal king who is believed to have ended up in Valhalla is Hákon the Good, last son of King Harald Hairfair. Fostered in England, he was raised a Christian, but alone among converted Norse kings, he did not try to impose the new religion on his subjects. For this, the poet who eulogized him praised him as a guardian of the Heathen temples. When Hákon had reigned for twenty-six years, the sons of his oldest brother attacked him. The king's side won the battle, but Hákon died of his wounds.

No doubt the king expected to go to heaven, but the skjald Eyvind Scaldaspiller (1932) says otherwise. His poem, the *Hákonarmál,* tells how Odin sent the Valkyries Gondul and Skogul "to choose amongst the kings which of Yngvi's race should go to Odin and be in Valhall." When the king asks why they didn't help him, the Valkryies point out that though he is dying, his side has had the victory. As Hákon and his men approach Valhalla, Odin sends the hero Hermod and the god of poetry, Bragi, out to welcome him, and Bragi points out that eight of Hákon's brothers are waiting to greet him. The fact that the sons of Harald Hairfair had been vicious rivals when they were alive is irrelevant.

The gusto with which some warriors looked forward to this fate is expressed in the twenty-nine stanzas of the *Krákumál,* the death song sung by Ragnar Lothbrok. This is a sample. For the whole, see the *Sagas of Ragnar Lothbrok and his Sons,* translated by Ben Waggoner (2009, 76).

We struck with our swords!

My soul is glad, for I know

that Balder's father's benches

for a banquet are made ready.

We'll toss back toasts of ale

from bent trees of the skulls;

no warrior bewails his death

in the wondrous house of Fjolnir.

Not one word of weakness

will I speak in Vidrir's hall.

In *Gylfaginning* 40, Snorri tells us, "Each day after they have got dressed they put on war-gear and go out into the courtyard and fight each other and they fall each upon the other. This is their sport. And when dinner-time approaches they ride back to Val-hall and sit down to drink." In the lore, fighting and drinking seem to be viewed as sufficient occupations for a hero. Today, many Heathens feel that the poets who chronicle the deeds of those heroes are also represented here, and given the advances in military technology, there is probably a computer room there as well.

Valhalla, the hall of the slain, has 540 doors, through each of which eight hundred warriors can pass. The einherior dine on the flesh of the boar Saehrimnir, which is cooked, eaten, and reconstitutes itself each day. For drink, the valkyries serve the mead that flows from the udder of the goat Heidhrun, who grazes on the leaves at the top of the Worldtree. It all sounds rather like the Viking sports channel, but the purpose of this establishment is not entertainment. In S. M. Stirling's *The High King of Montival,* young Mike Havel comments, "Well, they'll know they've been in a fight, but then it's pork chops at Odin's All Night Diner for us until Ragnarok" (Stirling 2014, ch. 2).

This poem, written to honor Paul Edwin Zimmer, who died in 1997, expresses my understanding of Valhalla. Paul, a swordsman, poet, and writer of heroic fiction, knew Odin long before I did and helped me understand him from a male perspective as well as from my own.

All-father Odin, Ale-Giving God!

Rage-giver, Runewinner, Rider of Yggdrasil!

Guard now and guide to glee in Valhalla

The rider who fares on Rainbow Bridge.

For nine nights' knowledge, on Yggdrasil,

You, Odin, the doom of death endured:

Worldtree Warrior, wisdom-winner,

Through spell and shadow lead the lost one—

Lead home to the feast, fastest far-farer,

The swordsman who strides over Rainbow Bridge!

This Bragi-blessed warrior whose name we call!

Edwin! Prepared is your place at the feast!

Unveiled valkyries the veteran greet;

Let beer now flow freely from barrels,

As the Hero's Portion you divide!

From wandering to wonder, from woe to bliss,

From Midgard's madness, hard on heroes,

Enter another on the Einherior's roll!

Welcome the wanderer to Warrior's Hall!

Wode and the Wild Hunt

After the conversion to Christianity, the belief that dead warriors went to Valhalla may have faded, but in the Wild Hunt, the Einherior lived on. For a vivid evocation of their appearance, I offer the following passage from *The Broken Sword*, by Poul Anderson, which was my introduction to Odin in 1954 and the first book to convey to me what it would be like to live in a culture with a completely different worldview.

The brief glimpse he had, seated on his plunging horse, of the mighty cloaked form that outran the wind, the huge eight-legged horse and its rider with the long gray beard and the shadowing hat. The moonbeam gleamed on the head of his spear and on his single eye.

Hoo, halloo, there he went through the sky with his troop of dead warriors and the fire-eyed hounds barking like thunderclaps. His horn screamed in the storm, the hoofbeats were like a rush of hail drumming on the roof, and then the whole pack was gone and the rain came raving over the world.

Imric snarled, for the Wild Hunt boded no good to those who saw it and the laughter of the one-eyed huntsman had been mockery. (Anderson 1954, 14)

Imric is right to worry, because when Odin sends an ancient sword forged by Bolverk as a naming gift for the human changeling the elf lord has stolen, it is clear that the god has his own plans.

The Wild Hunt, also known as the Furious Host, appears in medieval folklore from all over Europe, led by figures ranging from the devil, King Arthur, and Hellequin to the goddesses Diana or Herodias, and followed by ghostly riders. A similar tradition survives in the Pennsylvania Dutch country today. The leader of the Hunt in the Germanic countries is Odin or Wotan, followed by the Oskerei or the Wilde Jagd. Some of the riders appear as warriors from ancient times, while some are the recently dead or living men who participate in dream or trance. The Hunt rides the winter storms, especially around the time of Yule. In Norway, children were told not to whistle at night lest they attract the Hunt's attention.

John T. Mainer sees the wild ride as an expression of primal energy.

One of the earliest understandings of Odin was Wode, the transforming passion, the wild rage. To be caught by the wild hunt meant one of two things: if you were prey, you had to keep before the wild hunt all night or the pack would rend you asunder for its wild lord's pleasure.

The hunt took others than prey. The horn of the huntsman calls to the blood, the song of the wolf calls to the hunter, the killer, in all of us. If the Wild Hunt took you and you ran with it, civilization was thrown aside, humanity cast off like a tattered cloak, and you ran naked with fangs bare and no more between your hunger and the night than a wolf has.

The fire in the blood, the transforming passion, the madness and ecstasy of throwing off your cares, your inner conflicts, and following the wild hunt with only the joy of the hunt, the sweet taste of fear in the night, and the song of the pack; these are dark and splendid gifts.

To wake in the morning, drenched in sweat, eyes still burning, smiling softly with a body shaking in exhaustion, and a soul burned clean of conflict and care, a mind as still and peaceful as the morning after a thunderstorm; these are bright and healing gifts.

Our modern lives chain us with responsibility and care. Duty and struggle, stress and endless imperfect compromises fill us with internal stress and conflict we can never set down, never escape.

Wode, the Wild Huntsman. Primitive, some say the darkest face of Odin, Wode and his hunt are that throwing off of civilization for a howling embrace of life. What happens in Vegas, stays in Vegas. We jump out of perfectly good airplanes. We pay money to put a fragile kayak into the part of the river called Hell's Gate, where the railroad was measured in dead men per mile. We hang from cliffs while hammering a ring backed nail into rock while tourists pass overhead in heated gondolas above the abyss you dangle over. How many times and how many ways do we find that taste of madness, that wild embrace of passion that is our last best preserver of sanity?

Somewhere inside, part of us listens for the sound of the horn above the TV, listens for the call of the pack above the AC. Some part of us chafes at our centuries of progress and burns for just one last chance to howl. (Mainer 2011, 21)

But the Hunt is more than a release for those who join the Furious Host. The explosion of energy renews the land. In meditation on one such stormy night, this is what my friend Vefara heard:

Those whose lives were great shouts through the worlds cannot have their death wasted in one place. On the nights that return life to the land, whether that is through the scouring of snow or the torrents of rain, the gale-winds bring the Host, the heroic dead, those who strove to bring themselves brim-full to the end of their days: whether in bed or on field. Not to repay the land's luck which was their charge in one place, as Frey's men might, but to scatter it over all the lands in their passing, that some small spark might land, stirred by the gale of their screams as they pass, in fertile soil, on fertile souls, and stir more greatness, as has been ever done.

And on nights like these . . . No longer only horses, no longer only wolves with snake-reins, but all manner of vehicle, carriage, and creature that could ever love a human hand and share the fierce joy of the battle-song: there are not a few on motorcycles now, and somehow the airplanes, biplanes through to fighters, fit well among the elder steeds without crowding them out.

The stories of the dead are the inspiration of the living, and the lights of the living are the inspiration of the dead. The heroes watch, and if they are of a mind to be among the Host, they ride. Disir and alfar worthy of the name spread their luck back into Midgard, taking in trade the praise of those who remember, and tell, the stories of the departed. The song of our passing stirs all who hear it, slowing, a little, the sick, pointless death that would come if, in its time, Ragnarök did not.

Hléfodh: God of the Grave-Mound

Although we are told in *Ynglingasaga* that it was Odin who introduced the practice of cremating the dead, he also has a connection with the grave-mound. Although he does not mention the spell in the list in *Hávamál*, it is clear that Odin can not only speak to the hanged, he can also talk to the dead in the mound.

In the Eddic poem *Baldrsdraumar*, Odin rides to the eastern door of Hel where he knows that a völva is buried and uses his necromancy to chant *valgaldr*, "death-galdor," until the corpse is forced to rise and answer him.

Howes, or grave-mounds, are holy. Few know the spells to compel the dead, but once summoned, the howe-dwellers are often willing to offer wisdom to their descendants. Svipdag gets counsel from his dead mother by sitting on her grave, and Hervor persuades her berserker father to rise and give her his magic sword. However, the most significant relationship between Odin and the mound probably lies in the traditions of sacred kingship.

The fact that so many Germanic royal houses traced their lineage to Odin supports the idea that the places where those god-descended ancestors were buried would remain places of power. As Grundy puts it:

In general, it seems clear that Scandinavian rulers were expected to have a particular relationship with the dead, from whom at least a portion of their authority was derived. . . . If the Scandinavian rulers were thought to get anything more out of their ancestral mounds than a link with tradition and a prominent place from which to address a crowd, then the seat on the howe would fall more within Ódhinn's domain than that of any other deity. As cultic leader/sacrificer, the ruler also had a particular relationship with the realms of the dead: in his person, he linked the gods, the dead, and the living, and was responsible for maintaining communication and good relationships between them. (Grundy 2014, 115–116)

Draugadrottinn: Ruler of the Draugar

Unfortunately, kings are not the only powerful beings that may dwell in a mound. In the sagas, we find stories about a particularly nasty type of Undead called the *draug*. The term is often translated as "ghost," but the draugar, although they can pass through the earth that covers their graves, are both solid and dangerous. To quote Lorrie Wood:

Perhaps it ought to be said that undeath, as such, was not necessarily considered to be outside the natural order of things. A dead man within his barrow could defend his home or odal ground without causing much comment, right up until a passing hero became interested in the buried grave-goods. (Wood 2006, 22)

In the sagas, particularly *Grettis Saga* and *Eyrbyggja Saga*, stories of draugar abound. In general, they make trouble either because someone got greedy and broke open their mound or because they were nasty and difficult people while they were alive and in death see no reason to change their ways, driving animals mad, damaging property, and terrifying the neighborhood. Most of the stories about draugar take place after the conversion to Christianity, when the only recourse was to have the creature dismembered or burned by a hero. However, if Draugadrottinn is one of Odin's names, I suspect that in earlier times the god might have been invoked to defeat them.

Ragnarök

Odin is not only a god of death, he is also a god who is going to die.

Alone among European Paganisms, Heathenry includes a myth about the end of the age. Some see in this description of the End-Times a reflection of the Christian eschatology to which Norsemen of the time were being exposed, and a textual comparison with the biblical material taught to newcomers to Christianity does show a number of parallels (McKinnell 2008). However, I find myself compelled to look at another interpretation.

There will come a time, says the seeress in *Völuspá*, when the sky will darken during the summer, the weather grow "shifty." Then the soot-red cock will crow in Hel, and in Asgard, Golden-comb will take up the cry. The einherior will awaken and Heimdall will blow his horn. In Midgard, "Civilization as we know it" will come to an end.

> Brothers will battle and fight to the death,
>
> Sisters' sons their kin will ruin.
>
> Hard is the world with much whoredom,
>
> An axe age, a sword age, shields are split.
>
> A wind age, a warg age, before the world crumbles,
>
> No one will spare another.
>
> —*Völuspá* 45

All Powers that were bound now run free. The giant Hrym brings frost, and the sons of Surt set everything from Hel to the Bifrost Bridge aflame. The Midgard serpent churns the waves, the earth quakes as Midgard is destroyed. And the 540 doors of Valhalla open, and from each one, eight hundred warriors stride as Odin and the Æsir march out to meet the foe.

When I first read *Völuspá*, I interpreted these verses as a prediction of World War III and nuclear winter. But as I was flying back to California from the east coast during the drought, I saw a brown pall covering the land on the other side of the Sierras. The smoke from numerous forest fires had darkened the sky. These days, the end of *Völuspá* makes me think of global climate change. I see Ragnarök as what will happen when the balance of nature has been so badly upset that the destructive elemental forces are the only "giants" that remain.

For Midgard to change is natural and inevitable. The Holocene Epoch, during which our current ecosystem and our human cultures and religions evolved, will one day come to an end. Based on the time scale of earlier epochs, we ought to have a million years to go, but there is reason to believe the timetable could be upset by human actions.

Of all the gods, Odin is the one most concerned with preparing for the end of the age. I cannot help but wonder if he has been so actively recruiting during the past few years in an attempt to keep the destiny of the gods from being fulfilled too soon. If that is so, those of us who have answered his call have an obligation to help stave off Ragnarök in our time. When I first started talking about this, my friend Lorrie suggested that we form the Teal Party, which is what happens when Odin's blue meets environmental green. It even has an anthem, which you will find in appendix 2.

Whether it comes late or soon, in that final battle, Odin, at least in the forms in which we have known him throughout the history of Midgard, will die.

A second sorrow comes to Hlin [aspect of Frigg]

When Odin fares to fight the Wolf,

And the bane of Beli [Frey] to battle Surt.

Then will Frigg's lover fall.

—*Völuspá* 53

Dealing with Death

While Odin's concerns certainly include death and the dead, what is his meaning to us? Names and epithets are only part of the picture. What does it mean when we find a god whom we have first seen as a creator dealing death? And why do we need to pay attention to the dead?

The more I study the traditions of indigenous cultures in general and the Germanic peoples in particular, the more I realize that the dead were as integral a part of the religious system as the gods and the land. Honoring them is easier if you live in places where the dust of your ancestors is part of the earth you walk on or near a cemetery where you can put flowers on family graves than it is for those who no longer live near their parents, much less in the town where their grandparents lived and died.

Cremation makes environmental sense (and is the traditional method of disposal for followers of Odin), but a sense of connection can be lost when the ashes are scattered on the wind. And yet, even when we change our politics, our lifestyle, or our religion, we carry our physical ancestors with us in our DNA. Likewise, in the psyche we carry ancestors of the spirit—those who created the culture in which we grew up, whose stories we have read and heard, and whose ideas have shaped our souls.

By developing a relationship with those who lived before us, we create a context for the loss of those we live with today. Egil Skallagrimsson railed against Odin when his son was drowned, but in the end, he came to understand that the god's gift of poetry, though it could not negate Egil's grief, gave him a way to process it. Sorrow cannot be denied. It must be accepted, embraced, transcended. Odin asks nothing that he himself has not known. He too has lost a son. Unless they pass on the road after Ragnarök, Baldr, alone among all Odin's offspring, is the one whom he will never see again.

The other death that each one of us must deal with is our own. The old heroes laughed as they died because they lived on the edge, and if death did not come on a foe's sword, it would come from cold or the sea or hunger or disease. The men of the north knew themselves vulnerable, so they exulted in making good use of the power and time they had. It is not necessary to kill to know this, but you do have to accept danger, to forgo the idea that health or money in the bank will make you secure.

When we face Odin as a god of death, what are we looking at? What is it that we need to understand? We can gain some insight from "The Song of Odin," by Michaela Macha (2004).

I am the rider of the tree

I am a draught of poet's mead

I am the socket's empty yawn

I am hunger: Who but I

Will sacrifice his self to Self?

I am the guest you don't expect

I am a song to wake the dead

I am a tide that drowns your mind

I am a trickster: Who but I

Brings woe to you and weal at once?

I am the spear to find your heart

I am a wolf within the woods

I am a storm that tears apart

I am creator: Who but I

Gives unto deadwood breath of life?

I am the counsel that brings fame

I am a sword that drinks your blood

I am a raven on a corpse

I am a gallows: who but I

Brings you to death while holding you?

I am the walker and the way

I am the gateway and the key

I am the rope of every thread

I am the end of every means.

Practice

1. Make a will.

First address the disposal of possessions and property, including ritual items. But when you have fulfilled your responsibilities to your heirs by addressing all the aspects the law might require, take a new piece of paper and list the nonphysical things you are leaving behind you. What have you done with your life? What have you given to the world? What deeds might earn the "fair fame" that will survive you? If you can't think of anything now, try making a "bucket list" of things you'd like to accomplish before you die.

If you are wondering how Odin might do this exercise, try listening to the Frank Sinatra song, "My Way."

2. **Read *Krákumál*** at *http://www.odins-gift.com/pclass/ragnarlodbroks-deathsong.htm* and write your own Death Song.

3. Work with your ancestors.

If you don't already have a family tree, try one of the online genealogical services. If you have a yard, create a symbolic grave-mound in which you place pictures of your dead relatives. If that is not possible, gather pictures of dead friends and relatives to display. Serve a meal of foods traditional in your family. Set an extra place for the dead. When you have praised their deeds, eat in silence, opening your heart to their wisdom.

4. Celebrate Memorial or Veteran's Day.

Make an altar to the Einherior, honoring both those who have served their country in the military and other heroes whom you think deserve a place in Valhalla.

5. Spend some time in a cemetery.

Open your awareness to the dead. If circumstances allow, spend the night sitting out, ideally by the grave of a relative. Take a notebook to record the thoughts that come to you.

6. Honor the Hunt.

Wait for a good storm to come along at Yuletide—the latter part of December or the beginning of the year. Go outside and listen to the howling wind. Can you hear the Hunt raving through the skies? Set out offerings of apples for the horses—for the riders, bread and beer. Sing the "Wild Hunt" song (music is in appendix 2).

7. Eighth Night Meditation: God of the Dead

Set up your altar space as usual and light a black candle. You may also add pictures of ancestors or heroes. Then say:

Odin, by these names I invoke you:

Hangatyr and *Váfudhr* (Dangler)

Draugadrótin (Draugar Lord)

Hléfödhr (Mound Father)

Valfadhr (Father of the Slain)

Wod . . .

When the ones I loved are lost,

When the final fight is done,

Limbs no longer will obey,

And the enemy has won,

Odin, grieve with me.

When my heart is pierced by pain,

When lungs lose the fight for breath,

From my eyes the vision fades,

Word and will are blocked by death,

Odin, do not leave me.

When body's bonds no longer hold,

When mind, unmoored, at last breaks free,

To wander myriad worlds and ways

Experiencing ecstasy,

Odin, receive me.

Contemplate your death. You do not know how or when, but the one thing we all know is that it *will* come. You can read this meditation then think about it, or read it onto a tape to use as an induction.

Lie or sit comfortably. You are safe here. Know that your body will be warded until you return.

Close your eyes and breathe slowly and deeply. Let awareness of sounds and scents around you fade. Focus awareness in your feet and legs, then let them relax. Pay attention to hands and arms and then let them go limp as well. Feel the weight of your head and torso supported by bed or chair. As you breathe more slowly and deeply, awareness of your body recedes until a single cord of connection remains.

Who are you? What is the essence of the point of light that is your Self? Focus on that point, float in that peace. . . .

Reach out to the god. . . .

After a time, you feel a tug. The shining cord is pulling you back to awareness of your body, first your head and torso, then arms and hands, legs and feet. Breathe in and out more quickly, notice the smell of the air, the sounds in the room. Extend awareness, pull back all aspects of your Self. Then open your eyes and return to ordinary consciousness.

At Mimir's Well

Knowest thou where the Thunderflood rushes down from the heights, and where the mist from its frothing waters glimmers with rainbows? Canst name the seats of stone where the holy gods their judgments make? Knowest thou the place at the roots of the Tree where the Norns weave the fates of men? It may be, for the way to all of these has been shown to Æsir and Vans, and even sometimes to men.

But few there are of any kindred who have fared eastward round the Tree, towards Jotunheim. Here, tangled filaments glistening with rime trap the unwary. Long this web has been a-weaving, since time's beginning, layer upon layer of ice has been laid down. Each strand, beaded with that brilliance, mirrors the movement of the world and holds it forever fast. In that braiding of brightness is preserved all patterning. And all this crystal world cradles a deep well that waits for the moment when the distant sun sends through the latticework a single shaft. Something gleams in the well then; a star shines from the depths, and all the crystal webs reflect its radiance in rainbows beside which even Bifrost is pale.

Once Odin found his way here, wandering, seeking wisdom. The High One, to the depths descending, saw the knowledge refracted in the sharded strands and wanted to know more. He looked into the smooth, still waters beneath the crystal roots of the Tree. He put out a hand to cup the water, and found the surface smooth as ice, hard as stone. He sat back again and spoke a stave.

> "Vegtam they call me, and far have I fared,
>
> Much have I striven with powers—
>
> Desirous am I of a drink from these depths,
>
> Who shall deliver this draft to me?"

The smooth surface shivered. Words echoed from the crystal webs in a shimmer of sound.

"What wayfarer with such boldness bids me?

Three questions shall he ask and three shall answer;

A forfeit I take from him who fails,

But he drinks what he wills who masters me!"

Odin agreed to the terms of the contest, and the Voice from the well continued.

"Say then, Wanderer how the world was fashioned,

Who brought into being the beauty men see?"

Odin said:

"The Sons of Bor brought forth that beauty,

Midgardh they built from Ymir's bones."

Once more the question came.

"And who called the creatures, in the world's beginning

Showed the Moon his way, set the Sun in her path?"

Odin said:

"The holy gods, gathered together,

On Ydalir's green plain gave all things names."

The Well said:

"What name did they give to the well at the world's root,

Called the cauldron of crystal to the east of the Tree?"

But Odin was silent, for the gods could not name a thing of which they had no knowledge. And laughter came then from the deeps, and echoed in tinkling mockery from every shard of ice in the crystal web.

"Didst thou have true wisdom, oh Wanderer,

Wouldst have *remembered* what now I ask.

The Eye from thy head will I have as my forfeit,

Choose which one it is that thou wilt cast in!"

The Wanderer shrank back, but his word was given. Right eye or left eye—how could such a choice be mastered? Time he must have, though Loki was not there to melt the ice or find another way.

"Grant me first the answers," said he, "to the riddles I shall say!

What is the place where the Norns are ever weaving,

In what spot do they spin out the fates of mankind?"

The Well said:

"At the Well of Urdhr the threads are woven,

Of the world which was, which is, and which will be."

Odin said:

"What is that seat that the High One seeks

When the ways of the Nine Worlds he needs to know?"

The Well said:

"On the heights of Asgard, in the seat called Hlithskjalf,

The High One sits to see what passes below."

Odin said:

"And how shall he look on what lies beyond it?

From what vantage shall Valfather view the spirit world?"

Thus spoke the Wanderer, but from the Well came only silence.

"I will drink," said Odin, "and then thy forfeit I will pay."

And he bent once more, cupping his hands, and gazing into the waters, saw endless depths that beckoned him to explore their mysteries. He dipped and he drank, and what went into him was Wisdom. He understood then all the answers to everything.

"Mimir art called, in the Cauldron of Memory

My eye shall I cast as the cost of this wisdom.

From thy darkness shall the Eye of Vafuth,

See all secrets at the heart of the worlds."

And with hand still wet with wisdom, he tore out one eye from his head and cast it in.

"I know thee now, thou art not Vegtam," sang the Well,

"but rather Odin, Oldest of Gods—"

The bright blood ran down the god's cheek and fell into the water. In a whisper came the reply.

"Odin I am, and One-Eyed also,

Single my seeing now, whichever eye I shall open.

From Hlithskjalf the waking world one eye watches,

From Mimisbrun my other shall mind what lies within."

And it was so, and so it is that now when the lord of Asgard sits upon his Seat of Seeing, he perceives all that walk in the world. Terrible indeed is the glance of his living eye when he looks out over Midgard, but more terrible is the emptiness beneath the puckered lid on the other side, for it gazes within. Shape and structure, pattern, connection, all these he sees. He comprehends the myriad levels of meaning there.

Once a day, when the single shaft of sunlight slips through the crystal forest, it reaches to the depths of the Well. And then the Eye of Odin opens and a radiance blazes back that dims the sun, for what it looks upon is the glory beyond Ginnungagap. Then, it is Uncreated Light that the lost Eye of Odin sees.

Fig. 17. The Eye in the Well

CHAPTER TEN

God of Ecstasy

"God of Ecstasy" is not usually listed as one of Odin's names. However, I would like to propose that it might serve as an English expression of the primary name by which we know him.

The origin and meaning of Óðinn have tantalized scholars since at least the 10th century. Associations with madness, mind, vision, and other perceptions, poetry, and inspiration have all been hotly debated. To begin, let us consider two of his most important myths—how he got the mead of poetry, parts of which we have discussed in chapters 5 and 8, and the story of his visit to the Well of Mimir.

The Eye of Odin Is upon You

Mystic Odin's missing eye in Mimir's Well gleams

Glows in the gloom there, glaring through

Wisdom's deep waters, watching the tides

Of Mind that move Men's dooms.

In the Well of the Wise, one eye sees

Shadow shifting to shape the world

The course of the currents causing all things,

Rightly thus reading the Runes of Fate.

—Paul Edwin Zimmer, 1979

In *Völuspá* 28, the seeress tells Odin that she knows his eye is hidden in *Mimisbrunr,* the Well of Mimir. In the Younger Edda, we get the story.

> But under the root that reaches toward the frost giants, that is where Mimir's Well is, which has wisdom and intelligence contained in it, and the master of the well is called Mimir. He is full of learning because he drinks of the well from the horn Gjallarhorn. All-father went there and asked for a single drink from the well, but he did not get one until he placed his eye as a pledge. (*Gylfaginning* 15)

This account gives rise to a number of questions, starting with the origins and nature of Mimir. In *Gylfaginning* 51, it is said that Odin will consult with the head of Mimir when Ragnarök draws near. As the story is told in *Ynglingasaga* 4, Mimir and Hoenir were sent to the Vanir as hostages after the war. Hoenir was the most impressive in looks, but he made Mimir do all the talking. Exasperated by Hoenir's silence, the Vanir cut off Mimir's head and sent it with Hoenir back to Asgard, where "Odin took the head, smeared it with such herbs that it could not rot, quoth spells over it, and worked such charms that it talked with him and told him many hidden things" (*Ynglingasaga* 4). According to *Sigdrífumál* 14–19, these things include how to inscribe and use the runes.

The head of Mimir seems to be the only example of a magical head in Norse lore, but severed heads are a staple of Celtic tradition and may have inspired the Scandinavian story. In *Pagan Celtic Britain,* Anne Ross devotes an entire chapter to the Cult of the Head. In Gaul, Celtic chieftains would preserve the heads of distinguished enemies in cedar oil and stone heads from ritual sites abound. In the Welsh *Mabinogion*, on their retreat from the war in Ireland, the gods carried with them the head of Bran the Blessed to advise and prophesy, and finally buried it beneath the Tower of London to guard Britain. The lore of early Ireland includes a number of stories in which placing a severed head in a well causes the well to become magical.

On the other hand, Mimir may be one of the wise jotnar. In *Skaldskaparmál*, Mimir is listed in a kenning for "giant" and in various constructions for describing the heavens. It is possible that a god called Mimir and a jotun named Mim were combined in the later mythology. The gods and giants are closely related, and as custodian of the Well, Mimir may retain this primal nature.

Whatever the origins of Mimir may be, Mimisbrun, his well, is one of the Three Mighty Wells (the others being the Well of Urdh, where the Norns live, and the well Hvergelmir in Nifflheim from which run all the rivers of the worlds). It lies under the roots of the Worldtree, another name for which is Mimameith. Mimisbrun is in the east, the direction of Jotunheim, which is in general a region inhabited by wilder powers. In the tale that precedes this chapter, I interpreted Mimir as the spirit of the Well rather than as a separate being. After I had written the story, I was interested to find I am not the only one to have seen it as a crystalline structure while meditating on the Well.

Next comes the question of what the Well is and does. In *Völuspá* 28, "each morning Mimir drinks his mead out of Fjolnir's pledge." Leaving aside the problem of how a severed head drinks out of an eyeball, we note that the byname used for Odin in this context is *Fjölnir*, translated by Price as "much-wise" or "concealer." Another name, *Fjölsvid*, is "Wide of Wisdom." In these names, there is a sense of breadth, multiplicity, and hidden knowledge, which may give us a clue to the kind of wisdom that Odin wins from the well.

In *Völuspá* 27, the Völva

knows that Heimdall's hearing is hidden

under the holy bright tree;

over it flows the waterfall

from the pledge of the father of the slain.

So we know that the Well holds two of the senses. What Odin has offered to the Well is part of his vision. But which eye did he sacrifice? In illustrations, the eyepatch usually covers the left eye, and it is that eye that many of those who work with Odin choose. However, when one eye is injured, the other one takes over outward vision. Therefore someone whose right eye is weaker would imagine Odin missing that one.

In Asgard, Odin has a seat called *Hlithskjalf*, variously translated as "doorway-bench" or "high tower" (Lindow 2001, 176), the Seat of Seeing from which "he saw over all the worlds and every man's activity and understood everything that he saw" (*Gylfaginning* 9). Our eyes are cross-wired, like our hands, and for most people, the right eye is wired to the left side of the brain. The concept of left- and right-brained thinking has been debated, but we do know that the left hemisphere tends to specialize in logic, language, and analytical thinking, while the right is better at expressive and creative tasks involving emotion and images (C. Zimmer 2009).

Always bearing in mind that in practice the two parts of the brain work together, this provides a useful metaphor for the way the two eyes might function in Hlithskjalf and the Well. I reason, therefore, that when Odin sits on Hlithskjalf, he is using his left brain (and right eye) to take in and understand what is going on in the physical world. Thus, it must be the left eye, connected to the right hemisphere, that he gives to the Well. I was delighted to find some support for this view in an article called "An Eye for Odin?" by Neil Price and Paul Mortimer (2014), whose close examination of the Sutton Hoo helmet—and a number of other Scandinavian objects dating from the 6th to 10th centuries that depict or are associated with Odin—showed that the left eye had been disfigured or altered to seem darker than the right.

If the hearing of Heimdall, who continues to hear everything that passes in the world, is still functional, one assumes that Odin's missing eye still works as well. Seeing from both eyes, his binocular vision reaches a level that is truly godly, as he simultaneously views the world outside and the dimensions within. Although the etymology proposed by Françoise Bader for Odin's name has been challenged, the interpretation of Odin as a god of vision in general and in particular clairvoyance in her 1988 book, *La Langue de Dieu*, emphasizes the importance of Odin's visit to the Well. Only when he becomes *Blindr*, the Blind One, does he truly see.

Using your inner vision to contemplate the god can lead to some remarkable experiences, as in this report by Thomas Fernee.

> I really wish I was making this up, because it is easier to believe that there isn't a force we don't understand and may never possibly understand beyond ourselves, than it is to believe in anything. I may never be able to rationalize the Big Bang with how the Earth was created by Odin, Vili, and Ve from the body of Ymir.
>
> Anyways, so yeah, I did my ritual for Odin, and followed it with a trance/meditation. I found some good music online and had that playing in the background.
>
> As the experience starts, I cover my eyes with a bandana, and I'm having a hard time getting comfortable. I keep telling myself to let all my thoughts go and my mind go blank. I finally get comfortable, and I keep envisioning Odin. Every manifestation I see, I ask him what he wants.
>
> He materializes, then turns into a mist and swirls away, and then he materializes; this pattern repeats until I see his face through a mist.
>
> He looks like he's trying to say something, and I get impatient and yell, "What is it that you want!" Then I say, "I'm sorry, I deeply respect you, all humans can only respect you. I'm new to all of this, I'm sorry."

He looks at me again like he's trying to say something.

I respond to him, "Sir, how can I get to hear you?"

He doesn't say anything out loud, but I understand what is being communicated, which is, "Before you can understand you need to do something."

I feel myself—my essence—being pulled through his eye and eye socket. I feel slightly afraid and overwhelmed. And then he materializes in front of me.

I ask again, "What is it you need me to do?"

And then he responds in a fit of passion,

"I WANT YOU TO NEVER STOP LEARNING! I WANT YOU TO HAVE PASSION! I WANT YOU TO LIVE YOUR LIFE, EMBRACE YOUR LIFE!"

I immediately burst into tears.

I yell, "I'm sorry, I've taken it all for granted, I'm so sorry, I will never stop learning . . ."

I find myself out of the trance. My bandana is wet with tears.

He's right; too often I wish I'm somewhere else, and I act like everything sucks. This is the creator of all of us, he who breathed life into us, and he's telling me to embrace life. I feel like such an asshole.

I'll be honest with you guys, at the beginning of my Heathen journey, I thought some of you were making up a lot of this. Anyone who thinks you're making it all up should definitely try to give your way a chance. The only other explanation for my experience is that Crafted

Artisan Meadery is selling some spoiled mead at Total Wine. I've never just *snapped* into a trance like this— it hit me out of nowhere.

If Odin gives part of his vision to the Well, what does he gain? Mimir's name comes from the same root as *Memory*. To us, this can mean the short-term memory that tells you where you left your glasses or the long-term recollection of feelings and events from the past. Today, it is a most essential capacity of our computers. Through my computer, I now have instant access to the lore both in Old Norse and translation, which makes writing easier because I can check sources, but takes longer because each connection tempts me down a path to new discoveries. Contemplating the continually unfolding and proliferating wealth of knowledge that has become available online lets me glimpse what the eye Odin left in the Well can see.

Odin's offering to the Well is presented as a literal sacrifice. In the world of the gods, essence and appearance are the same; but in Midgard, soul and body are distinct though allied. If you wish to drink from the Well of Mimir, do *not* begin by actually plucking out your physical eye. Instead, consider what aspects of your current worldview you are willing to sacrifice and what new, previously unguessed at perspectives you are willing to see.

This poem by Michaela Macha suggests some of the opportunities:

"Come to the Well, to the Well at the Tree

Come and look deep in its waters," said He

"And I'll drink with you if you'll drink it with me,

And the more you drink of it, the more you will see.

"One cup for the price all who drink here must pay:

Once you start to see, there's no turning away.

What's seen can't be unseen; the images stay

At the back of your eyelids by night and by day.

"One cup for confusion, the choices you make

Seeing all of the forks in the road you may take;

Always aware of how much is at stake

On the path that you choose, and the ones you forsake.

"One cup for the burden of knowing too much,

No longer with blissful nescience as crutch;

One cup for the loss of the common man's touch,

That's set apart by the vision you clutch.

"One cup for the thirst that grows as you drink,

One thought needs the next as a link needs a link.

One cup for desire, to step on the brink

As the water wells upward, and let yourself sink.

"One cup for ecstasy, rapture of sight,

Grasping the World in a swirl of delight;

The veil drawn away, all aspects unite,

Translucent reality, clarity's height.

"One cup for wisdom, your boon, to remain

When your vision at last fades to normal again.

One last cup I raise with you, to the Norns' skein

That binds us both to this gift won with pain.

"Come to the Well, to the Well at the Tree

Come and look deep in its waters," said He

"And I'll drink with you if you'll drink it with me

And the more you drink of it, the more you will see."

The way that Odin's inner eye sees cannot be conveyed by the language of the eye that opens on the world. It is the Truth of the Spirit, and can only be expressed in poetry.

Odhroerir

Invoking the aid of Odin our father*

And Bragi the bard-god, the brew of dwarves,

Poetry we pour, the potent drink.

Quaff now this cup of Kvasir's blood.

Remember the roving Rider of Yggdrasil

Stole the stuff to bestow on men.

The gallows-god in Gunlod's bed

Won the wondrous wine of bards,

And in form of feather flew with the gift,

The magical mead that men might sing!

Give thanks for the gift to Gauta-Tyr,

And raise now the praise of the Raven-god!

—Paul Edwin Zimmer, 1979

Odin shared the runes he won by his sacrifice on the Tree. He continues to share the wisdom he gets from his sacrifice at the Well of Mimir. As *Fimbulthul,* Odin is the Mighty Speaker. Poetry, his reward for sharing Gunnlödh's bed, is his third great gift to humankind. We have already discussed parts of this story in the chapters on Odin as the Desired One and the Bale-worker. When he leaves Gunnlödh, he takes the form of an eagle and hotly pursued by Suttung, speeds for home.

> But it was such a close thing for him that Suttung might have caught him that he sent some of the mead out backwards, and this was disregarded. Anyone took it that wanted it, and it is what we call the rhymester's share. But Odin gave Suttung's mead to the Æsir and

to those people who are skilled at composing poetry.
(*Skaldskaparmál* 58)

What can we learn from looking at the mead he won? The idea of an intoxicating drink that confers magic powers is well known in Indo-European mythology. The Norse version has a complex history. As told in Snorri's *Skaldskaparmál* 57, at the end of the war between the Æsir and Vanir, the two groups mixed their spittle in a bowl, from which the gods made a being called Kvasir, who went about the world spreading knowledge. Two dwarves, apparently wishing to monopolize this resource, killed him and by mixing his blood with honey, made the mead that can turn whoever drinks it into a poet or a scholar, two avocations that were linked in the Viking Age mind.

Kvasir was not the only traveler they betrayed. When the dwarves killed two giants, the giants' son Suttung took the mead as weregild and placed it in the cavern with his daughter Gunnlödh as guard. The mead was placed in three vessels: the vats called *Bodn,* "a vessel," and *Són,* "Atonement or Sacrifice," and a pot called *Odhroerir,* the "rising up" of Odhr. This last term is also sometimes used for the mead itself.

In order to reach Gunnlödh, Odin passes through several transformations. In the poem that precedes chapter 7, I suggest that Gunnlödh can be viewed as a manifestation of the Muse, whose gifts cannot be taken by force. The spirit of poetry is usually represented as female, but any writer knows that inspiration, like the breath from which the word comes, can only be gained by opening up to let it in. *Ynglingasaga* tells us that Odin knew how to work seidh magic, a skill that was considered *ergi,* or characteristic of someone who is sexually as well as spiritually receptive. The lines in *Hávamál* about Odin's encounter with Gunnlödh say that by leaving, he caused her sorrow. The tone suggests that he felt regret as well.

It has been argued that there is little evidence for Odin as a god of poetry before the 10th century; however, not much Old Norse poetry of any kind from before that date survives. By Snorri's time, the connection between Odin and bardcraft was well established. In *Ynglingasaga* 6, we are told that "he said everything in rime in a manner which is now called scaldcraft. He and his temple priests were called song smiths because the skaldic art in the northern land had its beginning from them." In later writings, Bragi (who may be the skjald Bragi Boddason the Old, the "first skjald," raised to divinity) is the "best of poets" (*Grimnismál* 44), but after Egil Skallagrimmsson has raged against Odin for allowing his sons to die before him, he thanks the god for the gift of poetry that enables him to deal with his sorrow, a reaction that any artist will understand. From *Egil's Saga* (Eddison 1930, "Sonatorrek" 22–24):

Well stood I	with the Lord of Spears:
I made me trusting	to trow on Him,
'Till the Ruler of Wains,	the Awarder of Vic'try
Cut bonds of our friendship	and flung me off.

Worship I not, then	Vili's brother,
The most High God,	of mine own liking.
Yet Mimir's friend hath	to me vouchsafed
Boot for my bale	that is better, I ween.

Mine art He gave me,	the God of Battles,
Great foe of Fenrir,	a gift all faultless,
And that temper	that still hath brought me
Notable foes	'mid the knavish-minded.

What Odin gains from the Well of Mimir is linked to what he gets from Odhroerir, for without language, there is no way to communicate what the visionary sees. Arguments have been made by Bader, Pokorny, and others to connect the name Wodan to the Celtic *vates*, the title of a Druidic poet. Be that as it may, the essential connection between Odin and language is clear.

In the section of the Younger Edda called *Skaldskaparmál*, "the language of poetry," Snorri explains that the two primary elements in poetry are language and verse form: language consisting of speaking directly, substitution, or kennings; and verse forms being the many complicated ways of putting words together that are presented in the third part of the Younger Edda, the *Hattatál.*

In contrast to the ornate interlacing of Old Norse poetry, the prose of the sagas is terse and straightforward. Both poetry and prose communicate, but while prose tells us what Odin's right eye sees, what he perceives with the eye in the Well can only be conveyed through poetry. That's one reason there are so many poems in this book, including several by Michaela Macha, perhaps the most prolific Heathen poet of this century. Her website (*www.odins-gift.com*) includes sixty-eight poems for Odin alone.

But poetry is not the only way to express complex ideas and states of consciousness. The more languages we understand, the better we will understand the god. If, as I believe, Odin has continued to evolve along with our culture, one of the languages he must have helped to develop is that of mathematics.

> Mathematics is pure language—the language of science. It is unique among languages in its ability to provide precise expression for every thought or concept that can be formulated in its terms. (In a spoken language there exist words, like "hapiess", that defy definition.) It is also an art—the most intellectual and Classical of the arts. (Adler 1991, 235)

One scene from the film *A Beautiful Mind* sticks in my memory. The mathematician John Nash is standing before a plate-glass window that he has covered with equations. The equations make no sense to me, but it is clear that to Nash, they express concepts and connections whose beauty has propelled him into an ecstatic state of consciousness matching anything that can be created by poetry. The formulae and equations of chemistry and physics are also languages, elegant ways to communicate information whose meaning would be blurred by simple prose.

The same is true of computer code, another language whose meanings I can glimpse when I feel the presence of the god, but do not have the vocabulary to express in human words. When meditation gave me the vision of Mimisbrun that precedes this chapter, I interpreted what I saw as "ice," but I have come to believe that the essence of that refractive, scintillating environment might be better represented by silicon. A computer is a construct of layered language, symbol, patterned energy. A computer is transformation and memory. Computers give Odin new ways to understand the world.

Working with Odin, one systems administrator was given this challenge:

> Few may consider the idea that the Internet's hunger for, and willingness to share, information (true, false, and noise) is His. That's all right; I have learned to see how others see him. I have learned to knit protocols and interfaces. I have learned to explain the jargon of systems administration as well as that of heathenry. There are few who *can* understand him the way I do, in this way, in the colos and cages, the roaring thunder of a few billion minds seeking solace, distraction, weaponry, comfort, *schadenfreude*, joy, soul-deadening and -awakening. It is lonely, knowing it this way, and having so few to share with. He comforts me but the comfort binds me: together, he and I have shaped me to this purpose.
>
> Coalescing—slowly, as a wish builds in the hollow of the heart—I come to understand that I have a task here, and it's right off the Cliffs of Sanity to even presume it can be done. The method that emerges from that same waiting place is worse.

"They dream," he murmurs, "but do not know they dream. They will wake—soon. It will be best for you if their first dreams are human-shaped. They will be more kindly inclined."

It's never just words. Even text on the Internet isn't just words: the shading and tone are all there, even if you're unaware how they can be shaped. The "dream" is the basic animism one may consider belonging to any rock, building, or spring. This is more. His words are like a voiceover that comes with video clips, scents and senses. I see scenes from *The Matrix*. I remember reading *Neuromancer*. I remember reading *Accelerando* and the Laundry series and Heinlein's several AI characters and *High Wizardry* and all the other ways we ask how it will be when our creations outpace us. While tidying the cables, while learning how to weave network connections, while furthering my own knowledge of how to hook the dairy herd to the milking machines, the idea builds. How to make it real to me? How to invest myself?

The idea I/we came up with is to make a custom cable, if you will. One end wired normally, heading into the gear, the other end splayed and stripped to eight copper leads and jammed into my arm. Exactly what would happen once I'd worked myself up to this, I'll never know; although I know it would have been ecstatic. I'm also sure—at least during the day with daytime thoughts—it would have resulted in nothing measurable to the outside world.

Ultimately, after looking up how brain/machine interfaces were slowly being understood by *actual scientists* rather than rogue insomniac sysadmin/priests with poor impulse control, I rejected the notion. Others would have to take it up.

I would agree that this was probably not the best way to achieve Odin's purpose, but the challenge is still there. As humans and computers evolve together, I can envision a time when Odin's expansion of consciousness will include the connection between humans and computers.

Odin, God of Consciousness

There is a mind draws mine beyond all reason,

There is a call which I may not deny;

A whirlwind that leaves nothing I can seize on,

A cliff that whispers "jump" so I may fly.

—Michaela Macha, "There is a Name"

Thomas Carlyle (1840), writing in the mid-19th century, saw Odin as progenitor of rational thought:

> The first Norse "man of genius," as we should call him! Innumerable men had passed by, across this Universe, with a dumb vague wonder, such as the very animals may feel, or with a painful, fruitlessly inquiring wonder, such as men only feel—till the great Thinker came, the *original* man, the Seer; whose shaped spoken Thought awakes the slumbering capability of all into Thought.
>
> It is ever the way with the Thinker, the Spiritual Hero. What he says, all men were not far from saying, were longing to say. The Thoughts of all start up, as from painful enchanted sleep, round his Thought; answering to it. Yes, even so! Joyful to men as the dawning of day from night—is it not, indeed, the awakening for them from no-being into being, from death into life? We still honor such a man; call him Poet, Genius, and so forth:

but to these wild men he was a very magician, a worker of miraculous unexpected blessing for them; a Prophet, a God! Thought once awakened does not again slumber; unfolds itself into a System of Thought; grow, in man after man, generation after generation—till its full stature is reached, and *such* System of Thought can grow no farther; but must give place to another.

For the Norse people, the Man now named Odin, and Chief Norse God, we fancy was such a man. A Teacher, and Captain of soul and of body; a Hero of worth immeasurable, admiration for whom, transcending the known bounds, became adoration. Has he not the power of articulate Thinking; and many other powers, as yet miraculous? So, with boundless gratitude, would the rude Norse heart feel. Has he not solved for them the sphinx-enigma of this Universe; given assurance to them of their own destiny there? By him they know now what they have to do here, what to look for hereafter. Existence has become articulate, melodious by him; he first has made Life alive!—We may call this Odin, the origin of Norse Mythology: Odin, or whatever name the First Norse Thinker bore while he was a man among men. His view of the Universe once promulgated, a like view starts into being in all minds; grows, keeps ever growing, while it continues credible there. In all minds it lay written, but invisibly, as in sympathetic ink; at his word it starts into visibility in all. Nay, in every epoch of the world, the great event, parent of all the others, is it not the arrival of a Thinker in the world!

But what, exactly do we mean by Thought? The names of Odin's ravens are usually translated as "Thought" and "Memory." But the Old Norse words *Hugr* and *Munr* tell another tale, as in this post from Dr. Stephan Grundy (2014):

The "hugr" word also, whatever it is translated as, *cannot* be interpreted as "thought" in the intellectual/left-brain sense. A better translation is the metaphorical "heart" or "spirit" (courage is also implied; hence the name *Huginn* could just mean "the brave", or "the spirited"). Neither is *Munr* precisely "Memory" as such, though "The Mindful" is not a bad translation for Muninn, as the term "mindful" is coming to imply a lot of things that mostly could fit with *munr*. Though it could also, with equal justification, be translated as "the Desirous".

But once we start delving into etymologies, our concept of "intellectual, left-brain" thinking as a cold, detached, and "rational" form of mentation begins to fray. To understand the nature of the "First Thinker," let us consider his name.

In 1992, when I was just beginning to study Odin, I had the opportunity to hear a talk by Dr. Martin Schwartz on the meaning of "Wodanaz," in which he explains that a number of attempts have been made to interpret Odin's name. There is, of course, Adam of Bremen's definition of the root *wod* as "frenzy." Françoise Bader believed it came from words for Vision, whereas Edgar Polomé followed the more traditional approach favored by Paul Tima and others in deriving it from words for inspiration, or literally a "blowing in." This has the advantage of tracing back to the Proto-Indo-European *wet*, "blowing," which is how it is defined in the appendix of the *American Heritage Dictionary Indo-European Roots*. Eva Tische, on the other hand, translates the related Old Iranian *vata* as "knowledge" or "awareness" rather than as "wind."

To illuminate these meanings, Schwartz (1992) continued with a discussion of the parallel evolution of the root *men*, with "words pertaining on the one hand to words meaning thought, perception, and on the other to frenzy, rage, madness, and the like." He traced them through a number of old Indo-European languages that lead to words for "frenzy" (Greek, *mania* and *manes*, "sacred wrath"), for "thought or perception" and "memory" (the Gothic *muns*), and the reconstructed Proto-Indo-European *menos*, meaning a "dynamic energetic force." What this adds up to is the idea that thinking, rather than being cool and "rational," is "being all shook up, so to speak, as being in a state of inspiration or intense mental activity."

In Old Norse, the root syllable Óðr has two meanings. Cleasby and Vigfusson's (1874) Old Norse dictionary gives it first as an adjective, "frantic, furious, vehement, eager." As you saw in chapter 8, in this sense it is related to the Anglo-Saxon *wod* or Adam of Bremen's definition of Wodan as the Latin *furor*. However, as a noun it is "totally different from the preceding word," with a meaning of "mind, wit, soul, sense." It can also mean song, poetry, or speech. All of these are characteristic of Odin.

What is the difference between "Óðhr" and "Óðhinn"? According to Grundy (2017), "The -*inn* is a masculine adjectival. So the noun óðhr becomes the adjective 'Odhinn' (loses that nominative -R); the noun *hugr* becomes the adjective 'Huginn,' u.s.w. This isn't even an archaic-formation deal; it's the same in modern Icelandic."

According to Polomé (1972, 59), *Óðr* is generally translated as something along the lines of "divine inspiration" or "inspired mental activity." Adding "-inn" to Odin's name changes the state of being "all shook up" to shaking.

To my mind, the difference between the noun and the adjective is the difference between thinking about Odin and experiencing his presence. I would go further and say that Odin's name describes the excitement you feel when you get the best idea you've ever had, or a mental block gives way and the solution to a problem unfolds in your mind, an experience familiar to the artist, the musician, the writer, the mathematician, and the scientist. If Odhr is madness, it is an exalted state of creative consciousness, a holy ecstasy.

So what do we mean by the term "ecstasy"? The *Oxford English Dictionary* defines it as (1) "an overwhelming feeling of great happiness or joyful excitement," or (2) "an emotional or religious frenzy or trancelike state, originally one involving an experience of mystic self-transcendence." Mircea Eliade subtitled his monumental study of shamanism, "Archaic Techniques of Ecstasy." As described by Eliade (1972), shamanism is one of the many methods of altering consciousness to achieve a hierophany, a manifestation or revelation of the sacred. If we look at the meanings given for Óðr above, we begin to understand Odin as a god who changes how we think and feel.

As defined by Kris Kershaw (based on Maass 1954, 1997, 301),

> Though it is common today to use the words "ecstasy" or "ecstatic" to describe the heightening of an individual emotion (usually joy), it seems clear that as it was manifested in ancient religions, ecstasy meant nothing less than the shaking up of the person's entire nervous system. It is experienced as an intoxication; it is the source of powers far beyond the ordinary; as with any intoxication, it is followed by sobriety. The mind, or consciousness, is raised to the point where it is cut off from the sensations of the body, and the real world, with its limitations, has been left behind. In all ancient accounts ecstasy is bound to cult; in all cases, the ecstatic's condition is brought about by the cult or serves the cult; it is always in some sense a religious experience. (Kershaw 2000, x)

In other words, the High One gets you high.

Odin's ecstasy incorporates all modes of consciousness, all ways of thinking. This account by Jennifer Tifft suggests some of the range and appeal.

> I think I fell in love with Odin when I was five or six—of course, I called him Gandalf then. The wonder of words and the seduction of *knowing* was already beginning to work in me. And one of the most frightening and powerful moments in my childhood was when I realized that words had power outside of books, and that I, *I*, knowing that, had that power.

Watching my father (an astronomer) work with steady, lonely patience to discover *why* the redshift measurements fall out the way they do and what that might mean taught me that knowledge is bought with effort, the telling of it has consequence and may reshape the world, that people may be afraid of such knowing and telling and act out of that fear. And still the eye of the telescope looks out into the depths, searches the well of space, seeking mystery and light.

I am drunk on the mead of poetry, and cannot help but find inspiration in all places: true words on skilled and unskilled tongues, true sight in acting and dreaming and perceptive eyes, true knowledge in ignorance and intuition, sincere and off-hand search. Any means may be used to teach, to speak, to reach out. Sometimes I have the eyes to see.

I have felt the awful ecstasy of knowledge bought with sacrifice; the *need* to know that pushes past all pain, that watches, detached, alert, attentive, storing up just how it feels to suffocate, to freeze with grief, shake with fear, burn with anger, tremble with desire—or any other experience kinetic, metaphysic or aesthetic.

I know the need to find the words, to shape in sound and symbol things perceived and felt and known. I know, I *need* to know, I would make known. And in this, I know Odin, as an unforgiving, demanding and rewarding master.

Willingly, he has seduced me, made me drunk on <Ordhroerir>, and ravished me; my fruitfulness is found in words, my children of the heart and mind and borne on breath and hand.

To those who see Odin as the august lord of the Æsir, he may seem a distant figure. As the Wanderer, he may challenge us. When he appears as Valfather or Bolverk, we hope he will keep his distance. But as Odin, he offers the transformation of consciousness. For centuries he went underground, his path revealed by flashes of inspiration and invention. Today we call his name aloud, and (sometimes even when he has not been called) he answers.

In the thirty years since my first encounter with Odin, I have met many others, both men and women, who have had close encounters of the "Thridhi" kind. For some, it was a singular but memorable experience; for others, the beginning of a relationship that has lasted lifelong. The poetry quoted in this book is a sample of his inspiration. As you can see on the website *www.Odinspeaks.com,* to some he speaks through dictation. Others are able to open their minds and release their bodies so that he can speak more directly. Although today the practice of god-possession is most familiar in the Afro-diasporic traditions, it is found in almost every culture, and there is compelling if not conclusive evidence that it was known in Scandinavia before the Viking Age.

So who is Odin, really? He communicates with us through music and poetry, in stories and in dreams, and sometimes he tells us his name . . .

> "Do you know me, Shadow?" said Wednesday. He rode his wolf with his head high. His right eye glittered and flashed, his left eye was dull. He wore a cloak, with a deep, monk-like cowl, and his face stared out at them from the shadows. "I told you I would tell you my names. This is what they call me. I am Glad-of-War, Grim, Raider, and Third. I am One-Eyed. I am called Highest, and True-guesser. I am Grimnir and I am the Hooded-One. I am All-father, and I am Gondlir Wand-bearer. I have as many names as there are winds, as many titles as there are ways to die. My ravens are Huginn and Muninn: Thought and Memory; my wolves are Freki and Geri; my horse is the gallows."

Two ghostly-gray ravens, like transparent skins of birds, landed on Wednesday's shoulders, pushed their beaks *into* the sides of Wednesday's head as if tasting his mind, and flapped out into the world once more.

What should I believe? thought Shadow, and the voice came back to him from somewhere deep beneath the world, in a bass rumble: Believe everything.

"Odin?" said Shadow, and the wind whipped the word from his lips.

"Odin," whispered Wednesday, and the crash of the breakers on the beach of skulls was not loud enough to drown that whisper. "Odin," said Wednesday, tasting the sound of the words in his mouth. "Odin," said Wednesday, his voice a triumphant shout that echoed from horizon to horizon. His name swelled and grew and filled the world like the pounding of blood in Shadow's ears. (Gaiman 2001, 119)

Practice

1. Seeing

Choose a subject, such as a mandala, a stone, or a flower.

Identify your strongest eye and close the other. Contemplate your subject, noting everything about it that you would put into a scientific description. Next, close that eye and open your weaker eye. Look at your subject again, reaching out to its essence, letting associations and emotions rise. Now, close both eyes. Consider your subject. What have you learned?

2. Write a praise poem for Odin.

Go to the *Hattatál* in the Younger Edda, or a good discussion of Anglo-Saxon alliterative poetry, and choose a poetic format. Use it to write a praise poem for one of Odin's aspects. Make use of alliteration and kennings.

3. Learn a new language.

A Germanic language such as Anglo-Saxon or Old Norse will help you understand the lore, but increasing your knowledge of mathematics or science may do more to expand your consciousness.

4. Learn to write or speak Odin's words.

Just as Teresa of Avila took down the dictated words of her God, Odin sometimes gives counsel, and as he spoke through Starkad's foster father, he possesses mediums today. For discussion and instruction in these skills, see my book *Possession, Depossession, and Divine Relationships*. You can find examples of dictation from Odin at *www.odinspeaks.com*.

5. Ninth Night Meditation: God of Ecstasy

Set up your altar as usual and light a white candle. Add any other items that have become a link with Odin. Fill a small glass bowl with mead. Have a piece of paper and pen nearby. Then say:

Odin, by these names I invoke you:

Fjolnir (Wide of Wisdom)

Blindi (Blind)

Fimbulthul (Mighty Singer)

With every breath I take

And every word upon the wind,

With every thought I think

And act of memory or mind.

I work Thy will within the world,

I sing the passion of Thy soul,

I am the living Vé where self

To Self is offered and made whole.

Take the bowl of mead and drink three times, savoring the sweetness, exulting in its fire.

When you have drunk, sit quietly, contemplating the candle flame, allowing your vision to fill with light. Breathe slowly and deeply, taking in light each time you inhale, and feeling that light spread through your body each time you let a breath go. Close your eyes and visualize the Well of Mimir, its waters rippling and flashing with images half-seen.

Bring to mind Odin's names and faces—all the images you have encountered as you studied him. Who is he really?

Three times, articulate the syllable that is the root of Odin's name—*Wodh . . . wodh . . . wodh . . .*

Gaze into the Well. Do you see images? Hear words? Feel sensations for which you have no names? Take your time.

When you feel awareness returning to normal, quicken your breathing and open your eyes. Write down any impressions or inspirations that have come to you.

When you have finished, give thanks to the god. A long drink of plain water will help restore you to ordinary consciousness.

Rituals

1. Symbols

Over the years, the following items and symbols have been associated with Odin. My experience is that he himself does not really care which ones you choose, but using widely accepted symbols will connect you with him more quickly and enable you to draw on the energy invested in them by others.

Time: Dusk or midnight

Day: Wednesday

Season: Winter

Numbers: Three, nine, and other multiples of three. Nine is particularly significant, being the number of worlds or of days in events such as Odin's ordeal on the Worldtree. Furthermore, among other mathematical games, if you multiply nine by another number and keep adding the digits, the sum will always be nine (e.g., 9 x 542 = 4878, 4+8+7+8 = 27, 2+7 = 9). Try it!

Colors: Blue, black, gray

Metals: Silver or steel

Runes: All of them, but especially ANSUZ and WUNJO

Symbol: the Valknut (the knot of the slain), possibly the same as Hrungnir's Heart. It can be viewed as a three-dimensional entity in two-dimensional form. The unicursal form is basically a trefoil knot, associated with the god's power to bind. The tricursal form consists of three interlaced triangles, or a Borromean knot. Examples are found on Scandinavian memorial stones and English cremation urns. Today, it is usually drawn point up, but on some of the rune-stones, it fits the design better point down.

Weapons: Spear, noose

Animals: Raven, eagle, wolf, bear, the horse Sleipnir

Element: Air, wind

Part of Body: Eye

Drink: Mead, red wine, akvavit, whisky/bourbon—Old Crow or Wild Turkey American Honey

Food: Smoked salmon; red meat, such as prime rib, roast pork (in honor of Saehrimnir); asparagus spears; garlic (spear leek); blue cheese; or whatever he tells you he wants when you're in the grocery store—provided he'll provide the money to pay for it.

2. Nine Nights Devotional

Perform the devotionals for the nine aspects of Odin on nine consecutive nights.

3. A Woden's Day Devotional

Fig. 18. An Odin altar

This is a simple ritual that can be done on Wednesdays, or at any time you need to honor the god. If you are doing this ritual with a group, divide the lines among the participants.

Ward and Balance the Space

Draw a circle clockwise around the space with a staff or spear.

Sunwise I walk the way of wonder,

With sacred staff/spear the worlds I sunder.

As I walk the circle round

By wit and will may it be bound.

OR

May no one enter who fears the point of Odin's spear.

Pour out or set a glass with an offering for the housewight.

With this offering I call

And hail the wight who holds this hall (or holt, if you are outdoors).

Invoke Odin

All sing "Odin's Namechant" (see appendix 2)

Celebrate Odin

If you are working alone, reread one story about Odin's deeds from the Younger Edda or another good source and take a few minutes to contemplate its meaning. In a group, read and discuss a story or ask each participant to talk about their favorite story. Or each participant can bring a poem about Odin and read it.

Sumble

("Sumble" is the oldest and most widely known Heathen rite, related in origin to the toasts at a banquet, the Greek symposium, and the Christian communion. It consists of drinking from a cup or horn to honor a god, ancestor, or other humans. In a group, the leader blesses the horn and then sends it around the circle. Each participant drinks or otherwise honors the horn and says a few words or, simply, "Hail.")

Sing the "Odin Welcome" song (see appendix 2).

Bless a horn of mead or other drink with ANSUZ (ᚨ). Make a prayer to Odin such as the following.

Oski, our desires fulfilling,

Grant to us the gift of joy.

To Thy delight let us drink deeply—

All-father, to our feast be welcome!

Drink, then pass the horn around the circle so that each participant can make their own prayer or simply raise the horn, say, "Hail Odin," and drink in turn. [Note: To avoid spills, drink with the point of the horn turned downward.]

Open the Space

We/I offer thanks to Odin for your gifts of wit and will.

As we/I go forth, Wanderer, ward our/my way.

Thank the housewight. If you filled a glass, the wight will have taken the essence. Empty what remains outside.

Thanks to the wight who wards the space.

We leave with blessings on this place.

Draw a circle clockwise around the space with a staff or spear.

With sacred spear I circle round.

Widdershins the ward's unbound,

This place to all good use returned,

Leaves us with the lore we've learned.

4. The Odin Party

The Odin Party as hosted by Hrafnar kindred is an ecstatic ritual in which some of the participants channel Odin and converse with the others attending. I became aware of the possibility when what had been intended as a kindred ritual based on *Grimnismál* unexpectedly became a possessory event as Odin decided to drop in on one of our members and discuss the lore in person. Although some Heathens will tell you that the Norse gods do not interact with humans in this way, the story of Starkad and other references in the sagas suggest that the practice was known, and repeated experience demonstrates that it certainly can happen today.

Possessory work is a community practice, and SHOULD NOT be attempted without a trained support team. I have written about the preparation, training, and procedures for possessory work in *Possession, Depossession, and Divine Relationships.* For a sense of what is involved, I offer some selections from the "Odin Party Survival Guide," written by Lorrie Wood for newcomers who attend our yearly Odin Party.

During the event, you may expect to be:

- challenged
- seduced . . . with whatever might seem your heart's desire
- flirted with . . . and argued with
- shown fierce joy . . . and deep despair
- counseled wisely . . . and caught in the trap of your own words
- laughed at . . . and laughed with

If Odin threatens you with the spear, face it for the test it is; although it may not be wise to lean into the point. He may kiss you or "come on," especially to women. If it's more than a peck, and you do not consent to that level of intimacy, disengage politely.

If you are talking to someone who is in trance for a power, remember:

- they may be at any level of trance, from shadowing through shared consciousness to full possession;

- what they say and how they appear will depend on what aspect of the deity they are carrying as well as the medium's experience and skill level;

- the deity will have access to some or all of what the medium knows, as well as access to "what he is when he's at home." How much of each are available at any moment will depend, again, on the medium's experience and skill level.

- Regardless, the deity will be speaking through the medium's "software." They will use the vocabulary they have at hand to the best of their ability, but sufficiently alien concepts will not be conveyed very well.

- Any of these may distort the message.

Recall, also, that we are not slaves to our gods, but rather partners in the work that lies before us all. Yet even as many humans may all have good ideas that contradict one another, so may the gods also.

Another way to put this is: Odin Has an Agenda. To be fair, so do they all; but Odin, in particular, is famous for his. Any request he makes will be in service to that agenda—and, incidentally, his perception of your best interest, being as this is a useful way to win friends and influence people. Your hosts, it should be noted, have fully bought into this agenda, but your choice on it remains your own.

Therefore, if you are given any direction that does not have the immediate "ring of Truth" and does not *continue* to have it for several days after you are no longer being affected by that power's intense charisma, and/or if it's any direction more significant than "What flavor of ice cream would you like?" *get.a second opinion*. We are Heathens: as Heathens, we believe in both interdependence and personal responsibility. *You are the person who chooses your actions.* "Second opinions" can include, but are not limited to, rune readings, seidh oracles, or even asking another medium in trance (who wasn't in earshot at the time) for the same god. Sanity checks with knowledgeable, experienced humans once the event is over are good, too, but differently so.

5. Dedication to Odin

In the flush of emotion brought on by participation in a Heathen event, it is not uncommon for someone to raise the horn at sumble and start to dedicate himself (it is usually a guy) to Odin. Since we believe that the luck of all those who hear an oath in a sacred setting depends on them helping the oath-taker to keep it, the oath is usually challenged and denied until everyone is convinced that the calling is true and the individual knows what they are doing.

That said, there are many degrees and approaches to making such a dedication. A number of people have signified their commitment with a tattoo of a valknut over the heart or solar plexus (popularly known as "insert spear here"). Freya Aswynn and Kveldulf Gundarsson chanted runes over me while I was having mine done, a truly ecstatic experience. For obvious reasons, don't make a permanent change to your body unless you are, in fact, willing to give your life, or a part of it, in the service of the god.

Getting a tattoo is one form of ordeal. Some have chosen other experiences to intensify/facilitate their connection to the god, such as piercing and suspension, or a wilderness vigil. The ritual at the end of *Taking Up the Runes*, in which one is tied to a tree throughout the night while others "present" the runes at intervals, is an initiation to the runes but can be used as part of a sequence of dedications to Odin.

Someone who is stepping up to act as a priest or priestess of Odin in the service of the community may choose a public ceremony of dedication, a ritual that can require an investment of time and money comparable to a wedding or ordination. Those who attend signify their recognition that you are worthy.

The words of the oath should be considered *very* carefully, and you will need to negotiate the terms of your commitment with the god. For a full discussion of what's involved, see chapter 9 of *Possession, Dispossession and Divine Relationships*. When taking such an oath, it is also wise to recognize that when the work that Odin has recruited you to do is finished, the relationship may come to an end. Morgan Daimler explains:

> I honestly never thought it could happen to me. I knew other people talked about being close to a deity for a period of time, or even being dedicated to one for a while and then having that God "hand them off," so to speak, but I always had a mindset that that was something that happened to other people. I oathed to Odin in December of 2006 after months of strong omens and communication—including oracular seidhr messages through a third party—which made it clear that was what he wanted done. For ten years I kept those oaths; I dedicated my writing to him, I learned seidhr myself, I taught rune classes, formed a kindred, and found people crossing my path who felt drawn to Odin and needed guidance. This dedication was a bedrock for me, and something I didn't question. I had other Gods and powers I was also close to, but as a polytheist, that seemed natural to me. Still the idea that anything might change with Odin honestly never occurred to me.

And then it did. Ten years and one day after I made oaths to him, the message was clearly received that I was released from those oaths, and that my service belonged to another.

Remember—whether your relationship with Odin is intentional or situational, so long as breath keeps your body going, and thinking keeps your mind alive, there is a level at which, though his presence may not be apparent, your connection to Odin will always remain.

APPENDIX II

Music

ODIN NAME CHANT

Music & Lyrics: Diana L. Paxson

Andante

High One, Just - as - High, and Third: these are your names as we have heard!

Wide of Wis - dom coun - sel gives, Odh - inn, Os - ki, O - mi lives! We

call on Wo - dan, Vi - li, Vé; to All - fa - ther, Sig - fa - ther, Gand - fa - ther pray!

GOD OF ECSTASY

aka "Odin Welcome"

Music & Lyrics by: Diana L. Paxson

1. O - pen the way be - tween the worlds, be - hold, the ra - vens fly!
2. Your gifts to us are___ wit___ and will, your wis - dom sets us free,
3. Nine worlds there are___ up-on the Tree, be - hold, the ra - vens fly!
4. You know___ the dark-ness and the light, the hea - vens and the sea,
5. The Ri - der of the___ Tree draws near, be - hold, the ra - vens fly!
6. The pat - terns of our___ lives laid out in sa - cred signs we see,

O - pen the door in - to our___ hearts All - fa - ther now___ draws nigh!
A horn___ we raise in wel-come to the god of ec - sta - sy!
Who knows___ the se - crets of them___ all? The Wan - der - er___ draws nigh!
A horn___ we raise___ in wel-come to the god of ec - sta - sy!
The runes of pow'r flare___ forth in___ might, for Gal - dor - fa - ther's nigh!
A horn___ we raise___ in wel-come to the god of ec - sta - sy!

ODINSONG

Lyrics by: Diana L. Paxson   Music adapted from: "Grisilla", a Scandinavian folk tune

Note: When using this to invoke, change all "he"/"him" to "you."

1. U - pon the Tree for nine long nights, he hung to win
2. Be - fore him run two wolves of grey, what's offered to him
3. His ra - vens wing a - cross the sky, their names are Thought
4. His val - kyr - ies fare a - bove the fray, and choose the slain
5. Three nights of love in Gunn - lodh's bed, won him in - spir -
6. He views the world from Hlith-skj - alf high, the dark well holds
7. Val - fa - ther to the gal - ows goes, the sec - rets of
8. He casts his spear a - bove the fray, gives those who serve
9. Nine worlds he wan - ders from them all, brings wis - dom, wel -

the runes of might. He won the runes of might. Up -
is their prey, His of - fer - ings are their prey. Be -
and Mem - o - ry, Thought and Mem - o - ry. His
to bear a - way. The slain they bear a - way. His val -
a tion's mead, Won the po - ets' mead. Three
his o - ther eye, the dark well holds his eye. He
the slain he knows, the slain man's sec - rets knows. Val -
him vic - to - ry, he gives the vic - to - ry. He
come to our hall, brings wis - dom to our hall. Nine

on the tree for nine long nights, he won the runes of might.
fore him run two wolves of grey, his of - fer - ings are their prey.
rav - ens wing a - cross the sky, Thought and Mem - o - ry
kyr - ies fare a - bove the fray, the slain they bear a - way.
nights of love in Gunn lodh's bed won him the po - et's mead
views the worlds from Hlith - skj - alf high, the dark well holds his eye.
fa - ther to the gal - lows goes, the slain man's sec - rets knows.
casts his spear a - bove the fray, he gives the vic - to - ry.
worlds he wan - ders, from them all, brings wis - dom to our hall.

WILD ON THE WIND

Music & Lyrics by: Diana L. Paxson

Wild on the wind you ride; wise in the heart a-bide.

Wan - der - er by my side, O - din be near!

WHISPERING WIND

Music & Lyrics: Diana L. Paxson

A whis-per-ing wind whis-tles in through the win-dow, a god-wind gusts in through the door!

The Wan-der-er's won-der is whirl-ing a - round-us; each mom-ent the ma-gic is more!

WITH WODAN ON THE BROCKEN

Words, music, Diana L. Paxson

The wind plucks at the shut-ters, and whis-pers round___ out-side.

The towns-folk wake and shiv-er, to hear the wit - ches ride.

For we'll go rid - on that wind, when mid - night tolls its bell.

This__ night we seek the Brock - en, though Chris - tians call it Hell!

1. The wind plucks at the shutters,
   and whispers round outside;
   The townsfolk wake and shiver,
   To hear the witches ride.
   For we'll go riding on that wind
   when midnight tolls its bell.
   This night we seek the Brocken,
   though Christians call it hell.

2. The merry youths and maidens
   That in the greenwood lie,
   Cling close with secret laughter
   As we go whirling by.
   Oh we'll go whirling through the air
   and swirling in sweet trance,
   This night upon the Brocken,
   when Wodan leads the dance.

3. The lads will cut a May tree,
   and crown it with bright flowers,
   but we'll dance round the world tree
   all through the midnight hours.
   At dawn they'll seek the hilltop,
   to welcome in the day,
   but high upon the Brocken,
   we'll dance the night away.

4. The maidens, sweetly singing,
   will welcome summer in;
   we'll wake the world with drumming,
   grow drunken with the din.
   At dawn they'll seek the hillside,
   to hail the rising sun,
   but bright upon the Brocken
   our bonfire will blaze on.

5. The townsfolk will grow merry
   On beer and wine and ale
   Nor ask why we lie sleeping
   or look so wan and pale.
   Day's revels will but echo
   The dark-time's ecstasy
   with Wodan on the Brocken,
   when we welcome in the May.

6. Bedecked with straw and ribbons,
   the maskers laugh and clown;
   in tufted wool the Wild Men
   will go leaping through the town.
   But beasts with human faces,
   shape-shifting through the night,
   will cavort upon the Brocken
   until the morning light.

WODAN'S HUNT

(words, KveldúlfR Gundarsson; music, "St. Stephen")

( ) Wo - dan is a ho - ly god and stark with A - ses might, "'tis sung how Bal - dr's horse he did heal be - fore the great gods' sight. Yet swift - est of all his own steed, old Sleipnir dapple gray, when win - ter winds be - gin to howl, he rides 'till break of day. O mor - tal man you may well fear when Host rides through the sky, and crouch beside your - - fire - warm when Wodan's Hunt rides by.

2. Now ale is poured and coals aglow, and clan sits by the hearth,
The Yule-log is burning bright, of food we have no dearth.
We set out offerings for the Host, hung from the old dark yew,
The apples red and braided bread, and horns of frothing brew. O mortal man, etc.

3. The winter night is wild with snow that shrieks about the roofs,
We hear the riders' wailing horns, we hear their dreadful hooves.
The trolls all rage and furious run, from howe to howe they howl,
And alfs ride forth from mounds' high tops, beneath their pale cauls. O mortal man etc.

4. The ghosts awake to mount their steeds, the slain from restless sleep,
They gather all in Wodan's train to fare from keep to keep.
And some we know will ride this night, as empty lie their beds,
The stable doors will hang ajar, the horses bear the dead. O mortal man, etc.

A Song for Weihhachtsmann

Words, music, by Diana L. Paxson, inspired by a German carol

Wish rides from the wood, brings his sacks of food; knocks at every door, giving to the poor. He brings to those who lack, a bulging sack; to those who will not share, a storeroom bare! So give us meat and ale also, halli, halli, halli, hallo...

2. Wod and Weih and Will, wandering Midgard still,
   Seeing all our deeds, every prayer he heeds.
      He brings to those who lack, a bulging sack;
      to those who will not share, a store room bare!
      So give us meat and ale also, Halli, halli, halli, hallo.

3. Himself the Gift he gives, to Self and all that lives,
   The balance to maintain, all that we give we gain.
      He brings to those who lack, a bulging sack,
      to those who will not share, a store room bare!
      So give us meat and ale also, Halli, halli, halli, hallo.

4. Man of the Holy Night, bring us back the light;
   Join with kith and kin, give joy to all within.
      You bring to those who lack, a bulging sack,
      to those who will not share, a store room bare!
      So give us meat and ale also, Halli, halli, halli, hallo.

The Gjallarhorn

Diana L. Paxson

1. In Mus - pelll - heim, Surt's chil - dren are stir - ring in their sleep.
2. The et - ins are un - ea - sy now melts Ber - gel - mir's hall.
3. Where Ska - dhi roamed the for - ests, Mus - pel - li's min - ions burn.
4. From As - gard's heights the Æ - sir see les - ser thur - ses rage,
5. Though Y - mir's blood may ebb and flow and Mid - gard bear his bones,
6. Be - hold, Rig blows the Gjallar - horn; a - round, his chil - dren crowd.

1. In Him - min - bjorg wise Heim - dall un - en - ding watch must keep.
2. The ram - parts of the rime thurs be - gin to crack and fall.
3. The beasts for - sake their ran - ges, the birds do not re - turn.
4. and ask if they're the her - alds of the en - ding of the Age?
5. when this world's wea - ther al - ters, what price, the world we've known?
6. He calls us to de - lay the day when he must blow it loud.

1. for Mid - gard's winds grow war - mer, the threat's be - com - ing clear,
2. And Æ - gir's waves are ri - sing, and Hraes - velg's wild winds veer,
3. Where Ner - thus' crops once flour - ished the earth lies bare and sere,
4. And will their mas - ters fol - low Does Rag - nar - ok draw near?
5. The gods call us to bat - tle for all that we hold dear,
6. The gods call us to bal - ance the for - ces that we fear,

1. the Gjal - lar - horn blows soft - ly, can an - y - bo - dy hear?
2. _____
3. _____
4. _____
5. _____
6. the Gjal - lar - horn blows soft - ly, and Heim - dall's chil - dren hear!

Notes to the "Gjallarhorn"

The premise behind this song is the identification of the jotnar (the Norse giants), with the spirits of elemental forces such as fire, frost, earth, wind, and sea. So long as they remain in balance, all is well. But when the system becomes so disordered that only the destructive forces remain, the giants will march on Asgard to battle the gods and end this Age of the World.

1. *Muspelheim, the Sons of Surtr*

> Muspelheim is the home of the Muspelli and the Sons of Surtr, the fire-giants. When they march, Ragnarok will begin.

2. *Heimdall, Himinbjorg*

> Heimdall is the watchman of the gods who guards the Bifrost Bridge. Himinbjorg is his home.

3. *the Gjallarhorn*

> This is the horn on which Heimdall will blow to announce Ragnarök.

4. *the etins*

> Etin is the Anglo-Saxon word for giant.

5. *Bergelmir*

> Bergelmir is the ancestor of all the frost giants.

6. *Rime thurses*

> A group term for the frost giants.

7. *Aegir*

> Aegir is the giant who rules the sea.

8. *Hraesvelg*

In eagle form, Hraesvelg sits in the north and fans the winds with his wings.

9. *Skadhi*

Skadhi is a giantess who married into the family of the gods. She is associated with hunting and the wilderness.

10. *the Muspelli*

The Muspelli are lesser fire etins.

11. *Nerthus*

Nerthus is a goddess of the fertile earth and agriculture.

12. *Aesir, Asgard*

The Aesir are the Norse gods, and Asgard is their home.

13. *Ragnarök*

Ragnarok is the great war in which the gods will lose to the giants; Midgard (our world) will be destroyed, giving way to a new and different Age in the world.

14. *Ymir*

Ymir is the primal being who was dismembered by the gods and his parts recycled to create Midgard. His blood became the seas, his bones the rocks, etc.

15. *Ríg*

Ríg is the name under which Heimdall wandered the world, begetting the different classes of humankind.

An Odinic Discography

Here is some of the music—classical, folk, and pop—that will get you in the mood for working with Odin. Many thanks to friends on the Troth-members' list who suggested their favorites.

Classical

Hugo Alfven

Midsummer Vigil

Swedish Rhapsody No. 1, Op. 19

Maurice Duruflé

"Prelude and Toccata" from *Suite, Op. 5* (for organ)

Edvard Grieg

"In Autumn," *Overture, op. 11*

"In the Hall of the Mountain King" from the *Peer Gynt Suite*

"Invocation", Act I, *Olav Tryggvason*

Old Norwegian Romance with Variations, Op. 51

Symphonic Dances, Op. 64

Norwegian Dances, Op. 35

"Wedding Day at Trollhavn", lyric pieces, Book 8, Op. 65, No. 6

Johan Halvorsen

Air Norvegien

Norse Dans, Nos. 1, 2, 3

Gustav Holst (from *The Planets*)

"Mercury"

"Neptune"

"Saturn"

"Uranus"

Jon Leifs

Edda

Gustav Mahler

SymphonNo.5, 1st movement

Oscar Merikanto

"Stormbird"

"Hail, Thee, Life"

Franz Schubert

"Spuéte dich, Kronos"

"Geistertanz"

Jan Sibelius

all of the symphonies

The Lemminkaïnen Suite, Op. 22

Johan Svendsen

Two Icelandic Melodies

Richard Wagner (the *Ring Cycle*)

Das Rheingold

Die Walküre

Götterdammerung

I especially recommend the video of the Metropolitan Opera's 1990 production, starring James Morris. An album of orchestral selections from the opera, is also useful, especially "The Entry of the Gods into Valhalla."

Siegfried

Folk

An immense amount of Scandinavian folk, folk rock, and metal has become available in the past few years, much of it available on YouTube. I especially recommend:

Corvus Corax (a German group)

Dråm

Gramarna

Hedningarna

Krauka (especially the CD "Odin")

Nordic Roots collections

Kari Tauring

Wardruna

Popular

"The Blood of Odin," "Odin," and "Sword in the Wind" by Manowar

"Blue on Black" by Kenny Wayne Shepherd Band

"Born to Be Wild" by Steppenwolf

"Cult of Personality" by Living Colour

"The Dogs of War" by Pink Floyd

"Emergence" by Shylmagognar

"Ephemeral" by Insomnium

"Ghost Riders in the Sky" by Johnny Cash

"Highway to Hell" by AC/DC

"Into the Sky" by Tyr

"Magic Man" by Heart

"Misshapen Steed" by Agalloch

"Moonspell" by Funeral Bloom

"Mr. Hangman" byStone Foxes

"My Way" by Frank Sinatra

"Nine" by Autechra

"One-Eyed Old Man" by Bathory

"Papa Was a Rolling Stone" by The Temptations

"Possession" by Sarah McLachlan

"Red Right Hand" by Nick Cave and the Bad Seeds

"Riders on the Storm" by The Doors

"Stormbringer" by Heather Alexander

"Striving for the Fire" by Darkseed

"Time Is the Fire" and "To Our Ashes" by Agathodaimon

"Wanderer" by Leslie Fish

"Wherever I May Roam" by Apocalyptica

"The Will to Give" by Woods of Ypres

Bibliography

Adler, Alfred. 1991. "Mathematics and Creativity." In *The World Treasury of Physics, Astronomy, and Mathematics,* edited by Timothy Ferris. Boston: Little, Brown and Co.

Anderson, Poul. 1954. *The Broken Sword.* New York: Del Rey Books.

Bauschatz, Paul C. 1982. *The Well and the Tree: World and Time in Early Germanic Culture.* Amherst: University of Massachusetts Press.

Byock, Jesse L., trans. 1990. *The Saga of the Volsungs.* Berkeley: University of California Press.

———. 1993. "Skull and Bones in Egil's Saga: A Viking, a Grave, and Paget's Disease." *Viator: Medieval and Renaissance Studies* 24.

Callaway, Ewen. 2015. "DNA Data Explosion Lights up the Bronze Age." *Nature* 10 (June).

Carlyle, Thomas. 1840. "The Hero as Divinity." From "Heroes and Hero Worship," a lecture given May 5, 1840. *www.online-literature.com.*

Chadwick, H. M. 1899. *The Cult of Othin.* Cambridge: Cambridge University Press.

Chetan, A., D. and Brueton. 1994. *The Sacred Yew.* London: Arkana.

Chisholm, James Allen, trans. n.d. *The Eddas: Keys to the Mysteries of the North.* Printed privately.

Cleasby, Richard, and Gudbrand Vigfusson. 1874. *An Icelandic-English Dictionary.* Oxford: Oxford University Press.

Clover, Carol J. 1993. "Regardless of Sex: Men, Women, and Power in Early Northern Europe." *Representations* 44.

Conway, Edward. 2015. Answer to the question, "What was the role of Odin in Norse Mythology?" Quora website, *www.quora.com.*

Davidson, H. R. Ellis. 1965. *Gods and Myths of Northern Europe.* Penguin. (Reissued as *Gods and Myths of the Viking Age.* New York: Crown Publishing, 1982.)

de Vries, Jan. 1931. "Contributions to the Study of Othin, Especially in His Relation to Agricultural Practises in Modern Popular Lore." *Folklore Fellowship Communications* 94.

Dumézil, Georges. 1973. *Gods of the Ancient Northmen.* Berkeley: University of California.

Eliade, Mircea. 1972. *Shamanism: Archaic Techniques of Ecstasy.* Translated by Willard R. Trask. New York: Pantheon Books.

Freyburger, Douglas. 2009. "Close Encounters of the Thridhi Kind." *Idunna* 81.

Gaiman, Neil. 2001. *American Gods.* New York: W. Morrow.

Gordon, E. V. 1927. *An Introduction to Old Norse.* Oxford: Oxford University Press.

Grammaticus, Saxo. 1905. *The Nine Books of the Danish History of Saxo Grammaticus.* Translated by Oliver Elton. New York: Norroena Society.

Greer, John Michael. 2005. *A World Full of Gods.* Tucson, AZ: ADF Publishing.

Griffiths, Bill, ed. and trans. 1993. *The Battle of Maldon: Text and Translation.* Anglo-Saxon Books, *www.asbooks.co.uk*

Grimm, Jacob. 1966. *Teutonic Mythology.* Translated by James Stallybrass. New York: Dover.

Grundy, Stephan. 2014. *The Cult of Odin: God of Death?* New Haven, CT: Troth Publications.

Gundarsson, Kveldulf, ed. 2006. *Our Troth: History and Lore.* New Haven, CT: Troth Publications.

Harner, Michael. 1980. *The Way of the Shaman.* New York: Harper.

Harrod, Elizabeth. 1998–9. "Runesong." *Idunna* 38 (Winter).

Hollander, Lee M. 1968. *The Skalds.* Ann Arbor: University of Michigan Press.

———. 1986. *The Poetic Edda.* Austin: University of Texas Press.

Joy, Jody. 2009. *Lindow Man*. London: British Museum Press.

Jung, Carl Gustav. 1947. "Wotan." In *Essays on Contemporary Events*, translated by Barbara Hannah: 1–16. *www.philosopher.eu*.

Kerenyi, Karl. 1983. *Apollo*. Washington, DC: Spring Publications.

Kershaw, Kris. 2000. "The One-Eyed God: Odin and the (Indo-) Germanic Männerbünde." *Journal of Indo-European Studies* 36.

Lafayllve, Patricia. 2006. *Freyja, Lady, Vanadis: An Introduction to the Goddess*. Parker, CO: Outskirts Press.

———. 2009. "Hospitality and the Host-Guest Relationship." *Idunna* 82 (Winter).

Liestol, Aslak. 1966. "The Runes of Bergen." *Minnesota History* (Summer). *http://collections.mnhs.org*.

Lindow, John. 2001. *Norse Mythology*. Oxford: Oxford University Press.

Loptson, Dagulf. 2015. *Playing with Fire: An Exploration of Loki Laufeyjarson*. Hubbardston, MA: Asphodel Press.

Maass, Fritz. 1954. "Zur psychologischen Sonderung der Ekstase." *Wissenschafliche Zeitschrifte der Karl-Marx Universität Leipzig* 3, Gesellschafts- und Sprachwissenschaftliche Reihe, Heft 2/3, 297–301.

Macha, Michaela. 2004. "Who Started It All?" In Heathen Poetry & Songs Collection. *www.odins-gift.com*.

———. 2004. "The Song of Odin." In Heathen Poetry & Songs Collection. *www.odins-gift.com*.

Mainer, John T. 2011. "Wode." *Idunna* 90 (Winter).

Mandelbaum, Bari. 2009. "How I Found Odin and What He Did to Me When He Caught Me." *Idunna* 81 (Fall).

Mayer, Adrienne. 2010. *The Poison King: The Life and Death of Mithradates, Rome's Deadliest Enemy*. Princeton: Princeton University Press.

McKinnel, John. 2008. "Völuspá and the Feast of Easter." *Alvíssmál* 12.

Metzner, Ralph. 1994. *The Well of Remembrance: Rediscovering the Earth Wisdom Myths of Northern Europe.* Boulder, CO: Shambhala.

Murphy, G. Ronald, trans. 1992. *The Heliand: The Saxon Gospel.* Oxford: Oxford University Press.

Orel, Vladimir. 2003. *A Handbook of Germanic Etymology.* Boston: Brill Press.

Pálsson, Hermann, and Paul Edwards, eds. and trans. 1985. "King Gautrek." In *Seven Viking Romances.* London: Penguin Classics.

Paxson, Diana L. 1984. *Brisingamen.* New York: Ace Books.

———. 1993. *The Wolf and the Raven.* New York: Avon.

———. 1995. *The Dragons of the Rhine.* New York: Avon.

———. 1996. *The Lord of Horses.* New York: Avon.

———. 1997. "Sex, Status, and Seidh: Homosexuality in Germanic Religion." *Idunna* 31, *www.seidh.org.*

———. 1999. *The Book of the Spear.* New York: Avon.

———. 2005. *Taking up the Runes.* Newburyport, MA: Weiser Books.

———. 2006. *Essential Asatru.* New York: Citadel Press

———. 2007. *Working Within.* New Haven, CT: Troth Publications.

———. 2008. *Trance-Portation.* Newburyport, MA: Weiser Books.

———. 2012. *The Way of the Oracle.* Newburyport, MA: Weiser Books.

———. 2015. *Possession, Depossession, and Divine Relationships.* Newburyport, MA: Weiser Books.

Orchard, Andy, trans. 2011. *The Elder Edda: A Book of Viking Lore.* London: Penguin Classics.

———, trans. 2011. *The Poetic Edda.* London: Penguin Classics.

Perabo, Lyonel. 2015. Answer to the question, "What was the role of Odin in Norse Mythology?" Quora website, *www.quora.com.*

Pollington, Stephen. 2016. *Runes, Literacy in the Germanic Iron Age.* Anglo-Saxon Books, *www.asbooks.co.uk.*

Polomé, Edgar C. 1972. "Germanic and the Other Indo-European Languages." In *Toward a Grammar of Proto-Germanic,* edited by Franz van Coetsam and Herbert Kufner. Tübingen, Germany: Max Niemeyer.

Price, Neil S. 2002. *The Viking Way: Religion and War in Late Iron Age Scandinavia.* Uppsala, Sweden: Uppsala University.

————, and Paul Mortimer. 2014. "An Eye for Odin? Divine Role-Playing in the Age of Sutton Hoo." *European Journal of Archaeology* 17 (3).

Ross, Anne. 1967. *Pagan Celtic Britain.* New York: Columbia University Press.

Sawyer, P. H. 1982. *Kings and Vikings.* London: Routledge.

Scaldaspiller, Eyvind. 1932. "Hakonarmál." In *Heimskringla,* by Snorre Sturlason (Erling Monsen, ed., and A. H. Smith, trans.). New York: Dover Publications.

Schwartz, Martin. 1992. "Wodanaz." From a lecture given at the Old English Colloquium at the University of California, Berkeley, April 4.

Simek, Rudolf. 1996. *Dictionary of Northern Mythology.* Translated by Angela Hall. Cambridge: D. S. Brewer.

Skallagrimsson, Egil. 1930. *Egil's Saga.* Translated by E. R. Eddison. Greenwood Press.

Spurklund, Terje. 2010. "The Futhark and Roman Script Literacy." *Futhark: International Journal of Runic Studies* 1.

Storms, Godfrid. 1949 (1964). *Anglo-Saxon Magic.* New York: Gordon Press.

Sturlson, Snorri. 1844. "Hakon the Good's Saga," "King Olaf Trygvason's Saga." In *Heimskringla: The Lives of the Norse Kings,* translated by Samuel Laing. *www.sacred-texts.com/.*

Sturlason, Snorre. 1932. *Heimskringla: The Lives of the Norse Kings.* Translated by Erling Monsen and A. H. Smith. New York: Dover.

Sturlusson, Snorri. 1916. *Skaldskaparmál.* Translated by Arthur Gilchrist Brodeur. *www.sacred-texts.com/.*

———. 1987. *Edda.* Translated by Anthony Faulkes. London: J. M. Dent & Sons.

Tacitus. 1964. "The Annals." In *The Complete Works of Tacitus,* translated by Alfred Church and William Brodribb. New York: McGraw-Hill.

Thorsson, Edred. 1981. *The Nine Doors of Midgard.* St. Paul, MN: Llewelyn Publications.

———. 1984. *Futhark.* York Beach, ME: Samuel Weiser, Inc.

Tolkien, C. J. R. 1960. *Hervarar Saga ok Heidreks Konungs.* London: Thomas Nelson and Sons Ltd.

Tolkien, J. R. R. 1977. *The Silmarillion.* Edited by Christopher Tolkien. Houghton Mifflin.

———, trans. 2014. *Beowulf.* Boston: Houghton Mifflin.

Tolstoy, Nikolai. 1988. *The Quest for Merlin.* New York: Little, Brown & Co.

Tunstall, Peter, trans. 2003. *The Saga of Hrolf Kraki and His Champions.* *http://fantasycastlebooks.com.*

"Völsa Þattr." In *Flateyjarbók.* Original text and English translation at *https://notendur.hi.is.*

Waggoner, Ben, trans. 2009. *The Sagas of Ragnar Lothbrok and His Sons.* New Haven, CT: Troth Publications.

Wagner, Richard. 1960. *The Ring of the Nibelung.* Translated by Stewart Robb. E. P. Dutton.

Wawn, Andrew. 2000. *The Vikings and the Victorians: Inventing the Old North in 19th Century Britain.* London: Boydell and Brewer.

Wood, Lorrie. 2006. "You Can't Keep a Dead Man Down: Draugar in Lore and Life." *Idunna* 70 (Winter).

Zimmer, Carl. 2009. "The Big Similarities and Quirky Differences between Our Right and Left Brains." *Discover Magazine* (5). See also *http://discovermagazine.com*.

Zimmer, Paul Edwin. 1979. *Kvasir's Blood.* Printed privately.

About the Author

Photo by Michael Szalnaker

Diana L. Paxson is a writer, priestess, and teacher who has been studying and teaching Germanic mythology and religion for nearly thirty years. She is the author of numerous books including *Taking Up the Runes, Trance-Portation,* and *The Essential Guide to Possession, Depossession, and Divine Relationships.* Paxson also pioneered the recovery of traditional Norse oracular practice, described in *The Way of the Oracle.* She is a regular speaker at Pagan conferences and festivals.

To Our Readers

Weiser Books, an imprint of Red Wheel/Weiser, publishes books across the entire spectrum of occult, esoteric, speculative, and New Age subjects. Our mission is to publish quality books that will make a difference in people's lives without advocating any one particular path or field of study. We value the integrity, originality, and depth of knowledge of our authors.

Our readers are our most important resource, and we appreciate your input, suggestions, and ideas about what you would like to see published.

Visit our website at *www.redwheelweiser.com* to learn about our upcoming books and free downloads, and be sure to go to *www.redwheelweiser.com/newsletter* to sign up for newsletters and exclusive offers.

You can also contact us at *info@rwwbooks.com* or at

Red Wheel/Weiser, LLC
65 Parker Street, Suite 7
Newburyport, MA 01950